P9-EMD-912

WITHDRAWN

Modern Critical Views

Modern Critical Views

LEO TOLSTOY

Modern Critical Views

LEO TOLSTOY

Edited with an introduction by

Harold Bloom

Sterling Professor of the Humanities
Yale University

CHELSEA HOUSE PUBLISHERS
New York
Philadelphia

PROJECT EDITORS: Emily Bestler, James Uebbing
ASSOCIATE EDITOR: Maria Behan
EDITORIAL COORDINATOR: Karyn Gullen Browne
EDITORIAL STAFF: Perry King, Bert Yaeger
DESIGN: Susan Lusk

Cover illustration by Frank Steiner

Printed and bound in the United States of America

10   9   8   7   6   5   4   3   2

Library of Congress Cataloging in Publication Data

Leo Tolstoy.
    (Modern critical views)
    Bibliography: p.
    Includes index.
    1. Tolstoy, Leo, graf, 1828–1910–Criticism and
interpretations–Adresses, essays, lectures.
I. Bloom, Harold.   II. Title.   III. Series.
PG3410.L415   1986   891.73′3   85-28064
ISBN 0-87754-727-0

Contents

Editor's Note

This volume gathers together a representative selection of the best criticism devoted to Tolstoy that is available in the English language. The essays, reprinted here in the chronological order of their publication, cover a period from 1920 through 1983, and can be called a history-in-little of the twentieth-century reception of Tolstoy's work in Anglo-American criticism, although Continental and Russian commentaries are also included here. The editor is grateful to Ms. Olga Popov, without whose erudition he would not have known of some of these essays.

The editor's "Introduction" centers entirely upon Tolstoy's magnificent late short novel *Hadji Murad*, so as to intimate something of Tolstoy's Homeric powers in narrative. With the great Hungarian critic, Gyorgy Lukacs, we expect a social emphasis, but that emphasis is severely tested when Lukacs admits that Tolstoy transcended both romanticism and the form of the novel, and nearly renewed the Homeric or national epic, a renewal that Lukacs rejects upon Marxist historical grounds. Thomas Mann, who had portrayed Lukacs in *The Magic Mountain* as Leo Naphta, the Jewish Jesuit and Nietzschean terrorist, somewhat counters Lukacs here by comparing Tolstoy to Goethe. As Mann shrewdly notes, even the most social of Tolstoy's concepts and visions invariably originated as intense personal needs.

Viktor Shklovsky's brief excursus on Tolstoyan parallels provides a fine instance of twentieth-century Russian stylistic criticism. With Philip Rahv's ruminations upon Tolstoy's short novels, the startling *naturalness* of that cosmos is emphasized. Something of the same tribute is paid by George Steiner in his comparison of Tolstoy and Homer, which can be contrasted usefully to the editor's comparison in his introductory remarks.

In Isaiah Berlin's essay, Tolstoy is seen as a martyr of the European Enlightenment, sacrificing everything upon the altar of truth. In some sense, this is parallel to R. P. Blackmur's reading of *Anna Karenina*, which concludes that human life could not stand Anna's "intensity," perhaps a trope for Tolstoy's drive towards truth. In Barbara Hardy's very different analysis, Anna is seen as suffering from the disease of nihilism. When John Bayley, assessing Tolstoy's outrageous tract *What Is Art?*, concludes that

Tolstoy's answer is "My own novels," we receive a wry illumination upon Tolstoyan truth and Tolstoyan intensity.

War and Peace becomes the focus with the examination of that epic novel's varied narratives by W. Gareth Jones. In Gary Saul Morson's essay on the poetics of Tolstoy's "didactic fiction," there is an emphasis instead upon the first Sevastopol story, as an instance of the oxymoronic element in all didactic fiction, even Tolstoy's. With Edward Wasiolek's reading of *Resurrection*, we are given a salutary reminder of what is most positive in Tolstoy's fiction, his refusal to despair. This is akin to W. W. Rowe's tracing of fateful or overdetermined patterns in Tolstoy, patterns that his stronger and more flexible personages are able to transcend.

A reading of *Family Happiness*, by Natalia Kisseleff calls into question Tolstoy's positive and transcending tendencies, exposing their dangerous nearness to sentimentalism, while acknowledging that Tolstoy himself was aware of this unhappy proximity. Robert Wexelblatt defines an approach to Tolstoy's ultimate transcendence, the mystical vision of immortality in *The Death of Ivan Ilych* through a comparison with Kafka's *Metamorphosis*.

This volume ends with Martin Price's lucid analysis of moral character in *War and Peace* and *Anna Karenina*. Price's observations confirm Tolstoy's acuity as a tragic writer, a dimension so different from the epic heroism of *Hadji Murad* as to renew our sense of wonder at Tolstoy's range.

Introduction

*With God he has very suspicious relations; they sometimes remind me
of the relation of "two bears in one den."*

—MAXIM GORKY, *Reminiscences of Tolstoy*

I

Tolstoy, while at work upon his sublime short novel, *Hadji Murad*, wrote an essay on Shakespeare in which he judged *King Lear, Hamlet* and *Macbeth* to be "empty and offensive." Reading one of his few authentic rivals, Tolstoy "felt an overpowering repugnance, a boundless tedium." Homer and the Bible were equals he could recognize, but Shakespeare unnerved him. The customary explanation is that Tolstoy was morally offended by Shakespeare, but the truth is likely to be darker. *Hadji Murad* has a mimetic force difficult to match elsewhere. To find representations of the human that compel us to see reality differently, or to see aspects of reality we otherwise could not see at all, we can turn to only a few authors: the Yahwist or "J" writer (who made the original narratives in what are now Genesis, Exodus, Numbers), Homer and Dante, Chaucer and Shakespeare, Cervantes and Tolstoy and Proust. Of all these, Tolstoy most resembles "J." The art of Tolstoy's narratives never seems art, and the narratives themselves move with an authority that admits no reservations on the reader's side. Gorky wrote of Tolstoy that: "He talks most of God, of peasants, and of woman. Of literature rarely and little, as though literature were something alien to him." The *Reminiscences of Tolstoy* is continually astonishing, but perhaps most memorable when Gorky describes Tolstoy playing cards:

> How strange that he is so fond of playing cards. He plays seriously, passionately. His hands become nervous when he takes the cards up, exactly as he were holding live birds instead of inanimate pieces of cardboard.

That is the author of *Hadji Murad*, rather than of *What is Art?* Tolstoy holds Hadji Murad in his hands, as if indeed he held the man, and not a fiction. I read Tolstoy only in translation, and believe that I miss an immense value, but what remains in *Hadji Murad* overwhelms me afresh at every rereading. Tolstoy finished the novella in September 1902, shortly after his seventy-fourth birthday. Perhaps the story was his profound study of his own nostalgias, his return to his own youth, when he had participated as a volunteer in the Caucasian campaign (1851), at the age of twenty-three, and when he wrote *The Cossacks* (1858, published 1863).

Everything outward in *Hadji Murad* is historical, and Tolstoy evidently was precise and faithful in adhering to documented fact, and yet the inward story is a phantasmagoria so powerful as to devour and replace whatever we might yearn to call reality. Hadji Murad, like every other major figure in the narrative, was both a historical personage, and a living legend in Tolstoy's time, yet he is Tolstoy's vitalistic vision at its most personal, persuasive, and poignant, being a vision of the end. That is to say, *Hadji Murad* is a supreme instance of what the heroic Chernyshevsky, critic and martyr, praised as Tolstoy's prime gifts: purity of moral feeling, and the soul's dialectic, its antithetical discourse with itself.

Perhaps *Hadji Murad* can also be read as the return in Tolstoy of the pure storyteller, who tells his story as a contest against death, so as to defer change, of which the final form must be death. Tolstoy's ruinous meditations upon the power of death ensue from his awesome sense of life, a vitality as intense as his own Hadji Murad's. His crisis in the mid-1870s, when he wrote *Anna Karenina,* as set forth in his *Confession* (1882), supposedly turned upon a dread of nihilism, a conviction that no meaning of any life could be preserved once it ceased. But Tolstoy's famous refusal to divide life from literature, which could lead to the absurdity of his "Shakespeare" essay, led also to *Hadji Murad.* Consider the opening of the novella (I give the Aylmer Maude translation):

> I was returning home by the fields. It was mid-summer, the hay harvest was over and they were just beginning to reap the rye. At that season of the year there is a delightful variety of flowers—red, white, and pink scented tufty clover; milkwhite ox-eye daisies with their bright yellow centres and pleasant spicy smell; yellow honey-scented rape blossoms; tall campanulas with white and lilac bells, tulip-shaped; creeping vetch; yellow, red, and pink scabious; faintly scented, neatly arranged purple plantains with blossoms slightly tinged with pink; cornflowers, the newly opened blossoms bright blue in the sunshine but growing paler and redder towards evening or when growing old; and delicate almond-scented dodder flowers that withered quickly. I gathered myself a large nosegay and was going home when I noticed in a ditch, in full bloom, a beautiful thistle plant of the crimson variety, which in our neighborhood they call "Tartar" and carefully avoid when mowing—or, if they do happen to cut it down,

throw out from among the grass for fear of pricking their hands. Thinking to pick this thistle and put it in the centre of my nosegay, I climbed down into the ditch, and after driving away a velvety humble-bee that had penetrated deep into one of the flowers and had there fallen sweetly asleep, I set to work to pluck the flower. But this proved a very difficult task. Not only did the stalk prick on every side—even through the handkerchief I had wrapped round my hand—but it was so tough that I had to struggle with it for nearly five minutes, breaking the fibres one by one; and when I had at last plucked it, the stalk was all frayed and the flower itself no longer seemed so fresh and beautiful. Moreover, owing to its coarseness and stiffness, it did not seem in place among the delicate blossoms of my nosegay. I threw it away feeling sorry to have vainly destroyed a flower that looked beautiful in its proper place.

It does not matter at all that the thistle is so obviously a synecdoche for Hadji Murad himself. What is at work here is the authority of Tolstoy's own recalcitrance. Like the thistle, Tolstoy's stance is firm, rooted in the black-earth fields. "What reality!" we think, as we stare at Tolstoy's fictive cosmos. If in Balzac every janitor is a genius, in Tolstoy every object resists inanimate status, be it the "Tartar" thistle or the low ottoman that rebels against Peter Ivanovich at the beginning of *The Death of Ivan Ilych*:

Peter Ivanovich sighed still more deeply and despondently, and Praskovya Fedorovna pressed his arm gratefully. When they reached the drawing-room, upholstered in pink cretonne and lighted by a dim lamp, they sat down at the table—she on a sofa and Peter Ivanovich on a low pouffe, the springs of which yielded spasmodically under his weight. Praskovya Fedorovna had been on the point of warning him to take another seat, but felt that such a warning was out of keeping with her present condition and so changed her mind. As he sat down on the pouffe Peter Ivanovich recalled how Ivan Ilych had arranged this room and had consulted him regarding this pink cretonne with green leaves. The whole room was full of furniture and knick-knacks, and on her way to the sofa the lace of the widow's black shawl caught on the carved edge of the table. Peter Ivanovich rose to detach it, and the springs of the pouffe, relieved of his weight, rose also and gave him a push. The widow began detaching her shawl herself, and Peter Ivanovich again sat down, suppressing the rebellious springs of the pouffe under him. But the widow had not quite freed herself and Peter Ivanovich got up again, and again the pouffe rebelled and even creaked. When this was all over, she took out a clean cambric handkerchief and began to weep. The episode with the shawl and the struggle with the pouffe had cooled Peter Ivanovich's emotions and he sat there with a sullen look on his face. This awkward situation was interrupted by Sokolov, Ivan Ilych's butler, who came to report that the plot in the cemetery that Praskovya Fedorovna had chosen would cost two hundred roubles. She stopped weeping and, looking at Peter Ivanovich with the air of a victim, remarked in French that it was very hard for her. Peter Ivanovich made a silent gesture signifying his full conviction that it must indeed be so.

It has been remarked that the pouffle or ottoman here is more memorable, has more vitality, than the personages have in most other authors' fiction. Of *Hadji Murad* I am moved to say that everything in it—people, horses, landscapes—exuberantly is rammed with life. Isaak Babel, whose *Odessa Tales* are my own favorite among all modern short stories, reread *Hadji Murad* in 1937, and recorded his happy shock at his renewed sense of Tolstoy's vitalistic force:

> Here the electric charge went from the earth, through the hands, straight to the paper, with no insulation at all, quite mercilessly stripping off all outer layers with a sense of truth . . . .

Tolstoy, who moralized both abominably and magnificently, has little original to say concerning the pragmatics of literary representation. What might be called his theory of such representation is outrageous enough to be interesting:

> The art of the future will thus be completely distinct, both in subject matter and in form, from what is now called art. The only subject matter of the art of the future will be either feelings drawing men toward union, or such as already unite them; and the forms of art will be such as will be open to everyone. And therefore, the ideal of excellence in the future will not be the exclusiveness of feeling, accessible only to some, but, on the contrary, its universality. And not bulkiness, obscurity, and complexity of form, as is now esteemed, but, on the contrary, brevity, clearness, and simplicity of expression. Only when art has attained to that, will art neither divert nor deprave men as it does now, calling on them to expend their best strength on it, but be what it should be—a vehicle wherewith to transmit religious, Christian perception from the realm of reason and intellect into that of feeling, and really drawing people in actual life nearer to that perfection and unity indicated to them by their religious perception.

In the age of Proust and *Finnegans Wake*, of *Gravity's Rainbow* and "An Ordinary Evening in New Haven," Tolstoy's "art of the future" is still, thankfully, far in the unapparent. Yet there is a strength in Tolstoy's own attempts to write his art of the future that makes us hesitate, partly because Tolstoy seems at moments to have found his way back to an art that never quite was, even in the remote past, and yet something in us wants it to have existed. There is, in a tale like "How Much Land Does a Man Need?"

(1886), a balance between ethos and pathos that caused James Joyce to call it the finest story he had ever read. I myself give that tribute to *Hadji Murad*, but the tale is a dreadfully impressive nightmare, and yet a vision of reality, irresistible in its Biblical irony. I say "Biblical irony" with precise intention, because Tolstoy's ironies seem to me neither Classical (saying one thing while meaning another) nor Romantic (playing upon contrasts between expectation and fulfillment). Rather, they resemble the ironies of the Yahwist, and turn always upon the incongruous clash between incommensurate orders of reality, human and divine, eros and the spirit. It is not accidental that Tolstoy was obsessed with the Biblical story of Joseph and his brothers, because in some sense much of Tolstoy's greatest art is a transumption of that story. To read the tale of Joseph as Tolstoy read it may be a way of seeing what Tolstoy valued in literary representation, and may help us to appreciate more fully the greatness, almost beyond the reach of art, of *Hadji Murad*.

II

It is hardly invidious to say that *Hadji Murad* is the story that Hemingway always wished to write, but could not accomplish. If we could imagine an early twentieth-century story written by the author of the *Iliad*, then it would be *Hadji Murad*. Like Homer, Tolstoy neither loves battle nor hates it; both epic poets simply accept it as the condition of life. The world of *Hadji Murad*, whatever precise relation it has to the actuality that Tolstoy experienced as a young soldier in the Caucasus, is a scene where battle is the norm, and open warfare is morally preferable to societal treachery, whether the society be Russian or Tartar, the realm of czar Nicholas or the Imam Shamil. Overt battle is also nobler than the sad impingements of societal depravity upon those who fight, with the superb exception of Hadji Murad himself and his little band of followers, devoted to the death. In such a fictive cosmos, Hadji Murad the man combines in himself all the positive attributes divided in the *Iliad* between Achilles and Hector, while being free of the negative qualities of both heroes. Indeed, of all natural men of heroic eminence in Western literature, Hadji Murad is the most impressive.

How does Tolstoy so shape his representation of Hadji Murad as to arouse none of our proper skepticism (or his own) of the potential heroism of the natural man? No sensitive reader of Tolstoy's story would dismiss Hadji Murad as we are compelled to dismiss the fisherman in *The Old Man and the Sea* or Colonel Cantwell in *Across the River and Into the Trees.* Hemingway's natural vitalists are neither natural nor vital enough, and their sacred innocence is too close to ignorance. Hadji Murad is shrewder as well as more courageous than anyone else in his story. He dies in battle, knowing he must, because he has no alternative. But he dies without Achilles' rage against mortality, or Hector's collapse into passivity. He can die with absolute dignity because he knows that he is not only the best of the Tartars, but superior also in horsemanship, daring, fighting skill, and charismatic leadership to any of the Russians. Famous for all his exploits, his last stand will be not less famous, and yet he need not comfort himself with such a realization.. Perhaps his heroic completeness is implicit comfort enough.

Of the two chief Homeric heroes, Achilles excels in force and Odysseus in craft, but Hadji Murad is foremost in both qualities. Like Achilles, Hadji Murad has chosen immortal fame, and yet, like Odysseus, he wishes to return home, to rescue his women and his son. Unlike Odysseus, he fails, and yet Tolstoy's art makes it impossible to judge Hadji Murad's last exploit as a failure. The hero, in every phase leading up to his hopeless break-out and final battle, remains elemental, a force like wind, a kind of pure flame. That force and purity are not less elemental in the Tartar hero's dying:

> all these images passed through his mind without evoking any feeling within him—neither pity nor anger nor any kind of desire: everything seemed so insignificant in comparison with what was beginning, or had already begun, within him.

Elemental dying, strong process as it is, goes on simultaneously with the last spasm of Hadji Murad's sublime vitality:

> Yet his strong body continued the thing that he had commenced. Gathering together his last strength he rose from behind the bank, fired his pistol at a man who was just running towards him, and hit him. The man fell. Then Hadji Murad got quite out of the ditch, and limping heavily went dagger in hand straight at the foe.
>
> Some shots cracked and he reeled and fell. Several militiamen with trumphant shrieks rushed towards the fallen body. But the body that seemed to be dead suddenly moved. First the uncovered, bleeding, shaven head rose; then the body with hands holding to the trunk of a tree. He seemed so terrible, that those who were runninig towards him stopped short. But suddenly a shudder passed through him, he staggered away from the tree and fell on his face, stretched out at full length like a thistle that had been mown down, and he moved no more.
>
> He did not move, but still he felt.

When Hadji Aga, who was the first to reach him, struck him on the head with a large dagger, it seemed to Hadji Murad that someone was striking him with a hammer and he could not understand who was doing it or why. That was his last consciousness of any connection with his body. He felt nothing more and his enemies kicked and hacked at what had no longer anything in common with him.

The synecdoche of the mown-down thistle, called "the Tartar" in the novella's first paragraph, reminds us of Tolstoy's original tribute: "But what energy and tenacity! With what determination it defended itself, and how dearly it sold its life!" Hadji Murad also "stood firm and did not surrender to man" and marvelously demonstrated the vitality that will not submit. But why does this archaic heroism so captivate Tolstoy and, through Tolstoy, the readers of the story? Gorky said of Tolstoy: "He always greatly exalted immortality on the other side of this life, but he preferred it on this side." We should also recall Gorky's memory that Tolstoy liked to remark of *War and Peace*: "without false modesty, it is like the *Iliad.*" *Hadji Murad* is even more like the *Iliad;* uncannnily so, because its hero is Homeric to the highest degree, and yet something beyond even Homer, which remains to be explored.

It is totally persuasive that Hadji Murad is virtually without flaw, granted his context and his tradition. Tolstoy, as an artist, intends to transume the whole of the heroic concept, from all archaic sources, and in his Hadji Murad he fulfills that intention. The archaic hero falls somewhere between man and a god, but Hadji Murad is only a man. While the archaic hero of epic has as his special excellence what J. M. Redfield calls "not integration but potency," Hadji Murad is wholly integrated. What Redfield calls "the ambiguity of the hero" does not apply at all to Hadji Murad, whose elemental force, unlike that of Achilles, has in it none of the latency of the savage beast. Without in any way moralizing his hero, Tolstoy removes from him the childlike element that never abandons Achilles.

After Hadji Murad is dead, and even as his killers rejoice, Tolstoy renders his hero the tribute of a true threnody:

The nightingales, that had hushed their songs while the firing lasted, now started their trills once more: first one quite close, then others in the distance.

We can remember the universal adage, that if nature could write, it would be Tolstoy. His art itself is nature, and deserves that Shakespearean praise, despite his jealous dismissal of Shakespeare. He could not rival Shakespeare, but he came near to being Homer's equal.

GYORGY LUKACS

Tolstoy and the Attempts to Go Beyond the Social Forms of Life

The greater closeness of nineteenth-century Russian literature to certain organic natural conditions, which were the given substratum of its underlying attitude and creative intention, made it possible for that literature to be *creatively* polemical. Tolstoy, coming after Turgenev—who was an essentially Western European novelist of disillusionment—created a form of novel which overlaps to the maximum extent into the epic. Tolstoy's great and truly epic mentality, which has little to do with the novel form, aspires to a life based on a community of feeling among simple human beings closely bound to nature, a life which is intimately adapted to the great rhythm of nature, which moves according to nature's cycle of birth and death and excludes all structures which are not natural, which are petty and disruptive, causing disintegration and stagnation. "The muzhik dies quietly," Tolstoy wrote to Countess A. A. Tolstoy about his story *Three Deaths*. "His religion is nature, with which he has spent all his life. He has felled trees, sown rye, reaped it, he has slaughtered sheep and sheep have been born on his farm, children have come into the world, old men have died, and he knows this law from which he has never turned away as the lady of the manor has done, he knows it well and has looked it straight and simply in the eye . . . The tree dies

Translated by Anna Bostock. From *The Theory of the Novel: A Historico-Philosophical Essay on the Forms of Great Epic Literature.* Copyright © 1971 by The Merlin Press.

quietly, simply and beautifully. Beautifully because it does not lie, makes no grimaces, is afraid of nothing and regrets nothing."

The paradoxical nature of Tolstoy's historical situation, which proves better than anything else how much the novel is the necessary epic form of our time, manifests itself in the fact that this world cannot be translated into movement and action, even by an author who not only longs for it but has actually seen and depicted it clearly; it remains only an element of the epic work, but is not epic reality itself. The natural organic world of the old epics was, after all, a culture whose organic character was its specific quality, whereas the nature which Tolstoy posits as the ideal and which he has experienced as existent is, in its innermost essence, meant to be *nature* (and is, therefore, opposed, as such, to *culture*). This necessary opposition is the insoluble problematic of Tolstoy's novels. In other words, his epic intention was bound to result in a problematic novel form, not because he failed to overcome culture within himself, not because his relationship to nature as he experienced and depicted it was a sentimental one—not for psychological reasons—but for reasons of form and of the relationship of form to its historico-philosophical substratum.

A totality of men and events is possible only on the basis of culture, whatever one's attitude towards it. Therefore in Tolstoy's epic works the decisive element belongs, both as framework and as concrete content, to the world of culture which he rejects as problematic. But since nature, although it cannot become an immanently complete totality, is objectively existent, the work contains two layers of realities which are completely heterogeneous from one another both as regards the value attached to them and the quality of their being. And relating them to one another, which would make it possible to construct a work that was a totality, can only take the form of the lived experience of going from one reality to the other. Or, to put it more precisely, since the direction chosen is a given result of the value attached to both realities, it is the experience of going from culture to nature. And so, as a paradoxical consequence of the paradoxical relationship between the writer's mentality and the historical age in which he finds himself, a sentimental, romantic experience finally becomes the centre of the entire work: the central characters' dissatisfaction with whatever the surrounding world of culture can offer them and their seeking and finding of the second, more essential reality of nature. The paradoxy arising from this experience is further increased by the fact that this "nature" of Tolstoy's does not have a plentitude and perfection that would make it, like the relatively more substantial world at the end of Goethe's novel, a home in which the characters might arrive and come to rest. Rather, it is a factual assurance that an essential life really does exist beyond conventionality—a life which can be reached through the lived experiences of a full and genuine selfhood, the self-experience of the soul, but from which one must irremediably fall back into the world of convention.

With the heroic ruthlessness of a writer of historic greatness, Tolstoy does not flinch from the grim consequences of his world view; not even the singular position he allocates to love and marriage—a position halfway between nature and culture, at home in both spheres and yet a stranger in each—can mitigate these consequences. In the rhythm of natural life, the rhythm of unpathetic, natural growth and death, love is the point at which the dominant forces of life assume their most concrete and meaningful form. Yet love as a pure force of nature, love as passion, does not belong to Tolstoy's world of nature; passionate love is too much bound up with the relationship between one individual and another and therefore isolates too much, creates too many degrees and nuances; it is too cultural. The love which occupies the really central place in Tolstoy's world is love as marriage, love as union (the fact of being united, of becoming one, being more important than who it is that is thus united), love as the prelude to birth; marriage and the family as a vehicle of the natural continuity of life. That this introduces a conceptual dichotomy into the edifice would be of little importance artistically if it did not create yet another heterogeneous layer of reality, which cannot be compositionally connected with the other two spheres, in themselves heterogeneous from each other. The more authentically this layer of reality is depicted, the more strongly it is bound to be transformed into the opposite of what was intended: the triumph of such love over culture is meant to be a victory of the natural over the falsely, artifically refined, yet it becomes a miserable swallowing-up by nature of everything that is great and noble in man. Nature is alive inside man but, when it is lived as culture, it reduces man to the lowest, most mindless, most idea-forsaken conventionality. This is why the mood of the epilogue to *War and Peace*, with its nursery atmosphere where all passion has been spent and all seeking ended, is more profoundly disconsolate than the endings of the most problematic novels of disillusionment. Nothing is left of what was there before; as the sand of the desert covers the pyramids, so every spiritual thing has been swamped, annihilated, by animal nature.

This unintentional disconsolateness of the ending combines with an intentional one in the description of the conventional world. Tolstoy's evaluating and rejecting attitude extends to every detail he depicts. The aimlessness and insubstantiality of the life he describes expresses itself not only objectively, for the reader who recognises it, not only as the lived experience of gradual disappointment, but also as an a-prioristic, established, agitated emptiness, a restless *ennui*. Every conversation, every event bears the stamp of the author's verdict.

These two groups of experiences (the private world of marriage and the public world of society) are contrasted with the experience of the essence of nature. At very rare, great moments—generally they are moments of death—a reality reveals itself to man in which he suddenly glimpses and grasps the essence that rules over him and works within him, the meaning of his life. His whole previous life vanishes into nothingness in the face of this experience; all its conflicts, all the sufferings, torments and confusions caused by them, appear petty and inessential. Meaning has made its appearance and the paths into living life are open to the soul. And here again Tolstoy, with the paradoxical ruthlessness of true genius, shows up the profoundly problematic nature of his form and its foundations: these crucial moments of bliss are the great moments of dying—the experience of Andrey Bolkonsky lying mortally wounded on the field of Austerlitz, the sense of unity experienced by Karenin and Vronsky at Anna's deathbed—and it would be true bliss to die now, to die like that. But Anna recovers and Andrey returns to life, and the great moments vanish without trace. Life goes on in the world of convention, an aimless, inessential life. The paths which the great moments had revealed lose their direction, their reality, as the great moment passes. Such paths cannot be trodden, and when people believe they are treading them, their experience is a bitter caricature of what the revelation of the great moment had shown. (Levin's experience of God and his clinging to what he has thus attained—despite the fact that it is slipping from his grasp—stems more from the will and theory of Tolstoy the thinker than from the vision of Tolstoy the artist. It is programmatic and lacks the immediate conviction of the other great moments.) The few characters who are capable of really living their lived experiences—perhaps Planton Karatayev is the only such character—are, of necessity, secondary characters: events leave them unchanged, their essential nature is never involved in events, their life does not objectivise itself, it cannot be given form but only hinted at, only defined in concrete artistic terms in contrast to the others. They are not realities but marginal aesthetic concepts.

These three layers of reality correspond to the three concepts of time in Tolstoy's world, and the impossibility of uniting them reveals most strongly the inner problematic of his works, rich and profound as they are. The world of convention is essentially timeless; an eternally recurring, self-repeating monotony, it proceeds upon its course in accordance with meaningless laws of its own; eternal movement without direction, without growth, without death. Characters come and go, but nothing happens as a result of this constant flux because each figure is as insubstantial as the next, and any one can be put in the place of any other. Whenever one walks on to this stage, whenever one leaves it, one always finds—or has to reject—the same motley inessentiality. Beneath it flows the stream of Tolstoyan nature: the continuity and monotony of an eternal rhythm. That which changes in nature is the individual destiny, and this, too, is inessential. Individual destiny, caught in the current, rising or sinking with it, possesses no meaning founded upon itself; its relation to the whole does not assimilate its personality but destroys it; as an individual destiny, rather than as an element of a general rhythm side by side with innumerable other, similar and equivalent lives, it is completely immaterial. The great moments which offer a glimpse of an essential life, a meaningful process, remain mere moments, isolated from the other two worlds and without constitutive reference to them. Thus the three concepts of time are not only mutually heterogeneous and incapable of being united with one another, but moreover none of them expresses real duration, real time, the life-element of the novel.

Going outside and beyond culture has merely destroyed culture but has not put a truer, more essential life in its place; the overlapping into the epic only makes the novel form still more problematic, without coming concretely closer to the desired goal, the problem-free reality of the epic. (In purely artistic terms Tolstoy's novels are novels of disillusionment carried to an extreme, a baroque version of Flaubert's form.) The glimpsed world of essential nature remains an intimation, a lived experience; it is subjective and reflexive so far as the depicted reality is concerned; but in a purely artistic sense, it is nevertheless of the same kind as any other longing for a more adequate reality.

Literary development has not yet gone beyond the novel of disillusionment, and the most recent literature reveals no possibility of creating another type that would be essentially new; what we have now is an eclectic, epigonic imitation of earlier types, whose apparent productive force is confined to the formally inessential areas of lyricism and psychology.

Tolstoy himself, it is true, occupies a dual position. From the point of view purely of form (a point of view which, in Tolstoy's special case, cannot possibly do justice to what matters most in his vision or in his created world), he must be seen as the final expression of European Romanticism. However, in the few overwhelmingly great moments of his works—moments which must be seen as subjective and reflexive in respect of each particular work as a whole—he shows a clearly differentiated, concrete and existent world, which, if it could spread out into a totality, would be completely inaccessible to the categories of the novel and would require a new form of artistic creation: the form of the renewed epic.

This world is the sphere of pure soul-reality in which man exists as man, neither as a social being nor as an isolated, unique, pure and therefore abstract interiority. If ever this world should come into being as something natural and simply experienced, as the only true reality, a new complete totality could be built out of all its substances and relationships. It would be a world to which our divided reality would be a mere backdrop, a world which would have outstripped our dual world of social reality by as much as we have outstripped the world of nature. But art can never be the agent of such a transformation: the great epic is a form bound to the historical moment, and any attempt to depict the utopian as existent can only end in destroying the form, not in creating reality. The novel is the form of the epoch of absolute sinfulness, as Fichte said, and it must remain the dominant form so long as the world is ruled by the same stars. In Tolstoy, intimations of a breakthrough into a new epoch are visible; but they remain polemical, nostalgic and abstract.

THOMAS MANN

Goethe and Tolstoy

Turgenyev, in his last letter to Tolstoy, written on his death-bed in Paris, in which he conjured his friend to return to literature and stop tormenting himself and theology, Turgenyev was the first to give Tolstoy the title of "the great writer of Russia," which he has had ever since, and which seems to mean that he holds in the eyes of his countrymen the same rank that the author of *Faust* and *Wilhelm Meister* does in ours. Tolstoy himself was Christian through and through. Yet his humility was not so exaggerated as to prevent him from setting his name boldly beside the greatest, yes, beside the legendary great. He said of *War and Peace*: "Modesty aside, it is something like the *Iliad*." He was heard to say the same of his earliest work, *Childhood, Boyhood, Youth*. Was that megalomania? To me, frankly, it sounds like plain and simple fact. *"Nur die Lumpe,"* says Goethe, *"sind bescheiden."* A heathen saying. But Tolstoy subscribed to it. He saw himself always of heroic grandeur; and as early as at thirty-seven, writing in his diary, he ranked his own works, the finished and the still to write, with the great literature of the world.

In the judgment, then, of those competent to render it, the great writer of Russia; by his own estimate, the Homer of his time—but that is not all. After Tolstoy's death Maxim Gorky published a little book of reminiscences, the best book, in my humble opinion, that he has written. It closes with the words: "And I, who do not believe in God, looked at him timidly, for some dark reason looked at him and thought: The man is godlike." Godlike. Extraordinary. Nobody ever said or thought that of Dostoyevsky, nobody ever could have thought or said it. He has been called

Translated by H. T. Lowe-Porter. From *Essays of Three Decades*. Copyright © 1947 by Alfred A. Knopf, Inc.

a saint; and one might in all sincerity apply the word to Schiller, at least in the Christian sense which it must always connote, if without the specifically Byzantine flavour. But Goethe and Tolstoy, these two, have been found godlike. The epithet "Olympian" is a commonplace. It was not, however, only as a world-renowned old man of commanding intellect that Goethe had it applied to him; it was while he was still young, still the youth, of whose godlike, compelling gaze Wieland sang, that he had the attribute conferred upon him, a thousand times, by his own contemporaries. Riemer relates that at sixty the old man took occasion to make rather acridly merry over it. "The deuce take godlike," he cried. "What good does it do me to have people say: 'That is a godlike man,' when I go by? They behave just as they like, they impose on me just the same. People only call a man godlike when he lets them have their own way!"—As for Tolstoy, you could not say he was Olympian; he was not a humanistic god, of course. He was, Gorky says, more like some sort of Russian god, sitting on a maple throne under a golden lime tree; pagan, then, with a difference, compared with the Zeus of Weimar, but pagan none the less, because gods *are* pagan. Why? Because they are of the same essence as nature. One does not need to be a follower of Spinoza—as Goethe was, and had his own good reasons for it—to feel God and Nature as one, and the nobility that nature confers as godlike. "His superhumanly developed individuality is a monstrous phenomenon, almost forbidding, he was something in him of the fabled Sviatogor, whom the earth cannot hold." Thus Gorky, on Tolstoy. And I cite it in this matter of relative greatness. Gorky, for instance, goes on to say: "There is something about him which always makes me want to shout: "Behold what a marvellous man lives upon this earth!' For he is, so to speak, in general and beyond everything else, a human human being, a man. That sounds like something we have heard before. It reminds us of— whom?

No, the question of rank, the aristocratic problem, is no problem at all, within the grouping I have chosen. It becomes one only when we change partners: when we take saintly humanity and couple it, by means of the antithetic conjunction, with the godlike; when we say "Goethe and Schiller," "Tolstoy and Dostoyevsky." Only then, I think, do we pose the question of aristocracy, the problem in ethics and asthetics: Which is greater? Which is more aristocratic? I shall not answer either of these. I will let the reader come to his individual conclusion in this matter of value, according to his own taste. Or, less glibly put, according to the conception he has of humanity, which—I must add, *sotto voce*—will have to be one-sided and incomplete to admit of his coming to any decision at all.

Is it not strangely moving to hear that one man had known them both, the creator of *Faust* and the "great writer of Russia"? For certainly they belonged to different centuries. Tolstoy's life covered the greater part of the nineteenth. He is absolutely its son. As an artist he exhibits all of its characteristics, and, indeed, those of its second half. As for Goethe, the eighteenth century brought him forth, and essential traits of his character and training belong to it—a statement it would be very easy to substantiate. Yet on the other hand one might say that just as much of the eighteenth, Goethe's century, survived in Tolstoy as there had already come to birth of Tolstoy's, of the nineteenth, in Goethe. Tolstoy's rationalizing Christianity has more in common with the deism of the eighteenth century than it has with Dostoyevsky's violent and mystical religiosity, which was entirely of the nineteenth. His system of practical religion—the essence of which was a destructive intellectual force that undermined all regulations, human and divine—had more affinity with the social criticism of the eighteenth century than with Dostoyevsky's moralization, although those were, on the one hand, far more profound, on the other far more religious. And Tolstoy's *penchant* for utopias, his hatred of civilization, his passion for rusticity, for a bucolic placidity of the soul—an aristocratic passion, the passion of a nobleman—to all that, the eighteenth century, and indeed the French eighteenth century, can lay claim. And, on the other hand, Goethe. What most astonishes us in that masterpiece of his old age, the sociological novel *Wilhelm Meisters Wanderjahre,* is the intuition, the keenness and breadth of vision—they seem positively occult, but are simply the expression of a finer organism, the fruit of the most sensitive penetration—which anticipate the whole social and economic development of the nineteenth century: the industrialization of the old cultural and agrarian countries, the triumph of the machine, the rise of the organized labouring classes, the class conflict, democracy, socialism, Americanism itself, with the intellectual and educational consequences of all these.

But when all is said, and whatever the chronological affinity of these two great men, they cannot be called contemporaries. Only four years did the two of them inhabit this mortal sphere together: from 1828, when Tolstoy was born, to 1832, when Goethe died. Which does not prevent them from having one cultural element of their intellectual and spiritual make-up in common, and that a very real and positive one—to say nothing of universally human elements like Homer and the Bible. I mean the element Rousseau.

"I have read the whole of Rousseau, the whole twenty volumes, including the lexicon of music. What I felt for him was more than enthusiasm; it was worship. At fifteen I wore round my neck, instead of the usual cross, a medallion with his picture. I am so familiar with some of the passages in his works that I feel as though I had written them myself." These are Tolstoy's words, taken from his *Confessions*. And certainly he was Rousseauian more intimately, more personally, more damagingly, so to speak, than was Goethe, who as a man had nothing in common with poor Jean Jacques's enigmatic and not always ingratiating complexities. Yet hear Goethe (I quote from an early review): "Religious conditions, and the social conditions so narrowly bound up with them; the pressure of the laws, the still greater pressure of society, to say nothing of a thousand other factors, leave the civilized man or the civilized nation no soul of his own. They stifle the promptings of nature, they obliterate every trait out of which a characteristic picture could be made." That is, from the literary point of view, *Sturm und Drang*. But from the intellectual and historical, it is Rousseauianism. It bears the impress of revolution, even of anarchy; though in the Russian seeker after God that impress is religious and early Christian, whereas in Goethe's words the humanistic trend can be felt, the irradiation of a cultural and self-developing individualism which Tolstoy would have banned as egoistic and unchristian. But unchristian, egoistic, it is not: it means work on man, on mankind, on humanity, and it issues, as the *Wanderjahre* shows, in the social world.

What two ideas does the very sound of Rousseau's name inevitably evoke—aside, that is, from the idea of nature, which is, of course, first and foremost? Why, naturally, the idea "education" and the idea "autobiography." Jean Jacques Rousseau was the author of *Émile* and of the *Confessions*. Now, both these elements, the pedagogic and the autobiographic, are present in full strength in Goethe as in Tolstoy; they cannot be dissociated from the work or the life of either. . . . [Tolstoy] wrestled theoretically and practically to the very verge of exhaustion with the problem of the Russian primary school. As for Goethe, needless to say, his was a pedagogic nature in the fullest sense of the word. The two great monuments of his life, one in poetry and one in prose, the *Faust* and the *Wilhelm Meister*, are both creative treatments of the theme of education. And whereas in the *Lehrjahre* the idea is still that of the individual forming himself—"for to form myself, just as I am, was darkly, from my youth up, my purpose and my desire," says Wilhelm Meister—in the *Wanderjahre* the educational idea is objectivated, and issues in social, even in political concepts; while at the heart of the work is, as you know, the stern and beautiful Utopia of the *Pedagogic Province*.

The second association, the autobiographic, the confessional, is of course easy to attest in both authors. That all of Goethe's works represent "fragments of one great confession" we should know ourselves even if he did not tell us; and is not *Dichtung und Wahrheit*, next to the *Confessions* of Saint Augustine and Rousseau, the most famous autobiography in the world? Well, and Tolstoy too wrote confessions: I mean in the main a book with that title, laid down throughout on the line of the great self-revelations that runs from the African saint to Strindberg, the son of the servant. But Tolstoy is in the same case with Goethe: not by virtue of one book alone is he autobiographical. Beginning with the *Childhood, Boyhood, Youth*, throughout the whole body of his work, he is autobiographical to an extent that makes it possible for Merezhkovsky, the great Russian critic, to say: "The artistic work of Leo Tolstoy is at bottom nothing else than one tremendous diary, kept for fifty years, one endless, explicit confession." Yes, and this critic adds: "In the literatures of all times and peoples there will hardly be found a second example of an author who reveals his personal and private life, often in its most intimate aspects, with such open-hearted sincerity." Well—open-hearted. I may be allowed a comment upon the somewhat euphemistic epithet. One might, if one wanted to be invidious, use a different adjective to characterize this sincerity—an adjective that would suggest what Turgenyev had in mind when he once ironically referred to the shortcomings inevitable in a great writer: by which, obviously, he meant the lack of certain restraints, the absence of a customary reserve, discretion, decency, shame, or, on the positive side, the domination of a definite claim on the love of the world—an absolute claim, indeed, in that it is all one to the revealer whether he reveal virtues or vices. He craves to be known and loved, loved because known, or loved *although* known; that is what I mean by an absolute claim on love. And the remarkable thing is that the world acknowledges and honours the claim.

"A life that is romantic has always self-love at the bottom of it." I like this saying; and subjoin that self-love is also always at the bottom of all autobiography. For the impulse a man feels to "fixate" his life, to exhibit its development, to celebrate his own destiny in set literary form and passionately invoke the sympathy of his contemporaries and posterity, has for a premise the same uncommonly lively sense of his own ego which, according to that penetrating saying, is at the bottom of a life full of romantic happenings. Subjectively, for the man himself, but also objectively for the world at large. Of course, this love of self is something different, something stronger, deeper, more fruitful, than any mere self-complacency or self-love of the ordinary kind. In the finest instances it is what Goethe in the *Wanderjahre* calls *"Ehrfurcht vor sich selbst,"* and celebrates as the highest form of awe. It is the grateful and reverent self-absorption of the darling of the gods, that rings with incomparable sincerity from the lines:

Alles geben die Götter, die unendlichen,
Ihren Lieblingen ganz:
Alle Freuden, die unendlichen,
Alle Schmerzen, die unendlichen, ganz.

It is a proud and naïve interest in the mystery of high preferment, tangible superiority, perilous privilege, whose standard-bearer the chosen one feels himself to be; it is a craving to bear witness, out of the deeps of experience, how a genius is shaped; a desire to link together, by some miracle of grace, joy, and service; it was this desire that brought forth *Dichtung und Wahrheit* and in the truest sense inspires all great autobiography.

"I felt the need," writes Tolstoy of his youthful period, "to be known and loved of all the world; to *name my name*, the sound of which would greatly impress everybody, so that they would troop round me and thank me for something. . . ." That was quite early, before he had conceived any of his creative works or envisaged the idea of founding a new, practical, earthly, dogmaless religion—thought this idea, according to his journal, had occurred to him by the time he was twenty-seven years old. His name, he feels, his mere name, Leo Tolstoy, this formula for his darkly and mightily stirring ego, should, as it were, serve notice to the world; whereby, for some reason as yet unknown, the world should be greatly impressed, and feel impelled to surround him in grateful throngs. Long after that, in 1883—at about the same date that Tolstoy posed for an artist friend, sitting at his table and writing—he reads aloud to another friend and admirer, the one-time officer Tchertkov, from the manuscript of his just-completed personal revelations *What Does My Faith Consist In?* He reads from this manuscript a categorical reprobation of military service, on the gorunds of his Christianity; which so gratifies the ex-officer that he hears nothing else, ceases to listen, and only rouses out of his absorption when he hears, suddenly uttered, the reader's own name. Tolstoy, coming to the end of his manuscript, had, with particular distinctness, says Tchertkov, enunciated the name signed underneath the text: "Leo Tolstoy."

Goethe once played a little literary hoax with his own name, which I have always found singularly touching. You will recall that in the *Westöstliche Diwan* he selected for himself as the lover of Marianne-Zuleika the name of Hatem (the most richly giving and receiving one). The choice betrays a blissful self-preoccupation. Now, in one of the poems, a glorious one, he uses this name at the end of a line, where, however, it does not rhyme as according to the structure of the verse it should, and the name which would rhyme if it stood there is another, is Goethe's own; so that the reader involuntarily makes the substitution mentally as he reads. "Only this heart," says the already white-haired lover to the youthful beloved,

Nur dies Herz, es ist von Dauer,
Schwillt in jugendlichstem Flor;
Unter Schnee und Nebelschauer
Rast ein Ätna dir hervor,
Du beschämst wie Morgenröte
Jener Gipfel ernste Wand,
Und noch einmal fühlet Hatem
Frühlingshauch und Sommerbrand.

"And again, anew feels Goethe . . . ." With what delightful playfulness the poet makes the reader eliminate the name Hatem, which does not give the rhythm his ear expects! The Eastern masquerade is abandoned for autobiography, the ear confutes the eye, and Goethe's own name, beloved of men and gods, emerges with peculiar clarity, rhymed to perfection and irradiated by the most beautiful thing the world of sense can show: the rosy dawn.

May one call that "self-satisfaction," that awestruck sense of plenitude, of copious abundance, which pervades the consciousness of the darling of the gods? Goethe all his life had set his face against the affectation that might condemn such a feeling. He let it be known that in his opinion self-condemnation was the business of those who had no ground for anything else. He even openly spoke a good word for ordinary vanity, and said that the suppression of it would mean social decay, adding that the vain man can never be entirely crude. Whereupon follows the question: Is love of self ever quite distinguishable from love of humanity?

Wie sie sich an mich verschwendet,
Bin ich mir ein wertes Ich;
Hätte sie sich weggewendet,
Augenblicks verlör' ich mich.

And is not young Tolstoy's dream of glory, his craving to be known and loved, evidence of his love to the great *Thou* of the world? Love of the ego and love of the world are psychologically not to be divorced; which makes the old question whether love is ever altruistic, and not utterly egotistic, the most idle question in the world. In love, the contradiction between egotism and altruism is abrogated quite.

From which it follows that the autobiographical impulse scarcely ever turns out to be a mere dilettante trifling. It seems to carry its own justification with it. Talent, generally speaking, is a ticklish, difficult conception; the point of which is really less whether a man *can do* something than whether a man *is* something. One might almost say that talent is nothing more or less than a high state of adequacy to one's lot in life. But whose life is it that possesses this dignity in the face of destiny? With brains and sensibility anything can be made out of any life, out of any life a romantic existence can be made. Differing in this from the pure poetic impulse, which so often rests upon sheer self-deception, the autobiographic, as it seems, always presupposes a degree of brains and sensibility which justifies it beforehand; so that it need only become productive to be certain of our sympathy. Hence the conclusion I drew: that if the world sanction the love of self, which is at the bottom of the impulse, it will as a rule respond to it as well.

"Behold, what a marvellous creature lives upon this earth!" Gorky, contemplating Tolstoy, utters this inward cry. And this cry it is to which all biography seeks to move the world. Any human life, given brains and sensibility, can be made interesting and sympathetic, even the most wretched. J. J. Rousseau was not precisely one's idea of a darling of the gods. The father of the French Revolution was an unhappy wretch, half or three-quarters mad, and probably a suicide. Certainly the blend of sensibility and catarrh of the bladder displayed in the *Confessions* is not, aesthetically speaking, to everybody's taste. Nevertheless, his self-exposure contains and constitutes a claim upon the love of the world, which has been so abundantly honoured, with so many tears, that really one might call poor Jean Jacques the well-beloved, *le bien-aimé*. And this world-wide emotional response he owes to his bond with nature—rather a one-sided bond, it must be owned, for certainly this fool of genius, this exhibitionistic world-shaker, was a stepchild of the All-Mother rather than one of her pets, an accident of birth instead of a god-given miracle of favour and preference. His relation to nature was sentimental in the fullest sense of the word, and the tale of his life swept over the world in a wave of sentiment, not to say sentimentality. Poor Jean Jacques!

No, not in this tone does one refer to the two whom men called godlike, divine; in whom, as we have seen, important traits of Rousseau's character are reproduced. For they were not sentimental, scarcely had they occasion to yearn for nature, they themselves were nature. Their bond with her was not one-sided, like Rousseau's—or if it was, then it was nature who loved them, her darlings, loved them and clung to them, while on their side they drew away, and strove to free themselves from her heavy and earthbound domination; with indifferent success, it must be said, looking at them both singly and together. Goethe confesses: "So here I am, with all my thousand thoughts, sent back to be a child again, unacquainted with the moment, in darkness about myself." And to Schiller, the singer of the highest freedom, he writes: "How great an advantage your sympathy and interest will be to me you will soon see, when you discover in me a sort of sluggishness and gloom which is stronger than myself." And yet we may agree that Goethe's highly humanistic effort to "convert the cloudy natural product into a clear image of itself (i.e., of reason) and so discharge the duty and the claim of existence," as Riemer with extraordinary beauty expresses it, was crowned with a purer success than the attempt of Count Leo Nikolayevich Tolstoy to transform his life into the holy life of our blessed father the Boyar Lev, as Gorky says. This process of making a Christian and a saint of himself, on the part of a human being and artist so loved of nature that she had endowed him with godlikeness, was, as an effort at spiritual regeneration, most inept. Anglo-Saxondom hailed it with acclaim, but, after all, the spectacle is painful rather than gratifying, compared with Goethe's high endeavour. For there is no conflict between nature and culture; the second only ennobles the first, it does not repudiate it. But Tolstoy's method was not the enoblement but the renunciation of self, and that can quite easily become the most mortifying kind of deception. It is true that Goethe, at a certain stage in his development, called Götz the work of an undisciplined boy; but never did he so childishly and miserably calumniate his own art as the aging Tolstoy did, when he regretted having written Childhood, Boyhood, Youth, the fruit of his fresh youthful vigour, condemning it as insincere, literary, sinful; or when he spoke at large of "the artistic twaddle" that filled the twelve volumes of his works, and to which "people today ascribe an unmerited significance." That is what I call false self-renunciation, a clumsy attempt at spiritualization. Yet renounce himself as he would in words, his very existence gave him the lie; and Gorky looked at him, the patriarch with the "sly" little smile and the artist hands with their swollen veins, and thought to himself: "The man is like God." . . .

Tolstoy, in his Confessions, remarks that as a small child he knew nothing of nature, he had not even noticed her existence. "It is not possible," he says, "that I was given neither flowers nor leaves to play with, that I did not see the grass or the sunlight. And yet up to my fifth or sixth year I have no memory of what we call nature. Probably we have to get free from her in order to see her, and I myself was nature." From which can be deduced that even the mere seeing of nature, and our so-called enjoyment of her, are not only a specifically human condition, but one full of yearning emotion, in other words pathological, implying as it does our separation from her. Tolstoy's recollection is that he felt the pain of this separation for the first time when his childhood under the care of nurses came to an end and he moved over to his older brothers and the tutor Feodor Ivanovich in the lower storey. Never again, he assures us, did he feel so strongly what a sense of duty meant, and what, accordingly, moral and ethical obligation: "the feeling of the Cross, to carry which every one of us is called. It was hard for me to part from all I had known from everlasting. I was sad, sunk in poetical melancholy; less because I had to part from human beings, my nurse, my sisters, my aunt, than because I was leaving my little bed with its curtains and pillows. Moreover, I was apprehensive of the new life I was entering." The appearance of the word "Cross" in this connection is significant, not only with reference to Tolstoy, but also for the thing itself, the process of loosing oneself from nature. This process was felt by Tolstoy as painful and ethical: painful because ethical, and ethical because painful. He gives it a moral and an ascetic significance, as that which actually comprises all man's ethical obligation. To be humanized means, for him, to be denaturalized; and from that moment on, the struggle of his existence consists in this sort of humanizing process: in the divorce from nature, from everything that was natural and to him peculiarly so, for example from the family, the nation, the state, the church, from all the passions of the senses and the instincts, from love, the hunt, at bottom from all of physical life, and especially from art, which meant to him quite essentially the life of the body and the senses. It is quite wrong to think of this struggle as a crisis of conversion taking place suddenly in his later years; to make its inception roughly coincide with the beginning of old age. When the news came that the great Russian writer was as though stricken by a sort of mystical madness, the Frenchman Vogüé declared that he had long expected it. He was quite justified. The germ of Tolstoy's intellectual development had lain in *Childhood, Boyhood, Youth;* and the psychology of Levin in *Anna Karenina* plainly indicated what further course it would take. Besides, we have the evidence of Tolstoy's comrades-in-arms when he was an officer, the Sebastopol time. They give the clearest picture of the violence with which the struggle even then raged within him. But here we should note that his wrestling to break the strong bonds in which nature held him, regularly led up to disease, immediately assumed the form of illness. "Leochen is completely consumed by his writing now," so his wife, Countess Sophia Alexandrovna, puts it, about the year 1880, when he buried himself in theology and the philosophy of religion. It is a sight her love hates to see, and she constantly tries to call him back to creative work. "His eyes are strange and staring, he hardly speaks at all, he is like a being from another world, and is positively not capable of thinking of earthly things. . . ." "Leochen is quite sunk in his work. His head pains him all the time. He is very much changed, and become a rigid and practising Christian. But he has got grey, his health is weak, he is sadder and more silent all the time."—"Tomorrow we shall have been here a month," she writes in 1881 from Moscow, "and the first two weeks I wept every day without stopping, because Leochen was not only in a gloomy state, but fallen into a kind of despairing apathy. He ate nothing and did not sleep, sometimes literally wept—I honestly believe I shall lose my reason." And to her husband himself: "I am beginning to think that when a happy man suddenly begins to see only the horrible side of life, and has no eyes for anything good, he must be ill. You should do something for it, I say this in all seriousness. It seems so clear to me, I suffer so to see you. . . . Did you never know before that there were people in the world who were hungry, miserable, unhappy, and wicked? Open your eyes: there are also strong and healthy, happy and good ones. If God would only help you—what can I do? You must be ill," the poor woman wails—and is he not? He himself writes: "My health grows worse and worse, often I wish I could die. Why I am so reduced I do not know myself. Perhaps it is age, perhaps illness. . . ."

Compare with this the descriptions of him when he had sought in the holy animalism of married life a refuge from the insoluble riddles that his intellect set him; and then, with that power which the critics delighted to call "bearlike"—Turgenyev sought in vain to convince him that it came from the source whence all things come—created his two epic novels *War and Peace* and *Anna Karenina*. "He was always light-hearted then," his sister-in-law relates, "in high spirits, as the English say, fresh, healthy, and jolly. On the days when he did not write he went hunting with me or his neighbour Ribikov. We hunted with greyhounds. . . . Evenings he played patience in Tantchen's room." What happy days! Who can blame poor Countess Sophia Alexandrovna for scarcely containing herself for joy when she hears that her hollow-eyed Christian is planning a new imaginative work? Her happiness is touching. "What gladness suddenly filled me, to read that you mean to write something creative again! What I have so long awaited and hoped for has come to you. That is salvation, that is happiness, in it we shall come together again, it will console you and irradiate our life. This is the work you were made for, and outside this sphere there is no joy for your soul. God give you strength to cling to this ray of light, in order that the divine spark may flare up in you again. The thought fills me with ecstasy. . . ."

Goethe's and Tolstoy's biographies show that these great writers both alike suppressed for years their gift of plastic creation—for which, as Countess Sophia Alexandrovna says, they were born—and both in the service of a directly social activity—that is to say, on highly moral grounds.

Tolstoy suppressed the artist in him in favour of his activities as *mirovoi posrednik* (justice of the peace) and schoolmaster without pay. Goethe governed the dukedom of Saxe-Weimar, for ten years of his early manhood dedicated his powers to excise regulations, details of book manufacture, levies of recruits, construction of streets and water-conduits, workhouses, mines and quarries, finance, and other such matters—while Merck, in the style of Turgenyev, was constantly concerned to rescue him for literature, and he himself, with increasing resignation, steeling himself by inward exhortations to patience and fortitude, held himself to the heavy, hard, unrewarding, unnatural task. Added to all this, in Goethe's case, there was that somewhat seraphic affair with Frau von Stein. No doubt it was most beautifully instrumental in the process of civilizing the son of the Titans; but after all it did justice to but one of those famous two souls, which had, alas, their dwelling in his breast, and it let the other, the one with the *"klammernde Organen,"* the "avid organs," go empty away.—Well, in both cases, Goethe's and Tolstoy's, the result is illness. "My office as justice of the peace," writes Tolstoy, "has ended in destroying my good relations with the landowners, quite aside from the fact that it injures my health." Teaching the village children had the same result. True, in his pedagogical journal he claims that the exercises the children wrote were more accomplished than the writings of Leo Tolstoy, Pushkin, and Goethe; yet he discerns something evil and even criminal in his intercourse with them, it seems to him that he abuses and corrupts their souls. "It seemed to go very well," he says in the *Confessions*, "but I felt that I was mentally not healthy enough and that it could not go on so for much longer. I was more ailing mentally than physically; I threw it all overboard and drove out to the Kalmucks of the steppes to drink mares' milk and lead an animal life."— This absconding to the steppes vividly recalls the secret flight to Italy which was Goethe's salvation, after he too had seen that it could not go on so for much longer. The thirty-four-year-old man had become silent, taciturn, in plain words melancholy. He thought it was probably natural that a man should become serious over serious things. His health was actually undermined; by the time he was six-and-thirty his face was the face of a victim of exhaustion. For the first time he thought of taking a cure. He began to be aware of the ruinous perversity of his existence; expressed his view in the shrewd understatement that he was meant for private life. And fled before destruction. The parallel continues to hold: for Leo Nikolayevich, returned from the steppes and the mares'-milk cure, marries his Sophia Alexandrovna, who from then on finds herself almost continuously in the family way, and with epic and primeval power creates his two great novels.

While Goethe, back from Italy, takes Christiane Vulpius unto himself and, freed from the cares of office, gives his mind to his natural tasks. So much as a gloss upon a philosophy of disease.

Art is objective, creative contemplation, closely bound up with nature. Critique, on the other hand, is the moralizing, analysing attitude toward life and nature. In other words, critique is spirit; whereas creation is the preoccupation of the children of God and nature.

"In poetry my maxim was the objective principle," says Goethe. "I am a plastic artist (*ich bin ein Plastiker*)." Indeed, the contrast between Goethe's position and that of his great counterpart (Schiller standing for idealism, moralilzation, rhetoric—in short, for critique) is too well known to need labouring. Goethe regarded his own inborn poetic gift "quite as nature." His tolerance, his attitude of live and let live, the complaisance of his character, are all consonant with this view. They are based on the Spinozan concept of the perfectitude and necessity of all being, on the idea of a world free from final ends and final causes, in which evil has its rights like good. "We struggle," he declares, "to perfect the work of art as an end in itself. They, the moralists, think of the ulterior effect, about which the true artist troubles himself as little as nature does when she makes a lion or a humming-bird." It is a primary maxim with him that art is as inimical to purpose as nature herself; and this is the point where the follower of Spinoza sympathizes with Kant, who conceives detached contemplation as the genuine aesthetic state, thus making a fundamental distinction between the aesthetic-creative principle and the ethical-critical one. "When," says Goethe, "philosophy confirms and enhances our original feeling of our oneness with nature, turning it into a profound and tranquil contemplation, then I welcome it." I could cite ten or twelve other places in his works where in the name of art he repudiates the moral sanction—which indeed is always social as well. "It is possible, I suppose, for a work of art to have a moral effect; but to demand from the artist a moral purpose and intention is to spoil his craft for him."—"I have, in my trade as a writer, never asked myself: How shall I be of service to the world at large? All I have ever done was with the view of making myself better and more full of insight, of increasing the content of my own personality; and then only of giving utterance to what I had recognized as the good and the true."

When we contrast the Christian-social ethics of Tolstoy as an old man with Goethe's pagan and cultural idealism, we must not forget that the Tolstoyan socialism had its origin in the most private and personal need, the profoundest concern with the salvation of one's own soul. A permanent dissatisfaction with self, a tortured seeking for the meaning of life, was the source of this socialism. The moralist began all his teachings and reforms with a self-discipline (the *Confessions*, that is) such as the true and proper social critic never demands of himself. Revolutionary in the real and political sense of the word he can by no means be called. "The significance of the Christian doctrine," he declares, "is not that in its name society shall forcibly be reformed. It is that one shall find a meaning to life." And it should be pointed out that Tolstoy's original conception of art corresponded precisely to Goethe's—a fact that will surprise none but those who in all good faith accept him as a child of spirit, like Schiller and Dostoyevsky, on the ground of his naïve and clumsy efforts at spiritual regeneration, and fail to recognize in him a natural nobility akin to Goethe's own. Tolstoy's hatred of Shakespeare, which dates from much earlier than is generally realized, undoubtedly has its roots in antagonism against that universal and all-accepting nature: in the jealousy which a man enduring moral torment was bound to feel in face of the blithe irony of an absolutely creative genius. It was a reaction against nature, against the simple, against indifference to the moral point of view; and an impulse toward spirit—that is, toward an ethical and even social revaluation—a reaction so whole-souled, indeed, that it ended in his playing off against Shakespeare Mrs. Harriet Beecher Stowe, the creator of *Uncle Tom's Cabin*—an absurdity that only goes to show how very much the child of nature he was. Genuine sons of spirit and of the idea, like Schiller and Dostoyevsky, do not go aground on such fantastic coasts. Tolstoy's critical and moral faculty, in short his bias toward spirit, was but secondary, an act of will, and a feeble will at that. It always balked at organic union with his mighty creative gift; we have unequivocal declarations from him to the effect that, in his view, pure creative power stood higher than talent with a social coloration. As an old man he criticized Dostoyevsky for going in for politics, much as Goethe had criticized Uhland's activities in that line. At the age of thirty-one, in 1859, as a member of the Moscow society of the Friends of Russian Literature, he made a speech in which he so sharply accented the superiority of the purely artistic elements in literature over merits due to ulterior or ephemeral causes that the president of the society, Khomyakov, reminded him in a sharp rejoinder that a servant of pure art might very well, without knowing or wishing it, find himself indicting society.

An outburst of intellectual misgivings, of that humility of spirit to which the sons of nature are prone, occurs at the end of Tolstoy's novel *Lucerne*. Here is a splendid lament over the fate of man, who, with all his need of positive redemption, is flung into an ever billowing and shoreless ocean of good and evil. "If man," cries Tolstoy, "had only once learned not to judge and think so sharply and decisively, and not always to give answers to questions which are only put in order that they may remain forever questions! If he would only comprehend that every thought is at once false and true! . . . Men have divided up into sections this ever-rolling, boundless, eternally mingled chaos of good and bad; they have drawn themselves imaginary boundary-lines in this sea, and they expect the sea to divide according to their lines. As if it were not possible to make millions of other divisions, from other points of view, and on different planes! . . . Civilization is good, barbarism evil; freedom is good, unfreedom evil. This imaginary knowledge destroys in human nature the *original blissful and instinctive striving towards good.*" And asking himself whether in the souls of the poor there may not be more happiness and affirmation of life than in that of the callous rich man against whom, for his own part, his heart revolts, he bursts out with the words: "Endless is the goodness and wisdom of Him who has permitted and commanded all these contradictions. Only to you, poor worm, so presumptuously struggling to accomplish your schemes and devices, only to you do they seem contradictory. He looks mildly down from His radiant, immeasurable height and rejoices in the endless harmony wherein in endless opposition you all do move!"

Could one express oneself more "Goethically"? Even the *"Harmonie des Unendlichen"* is here. This is not mere philosophical or moral doubt; such words are too light, too thin, too intellectual to characterize the piety, the religious acceptance, the adoration of nature, that breathe from Tolstoy's page. This is not the voice of the prophet, schoolmaster, and reformer; here speaks the child of this world, the creative artist. Nature was his element, as she was the element, the beloved, kindly mother, of Goethe— and his constant tearing at the bond that held him fast to her, his desperate urging away from her in the direction of spirit and morality, from creation to critique, has much to command our respect and reverence, though at the same time there is about it something painful, tormenting, and humiliating, which is not present in the character of Goethe. Look at Tolstoy's attitude toward music, it is most instructive. When he met Berthold Auerbach in Dresden, that not too profound moralist told him that music is an irresponsible enjoyment, and added that irresponsible enjoyment is the first step toward immorality. Tolstoy, in his journal, made this clever and abominable phrase his own. His hatred and fear of music had the same moral and social basis as his hatred and fear of Shakespeare. We are told that at the sound of music he grew pale and his face became drawn with an expression very like horror. Notwithstanding, he was never able to live without music. In his earlier years he even founded a musical society. Before beginning work he habitually seated himself at the piano—that means a good deal. And in Moscow, when he sat beside Tchaikovsky and listened to the composer's Quartet in D major, he began to sob at the *andante*, before everybody. No, unmusical he was not. Music loved him, even though he, great moralizing infant that he was, felt that he ought not to return her love.

There is that legend of the giant Antæus, who was unconquerable because fresh strength streamed into him whenever he touched his mother earth. The lives of Goethe and Tolstoy irresistibly recall that myth. Both sons of mother earth, they differ only therein, that one of them was aware of the source of his nobility, the other not. There are places in Tolstoy's remorseful confessions where he touches the earth, and all at once his words, which, so long as they dealt in theory, were wooden and confused, are imbued with the most penetrating sensuousness, with an irresistible force and freshness of life. He recalls how once as a child he went nutting with his grandmother in the hazel wood. Lackeys instead of horses draw the grandmother's little carriage into the grove. They break through the undergrowth and bend the boughs, full of ripe, already dropping nuts, down into the old lady's lap and she gathers them into a bag. Little Leo marvels at the strength of the tutor, Feodor Ivanovich, who bends the heavy branches; when he lets go they spring up again and slowly mingle with the others. "I can feel how hot it was in the sun, how pleasantly cool in the shade, how we breathed the sharp scent of the foliage, while all round us the girls were cracking nuts between their teeth; we munched the full, fresh, white kernals without stopping."—The fresh, full, white kernals cracking between the girls' teeth: that is Antæus-Tolstoy, and the strength of his mother the earth streams through him, as it did when he wrote *War and Peace*, where his rather vague, fine-drawn, not very convincing philosophical digressions are followed by pages of which Turgenyev wrote: "They are glorious, they are the very best there is, everything original, everything descriptive, the hunt, the night boat-ride and all—nobody in Europe can touch him."

And Goethe: how the Antæus-consciousness governed his whole existence! How constantly it conditioned his seeking and shaping! Nature is to him "healing and comfort" after the visitations of passion; and while he well knows that to know her "one must have moulded all the manifestations of the human being into one definite and distinct entity," that true research is unthinkable without the gift of imagination, he is wary of the fantastic, avoids speculative natural philosophy, guards himself against losing touch with the earth, and calls the idea "the result of experience." The imagination that guides his research is intuitive, it is the inborn sympathy of the child of nature with the organic. It is Antæan, like the imaginative power which conditions his creative art, nor is that, either, capricious in its nature, but precise and based on the sense-perceptions. Such is the imagination of the creative artist. The sons of the thought, of the idea, of spirit, theirs is another kind. We will not say that the one creates more reality than the other. But the figures created by the plastic fancy possess the realism of sheer being; while those created by the "sentimental" artist evince their actuality by action. Schiller himself makes this distinction. Apart from the things they do, he himself confesses, they have something shadowy—"*etwas Schattenhaftes*" is his expression. Translate this from the sphere of German idealism into the Russian and revelational, and you get, as a sort of national pendant to Schiller's world of idea, rhetoric, and drama, the shadow-world of Dostoyevsky, over-life-size and exaggeratedly true. A catchword occurs to one from the philosophy of art, that is in everybody's mouth today, or at least was yesterday: the word "expressionism." Really, what we call expressionism is only a late form, strongly impregnated with the Russian and revelational, of romantic idealism. Its conflict with the epic attitude toward art, the conflict between contemplation and ecstatic vision, is neither new nor old, it is eternal. And it finds complete expression in on the one side Goethe and Tolstoy, on the other Schiller and Dostoyevsky. And to all eternity the truth, power, calm, and humility of nature will be in conflict with the disproportionate, fevered, and dogmatic presumption of spirit.

Very much, yes, precisely as Goethe's "profound and tranquil contemplation," his precise and sensuous fancy, the lifelikeness of his characters, stand in relation to the ideal visions of Schiller and the activism of his creations, so the mighty sense-appeal of Tolstoy's art stands to Dostoyevsky's sickly, distorted dream-and-soul world. Indeed, the contrast becomes even more pointed by reason of differences between nations and periods. Tolstoy, the realistic novelist, the prince-and-peasant scion of a race still young, displays in his art a sensuousness more powerful, more immediately fleshly in its appeal, than does the German humanist and classicist, bourgeois-born and patrician-bred, in his.

Compared with Eduard and Charlotte, the lovers in the *Wahlverwandtschaften*, Vronsky and Anna are like a fine strong stallion and a noble mare. The comparison is not mine; it has often been made. A certain school of Russian criticism, hostile, of course, and on a low plane, found most offensive Tolstoy's animalism, his unheard-of interest in the life of the body, his genius for bringing home to us man's physical being. These critics wrote, for instance, that *Anna Karenina* reeked with the classic odour of babies' diapers. They raved at the salaciousness of certain scenes, and ironically reproached Tolstoy for omitting to describe how Anna takes her bath and Vronsky washes himself. They were wrong even in the fact; for Tolstoy does tell us how Vronsky washes, we see him rubbing his red body. And in *War and Peace* we are vouchsafed a glimpse of Napoleon naked, in the scene where he has his fat back sprayed with eau-de-Cologne. A critic wrote in *Die Tat* about this book: "Its main theme is the satisfaction of any and every human being within the fold of wedded bliss, conceived in the grossest sense." And then the same critic, parodying Tolstoy's style, proposed to him that he write another novel treating of Levin's love for his cow Pania.

All this, of course, is on a lower plane than the criticism of Goethe which Caroline Herder wrote to Knebel: "Oh, if he would only give some soul to his characters! If only there were not so much philandering in everything that he writes, or, as he himself so likes to call it, so much 'good feeling.' " But unenlightened comment such as this may very well be illuminating none the less, even though unawares and as it were on false pretences; and these remarks, in their folly, do undoubtedly contain a grain of truth. Caroline's "philandering" is a mincing, sentimental word to characterize what Goethe wrote; yet it has a certain aptness, if the comparison is between his frank realism and the lofty insubstantiality of Schiller's world. It is not such a bad joke, either, to make Levin fall in love with his cow. It hits off the fleshliness of Tolstoy's art as contrasted with the holy soulfulness of Dostoyevsky's—especially when we remember Tolstoy's personal passion for one of the preoccupations of farm life— namely, the breeding of cattle and pigs. It is an interest quite proper, of course, to a landed proprietor; yet where so strongly marked as this surely not quite without deeper meaning. . . .

My subject is still the aspiration of the children of nature toward spirit; which is just as sentimental in kind as is the converse striving of the sons of the spirit toward nature, and may function with varying degrees of aptitude or success, with more or less naïveté or subtlety. Compared with Goethe's majestic work of spiritualization, I cannot find that Tolstoy's struggles to throw off nature's yoke were crowned with great success. But I am whimsical enough to relish putting my finger on the mighty kernel of racial loyalty which dwelt at the heart of the Christianity of the one and the humanity of the other. And that kernel was, of course, in other words, their aristocratic integrity; for racial loyalty is aristocratic by nature, while Christianity, humanity, and civilization all represent the conflicting principle of the spirit of democracy, and the process of spritualization is at the same time one of democratization. What Tolstoy aptly calls his "democratic trend"—aptly, because the word "trend" implies a will and a direction somewhither, indicating an effort and not mere being—finds emphatic expression now and again in Goethe as well. "One would have," he says, "to become *Catholic* at once, in order to have a share in the lives of humanity!" To mingle with humanity, on equal terms, to lead the life of the people, and in the market-place, seems at such moments happiness to him. "In these small sovereign states," he cries, "what wretched, isolated men we are!" And he praises Venice as a monument to the power, not of a single despot, but of a whole people. But such phrases, clearly, are meant more correctively than absolutely; they are self-critical comments, meant to redress the balance of his German and Protestant aristocratism—"tendencies," then, sentimental leanings, of the same kind as the radical and pacifistic bent of the Russian giant, in whose "holiness" a penetrating eye can see so much self-deception, childishness, and "let's pretend."

A close observer like Gorky, or a shrewd critic like Merezhkovsky, felt at once and keenly the patriarchal and sensual quality, the life-bound animalism, which lay beneath the sanctification. Tolstoy married at thirty-four the eighteen-year-old Sophia Alexandrovna Behrs, who from then on was scarcely ever anything but "expectant," and was confined thirteen times. Through long, creative years his marriage was an idyll of family life, full of healthy, God-fearing animal pleasure, against a lavish economic background of agriculture and cattle-breeding. The atmosphere was Judaic Old Testament rather than Christian. Tolstoy knows the same great simple love of existence, the everlasting childlike joy of life, that possessed Goethe's soul. When he "praises each day for its beauty," when he "marvels at the richness of God's kingdom" expressing itself therein, how "each day He sends some new thing to distinguish it," we are reminded of what may have lain at the bottom of Goethe's conception of *"Behagen."* Waves of piercing sensuous enjoyment of nature break upon him even in the years of gloom, when he meditates suicide, plans the *Confession*—in short, conjures up that misunderstanding to which his sanctification falls prey, and dehumanizes and shrinks the majesty of the patriarch, Christianizes and conventionalizes it into the Anglo-Indian model.

Merezhkovsky called him the great seer of the body, in contrast to Dostoyevsky the visionary of the soul; and truly it is the body to which his love and deepest interest belong, to which his knowledge refers, by which his genius is conditioned. We see this so clearly in his reaction to old age. In 1894 he writes: "Age is approaching. That means the hair falls out, the teeth decay, the wrinkles come, the breath gets bad. Even before the end, everything turns frightful, disgusting; sweat, rouge, powder, all sorts of beastliness. Then what has become of that which I have served? Where has beauty gone? It is the essence of everything. Without it there is nothing, no life."—This description of dying while the body still lives may pass for Christian, by virtue of its insistence on misery and its characterization of the flesh, revolting and insulting on the spiritual side. But the physical apprehension of old age and death is through and through pagan and sensual.

Aksakov says of Tolstoy: "His gift is *bearlike* in kind and degree." And is it not this "bearlike" quality of his genius that made Tolstoy "the great writer of Russia," the author of *War and Peace*, the epic poet of the people's struggle against Rome, against Napoleon? I openly declare my deliberate intention to cast doubt on the pacifism which the prophet of humanity so didactically professed. Not, I hasten to add, from any anti-pacifistic sentiments on my own part; merely out of a sense of humour. That Tolstoy was in his youth a soldier and an officer we know. From his biography we learn that he was heart and soul a soldier; and we have evidence of his heroic and warlike enthusiasm in the Sebastopol days— that "splendid time," that "glorious time," that time of touching pride in the Russian army, when he was confessedly saturated with patriotic feeling and thrilled by his experience of comradery under arms, first felt when the serious moment is at hand. His attitude toward the Serbo-Turkish war of 1877 is still full of conviction. It is a *real* war, he says, and it moves him. The distinction between "real" and "unreal" doubtless indicates some progress in the direction of pacifism. But is pacifism "real" so long as it is conditional and must progress in order to exist?

In 1812, at least, there *was* a "real" war, and its history occupied Tolstoy long before he became the great writer of Russia by dint of it. He treated of it, quite in the patriotic key, in his school at Yasnaya Polyana. From all we hear, he dealt with it on a mythical rather than a historical basis; but he expressly declared that he presented his pupils with these legends of a warlike mythology in order to rouse their patriotic feeling. And then the root-and-branch Russianism, the fundamental folk-character of his peasant-patrician nature, comes out strong in his epos, whose theme is a defensive war waged against the invasion of Latin civilization. *War and Peace* had a huge popular success, though the critics and military men had some fault to find. *On the intellectual side it was weak,* they said; its philosophy of history was narrow and superficial; it was mysticism and sophistry to deny the influence of individuals on events. But the creative power, the "bearlike" strength of it, were unanimously declared to be beyond all discussion, as well as its enormous genuineness as a folk-epic. The liberal criticism of Russia admitted that it was "Russian to the core," that it "presented the soul of the Russian people, in its whole range and variety, in all its lofty simplicity, with a sheer creative power that had never been equalled." But the critics took in bad part Tolstoy's "wilful remoteness from all contemporary *currents of progress*"—a phenomenon and a reproach which were to recur with the appearance of *Anna Karenina*. "*Anna Karenina* I don't like," Turgenyev wrote, "though there are splendid things in it: the race, the mowing, the hunt. But the whole thing is soured; it *smells of Moscow,* and old maids and incense and Slavophils and high life and all that." In a word, Turgenyev, the *Sapadnik,* rejected with horror the Oriental element in the novel, and with him went the whole liberal-radical party; some ignored *Anna Karenina,* others sneered or called names, while the Slavophils and the aristocrats and court party rubbed their hands in glee. In fact Tolstoy, in an intellectual and political sense, had the reactionaries on his side; and they could have little appreciation of the artistic qualities of his work. The liberals were liberal enough to know how to value these, and they did so, albeit in that state of bewilderment into which people always fall at the sight of genius in the camp of reaction. Witness the bewilderment of Europe over Bismarck.

The paradox is worth a little attention. Our idealists would have us believe that genius, the creative power, must, as a living force, act only in the service of progress and human purpose, and be justly denied to the forces that side against life, show sympathy with death, and are inimical to freedom and progress and thus bad in the human sense. We would almost accept it as metaphysical evidence for the goodness of a thing if a capital piece of writing were done in its name. And really, it does seem that, as a rule, the reactionary camp suffers from lack of talent. But not invariably. The reactionary genius does occur, the brilliant and conquering ability does act as attorney for retrograde tendencies—and nothing dazes the world more than the sight of this paradoxical phenomenon. Sainte-Beuve said of Joseph de Maistre that he had "nothing of a writer but the gift"—a comment which perfectly expresses this bewilderment and precisely indicates the thing I mean.

Liberal and progressive Russia must have seen in Tolstoy just this— a case of a great gift in the service of reaction. But it is clear enough that this great gift is of one essence with his fundamental Russianism, his immense integration with the people, his pagan and natural aristocracy; and that the tendency toward democratic spiritualization was—just tendency, romantic in its nature and crowned, after all, by such strikingly indifferent success! His tremendous Orientalism found intellectual expression in this mockery at and denial of European progress; and this it was which must necessarily and profoundly alienate all the Westernizing and liberalizing, all the "Petrinic" elements in Russia. Actually, he quite frankly scouted the Western belief in progress, which, he said, had been accepted by the Russia of Peter the Great. They had, he said, observed the operation of the law of progress in the Duchy of Hohenzollern-Sigmaringen, with its three thousand inhabitants. But then came China, with its two hundred million inhabitants, and knocked the theory of progress into a cocked hat. Which did not for one moment prevent them from believing in progress as a general law of mankind; they took the field with cannons and guns to instruct the Chinese in their thesis. Yet ordinary human understanding tells us that if the history of the larger part of mankind, which we call the Orient, does not confirm the law of progress, then this law does not obtain for the whole of mankind, but forms at most an article of faith for a certain part of it. Tolstoy vows that he himself is unable to find a universal law in the life of mankind, and that history might be co-ordinated just as well in the light of any other idea or "historical whimsy" as in that of progress. And more than that, he does not see the slightest necessity of finding laws for history—quite apart from the impossibility of the thing. The universal, eternal law of perfection, he says, stands written in the soul of every human being; it is only an error to carry it over into the field of history. So long as it remains personal, this law is fruitful and accessible to all; applied to historical conceptions, it is idle talk. The general progress of mankind is an unproved thesis. It does not exist for any of the nations of the East; hence it is just as unfounded to assert that progress is a primary law of mankind as it would be to say that blondness is—all people being blond save those with dark hair.

It is remarkable to see how ideas from the sphere of an idealistic individualism, which is German, and places human perfection within the individual soul, are here found in the company of others which constitute the most decisive challenge to an arrogant Europe setting itself up as intellectual arbiter of the world. Tolstoy protests against what he considers the childishness of this attitude, which confuses western Europe with humanity as a whole; and the protest betrays that his gaze is directed eastward. It betrays, in a word, his Asiatic bias: anti-"Petrinic," primitive Russian, anti-civilization—in short, *bearlike*. What we hear is the voice of the Russian god on the maple throne under the golden lime tree. . . .

"I am reading Goethe. My mind teems," Tolstoy wrote in his journal at the beginning of the sixties. He was then a man of some thirty years and had not long returned to Russia and begun his work as a preaching and practising pedagogue. What was he reading? Was it contact with German idealism and humanism that made his mind so to "teem"? It was an alien sphere to him. For in Tolstoy (otherwise than in Goethe) the origin of the pedagogic impulse was immediately social and ethical. A man of parts and attainments, said he, must share with those who lack such blessings before he can derive pleasure from them himself. The motive seems a poor one to me; rationalizing and humanitarian, like all the conscious thought of the great artist just then, I find it deeply inferior to the beautiful humanity of Goethe, in whom the social ideal was an organic outgrowth of the cultural and educational. But what Tolstoy thought was usually smaller than what he was. And to come back to our starting-point: what was it made his mind "teem" when he read Goethe and at the same time set to work as singlehanded schoolmaster and founder of a primary school to put into practice the pedagogic ideas that rumbled in his belly?

Or, rather, to experiment with them. For he had made up his mind to settle, by actual experiment, what it was that the people, and in particular youth, wanted to be taught; it had not been settled, and that it had to be settled was his primary pedagogical thesis. "The people," he said, "this most interested party in the whole situation, party and judge in one, listens quietly to our more or less ingenious exposition as to the best way of preparing and presenting its mental fodder. It is not disturbed; for it perfectly knows that in the great business of its mental development it will never take a false step, or accept anything that is false; and that all efforts to force it into paths unsuited to it, for instance German paths, will be like water on a duck's back." One must recognize, Tolstoy declares in writing and controversy, that the German type of school is a desirable one; that is a fact for which history vouches. But, even so, one may as a Russian hesitate to enter the lists in favour of a primary school which does not yet exist there. What historical argument can be brought for the assertion that Russian schools must be like those in the rest of Europe? The people, he says, need education, and every human being seeks it unconsciously. The more highly cultivated classes, society, and government officials, seek to extend the benefits of their knowledge and to educate the less educated masses. One would suppose that such a concurrence of the needs of both classes, the giving as well as the receiving, would suffice. But no. The masses steadily oppose all efforts made in their behalf to educate them, so that these are often entirely futile. Whose is the fault? Which is more justified: the opposition, or the system against which it is directed? Must the opposition be broken or the system altered? The latter, Tolstoy decides, is the case. "Shall we not," he asks, "confess honourably and openly that we do not, cannot, know what the needs of the coming generations will be; but that we feel none the less bound to investigate? That we will not charge the masses with ignorance because they will not accept our education; but rather accuse ourselves of both ignorance and arrogance if we go on trying to educate them on our own lines? Let us at least cease to see hostility in the resistance of the people to our system; and find in it the expression of the people's will, which alone should guide us. Let us at last accept the fact, so clearly evinced by the whole history of pedagogics, that if the educating class are to know what is good and what bad, the class to be educated must have full power to register dissatisfaction, and opportunity to reject a system which they instinctively find unsatisfying; that, in short, *freedom* is the sole criterion of educational methods."

"The sole criterion of education is freedom, the sole method experience, experimentation." This is Tolstoy's first and highest pedagogic maxim. According to him, the school should be at once a means of education and an experiment performed on the rising generation, an experiment productive of ever new results. It should, in other words, be an educational laboratory, where the experiment of pedagogic science seeks to create a firm basis for itself. To do this, it is necessary that it function under circumstances that ensure the value of its results—that is, in freedom. The school as it is, Tolstoy declares, enfeebles the children by distorting their mental faculties. During the most precious period of development it wrenches the child out of the family circle, robs him of the joy of freedom, and makes of him a jaded, suppressed creature, upon whose face rests an expression of weariness, fear, and boredom, while with his lips he repeats strange words in a language he does not know. But if we give the people freedom during their training, then we also give them the chance to speak out on the score of their necessities, and furthermore to choose among the kinds of knowledge offered. Philosophers from Plato to Kant have unanimously striven to free the school from the feters of tradition. They have sought to discover wherein the intellectual needs of man consist, and to build up new schools on these more or less correctly envisaged needs. Luther demands that the masses shall study the Scripture from the original text, and not from the commentaries of the Fathers. Bacon advises the study of nature from nature herself and not from the works of Aristotle. Rousseau wants to teach life *from life*, as he conceives it, and not from outworn experience. All philosophy stands for freeing the school from the idea of instructing the younger generation in that which the older generation held to be science; and in favour of the idea of teaching them what they themselves need. And we can see by the history of pedagogic science that every step forwards consists in greater natural *rapport* between pupil and teacher, in less compulsion and greater facilitation of the process of learning.

Tolstoy, then, an anarchistic pedagogue, sets his face against discipline. "The school in which there is less compulsion," he says, "is better than the one in which there is more. The method which can be introduced without increased disciplinary strain is good; one which requires greater severity is surely wrong. Take a school like mine and try to carry on conversations about tables and corners of rooms or shove little dice to and fro. A frightful disorder will reign at once, and it will be absolutely necessary to restore order. But tell them an interesting story or set them an interesting task, or let someone write on the board and the others correct, and *let them all out of their benches,* and they will all be busy, and there will be no mischief, and no increased discipline will be necessary. We may safely say that this way is good."

"The children bring nothing with them," thus Tolstoy describes the procedure at Yasnaya Polyana, "neither primers nor copy-books. These are no tasks to take home. They need not remember anything—nothing of what they did the day before. They need carry nothing, either in their hands or in their heads. They bring nothing with them but their receptive natures and the conviction that school will be just as jolly today as it was yesterday; they only think of the instruction when it has begun. No one who comes late is ever scolded, and they never come late, except some of the older ones, whose fathers occasionally keep them to work. When that happens, they run as fast as they can to school and get there breathless."

Lucky village children of Yasnaya Polyana! But it is comprehensible that Tolstoy tries to make the school at least pleasant for his pupils; his faith in its educational value is weak, and he makes in the end no secret of his conviction—which he declares he derived from personal observation in the schools of Paris, Marseille, and other cities of western Europe—that the greater part of popular education is gained, not from school, but from life; and that free public instruction, by means of lectures, clubs, books, exhibitions, and so on, remains far superior to any teaching in schools. But be that as it may; what interests us here is not the rightness or wrongness of Tolstoy's ideas, but rather what is characteristic in them; and characteristic they certainly are, in the highest degree, and from every point of view, not only in a personal sense, but also as a sign, even as an augury of his time.

What strikes one first of all, then, is a note that sounds in clearest contradiction to certain other of his doctrines: to the pacifistic and antinational ones, to the thesis of democratic equality he preached in his latter days. It is the national note. He emphasizes the right of the Russian people to an education suited to their genius, independently of the foreign spirit. His root-and-branch Russianism, at this time still quite unregenerate, denies the right of the upper and official classes, with their west-European liberal education, to force upon the masses an education not suited to their actual needs. Here he is turning against Peter the Great, who created these official classes and gave them their orientation toward liberalism and the west. Tolstoy's educational ideas are all extreme anti-"Petrinic," anti-western, anti-progressive. He openly declares that the educated class is not capable of giving the masses their proper training, conceiving, as it does, that the well-being of the people lies in the direction of civilization and progress. What speaks out of Tolstoy's mouth, what rules his thinking, is Moscow. It is that leaning toward Asia which so alarmed Turgenyev and others like him in Tolstoy's writings and which here is elevated to a pedagogic principle. His anarchism, his faith in the anarchistic principle as the single reasonable basis of communal human life; his doctrine that absolute freedom makes all discipline superfluous—all these are part of it, and it and they are expressed in Tolstoy's prescription to "Let all the children out of the benches" and free them from every oppressive sense of duty.

This *"letting all the children out of the benches"*—a picturesque and stimulating formula—is a perfect symbol for Tolstoy's social and political (or, rather, his anarchistic, antipolitical) views. His famous letter to Czar Alexander III develops these most concisely. The new Czar's father had been murdered on the 13th of March 1881; and Tolstoy wrote begging him to exercise clemency toward the murderers. He here sets down for the Emperor, in words so compelling that one almost wonders at their not prevailing, the two *political* expedients that had been applied up to date against increasing political disorder: first, force and terror; and second, liberalism, constitution, parliament. Both these have finally shown themselves impotent. There remains, however, a third expedient, which is not of a political nature and which has at least the advantage of having never yet been tried. It consists in the fulfilment of the divine will regardless of consequences, without any cautious reservations of policy; quite simply in love, forgiveness, the requital of evil with good; in mildness, in non-resistance against evil, in freedom. . . . In a word, Tolstoy advises the Czar to "let all the children out of the benches"; he counsels anarchy—I am not using the word in a derogatory sense, but quite objectively, to specify a definite social and political gospel of salvation.

The Asiatic bias of this great Russian genius has already been shown to be a mixture of various psychical elements: Oriental passivity, religious quietism, and an unmistakable tendency to Sarmatian wildness. Here, in this anarchistic theory, it lies down with quite different company: with the revolutionary ideals of western Europe, with the educational and political conceptions of Rousseau and his pupil Pestalozzi, in both of whom there is present the element of wildness, the return to nature—in short, the anarchistic element in another form and under other colours. Here, then, we are arrived at the common factor in the education of our two protagonists—but with a difference. On the educational side, Goethe fell away from his allegiance to Rousseau. Pedagogic Rousseauianism, as preached and practised by its founder, revolted him. Furiously, even desperately, he rejected it, and the anarchical individualism of the revolutionary education.

Boisserée tells how Goethe expressed to him his distress on the score of Pestalozzi and his system. For its original purpose and in its original setting, where Pestalozzi had only the children of the people in mind, the poor who lived in their isolated huts in Switzerland and could not send their children to school, it might be a capital idea. But it became the most destructive one in the world so soon as it ceased to confine itself to elementary teaching and went on to language, art, the general field of knowledge and power, which of course presupposed a *previous tradition*. . . . And then the insubordination this cursed kind of education aroused: look at the impudence of the little school-urchins, who feel no awe of any stranger, but rather put him in a fright instead. All respect gone, everything done away with that makes human beings human beings in their relations with each other. "What should I have been," cried Goethe, "if I had not always been obliged to show respect for others? And these men, in their madness and frenzy, to reduce everything to terms of the single individual and be simply gods of self-sufficiency! They think to educate a nation which shall stand against the barbaric hordes, just as soon as the latter shall have mastered the elementary tools of understanding, which Pestalozzi has made it so very easy for them to do."

Tradition, reverence—which "makes human beings human beings in their relations with each other"—conformity of the ego within a noble and estimable community; do you not feel the nearness of the Pedagogic Province? Let me recall a moment that dream so wise and splendid, at once austere and blithe, in which can be traced much of the humanism of the eighteenth century, much of the spirit of the *Zauberflöte*, of Sarastro and the "moving toward good with one's hand in a friend's"; and which at the same time contains so much that is new and bold and, humanly speaking, advanced that it cannot be called less revolutionary than Tolstoy's educational ideas. Only, of course, the anarchistic flavour is utterly lacking;

while its conception of humanity and human dignity, culture and civilization is so consonant with solemn regulation and gradation, with such a pronounced sense of reverence, of traditions, symbols, mysteries, and rhythm, with such a symmetrical, almost choreographic restraint in its freedom, that I may be permitted to call it statesmanlike in the best and finest sense, by way of pointing the contrast to Tolstoy's letting the children out of the benches. However, the boys and youths of Goethe's dream-province do not sit glued to their benches either; at least we do not see them thus. The basis of their education is quite in the Pestalozzian style: it is husbandry. And their training goes forward in the open air, work and play constantly accompanied by singing. We are told, quite explicitly, what its essence is: "Wise men lead the boys to find out themselves what is fitted for them; and shorten the by-ways into which man will often too readily turn aside." Every well-marked bent to a pursuit is fostered and cultivated, for "to know and practice one thing rightly gives higher culture than half-way performance of a hundred things." But if the education is thus adapted to the individual, it is not thereby in the very least individualistic—so little, in fact, that respect for convention is insisted upon, and regarded as a conspicuous characteristic of genius; for genius understands that art is called art just because it is not nature; and easily accommodates itself to paying respect to the conventions, in the view that they represent "an agreement arrived at by the superior elements of society, whereby the essential and indispensable is regarded as the best." That is hostility toward the voluntary, with a vengeance; and the Head is at pains to define and interpret it by a musical parallel. "Would a musician," he asks, "let a pupil make a wild attack on the keyboard or invent intervals to please himself? No, the striking thing is that nothing is left to the choice of the learner. The element in which he is to work is fixed, the tool he must use put into his hand, even the way he shall use it is prescribed—I mean the change of fingers, in order that one get out of the other's way and make the path plain for its successor; until by dint of this regulated co-operation and thus alone the impossible at last becomes the possible."—It is not by chance, I insist, that the Heads of the Province draw their parallel from the field of music: is she not truly the most spirited symbol for that regulated co-operation of manifold elements toward an end and goal which is culturally noble and worthy of humanity? In the Pedagogic Province song presides over all the activities, everything else is linked with it and communicated by it. "The simplest pleasures as well as the simplest tasks are animated and impressed by song; yes, even our instruction in morals and religion is communicated in this wise." Even the elements of knowledge, reading, writing, reckoning, are derived from song, notewriting, and putting text beneath, and from observing the basic measures and notation—in short, as agriculture is the natural, so music is the spiritual element of education, "for from it level paths run out in all directions."

Another great German and shaper of German destiny comes to mind here: Luther's view of music as an instrument of education was very like Goethe's. *"Musicam,"* he says, "I have always loved. One should accustom youth to this art, for it makes fine, capable people. A schoolmaster who cannot sing I will not look at." And in the schools under his influence there was almost as much singing as in the Pedagogic Province—whereas no one would know whether they sang in Tolstoy's school or not. To the wanderer through the Pedagogic Province it seems as though none of its inhabitants did anything of his own power, but as though a mysterious spirit animated them through and through, leading them on toward one single great goal. This spirit is the spirit of music, of culture, of "regulated co-operation," whereby alone at length "the impossible"—that is to say, the state as work of art—becomes possible; it is a spirit remote from and hostile to all barbarism; one would like to be allowed to call it a German spirit.

The salutation in three degrees, whose meaning, the threefold reverence, is kept secret from the boys themselves, because mystery and respect for the mysterious is a moral and civilizing influence; the insistence upon modesty and decorum; the lining up and standing at attention of the young human being in face of the world, and his honourable comradeship with his kind; the enhancing of his own honour through the honours he renders; all this militarism so highly imbued with the spirit and with art— how far it is from the rational radicalism of Tolstoy's Christianity, with its heart of wildness! Is it anyway credible that, in essentials, a remarkable likeness subsists between the educational conceptions of our two geniuses?

Tolstoy in all pious simplicity once declared that the world can find salvation simply by no longer doing anything which does not seem inherently reasonable: that is to say, anything which our whole European world is doing today; for example, teaching the grammar of dead languages. What finds utterance, what bursts forth, in this polemic against the study of ancient tongues is the revolt of the Russian people against humanistic civilization itself. Tolstoy's unclassic paganism stands revealed, his ethnic godhead, which, according to Gorky, was not Olympian, but more like that of a Russian god, "sitting on a maple throne, under a golden lime tree." Tolstoy's pedagogic writing betrays an extremely anti-humanistic, anti-literary, anti-rhetorical conception of the relative importance of different branches of study. He has anything but the traditional European view of the importance of the discipline of reading and writing; entertaining not the faintest humanistic fear of "analphabetism," but rather openly defending what to our way of thinking would almost amount to a state of barbarism. "We see people," he says, "who are equipped with all the knowledge necessary for farming; who perfectly comprehend all its bearings, though they can neither read nor write; or capital military leaders, tradespeople, foremen, machine-overseers, labourers, all people who got their training from life, not books, and stored up large resources of information and reflection, but who, again, can neither read nor write. On the other hand we see people who can both read and write, but who have not profited by this advantage to learn any new thing." When he dwells upon the conflict between the needs of the people and the learning forced upon them by the ruling classes, he has in mind the fact that the elementary schools are an outgrowth of the higher ones. First the church school, then the higher education, then after that the primary school—a false hierarchy, for it is false that the primary school, instead of conforming to its own needs, should conform—only on a smaller scale—to the demands of the higher education. His meaning is clear. He finds the folk-school too literary, too much subordinated to the classical ideal of education, not practical or vital enough, not guided by the principle of training for a calling in life. But we shall be mistaken in expecting from him any greater kindness for either the system or the spirit of the higher institutions of learning. He accuses them of being "entirely divorced from actual life." He compares the true education derived from life itself with that offered to the academic student, and finds that the former produces men capable in their calling, the latter merely "so-called people with a university education—advanced, that is to say irritable, sickly liberals." He gives "Latin and rhetoric" another hundred years of life, not more, and so much only for the reason that "when the medicine has once been bought, one must take it." The phrase betrays plainly enough his attitude toward classical education, toward the traditional European culture, toward humanism. It betrays at the same time his attitude toward the west and civilization, his folk-hatred of all that is not of the people, that is foreign, that comes from abroad, that has merely a cultural value—in short, the anger of primitive Russia against Peter the Great.

It is time we looked round in the Pedagogic Province for the place where youth busies itself with the ancient tongues. And, after all, it is rather a shock not to find it. Goethe is not such a barbarian as to despise the study of language or languages, as a cultural instrument. He calls it enthusiastically the most sensitive in the world, and emphasizes its value as a civilizing agent, by having his imaginary pupils take it in connection with the rude tasks of stable-work; so that, caring for and training animals, they do not become like animals themselves. But the langauges here are modern languages. The tongues of various nations are studied in turn—but Latin and Greek, it will be noted, are not in the curriculum.

Well, there are other things which are not expressly mentioned either. But that precisely these subjects should be absent is after all rather striking. Was Goethe a humanist, or was he not? In the first place, his humanism was always of another and a broader kind than merely the philological. And in the second place, the impress of a certain high austerity lies upon all the regulations of the Pedagogic Province, despite the Parnassian blitheness that reigned there. There is no doubt that Goethe, in his consciously pedagogic period, felt toward the humanistic, Winkelmannian ideal of education much as Tolstoy and Auerbach did about music: a moral severity against the sybaritic, dilettante, the roving and ranging, sipping and changing, which he considered the danger of the "universally human" ideal as applied to pedagogy. He considered this danger more threatening than the peril of specialization and its consequent narrowness and inpoverishment—the horrors of which we later comers, to be sure, have learned to know. He espouses the cause of vocational against verbal training, out of the same anti-literary tendency which we observed in Tolstoy; sharing with him the conviction that human culture makes sounder progress by the method of limitation; he is radical enough to use the *Wanderjahre* as a mouthpiece through which to shout "*Narrenpossen* (Stuff and nonsense)!" at the "universally human" educational ideal and "all its works." That is severe. But today, when nobody any longer can live on his income, does it not sound like an uncommonly clear-sighted prophecy when he declares: "Whoever from now on does not take to either an art or a trade will have a hard time of it"?

I have made no secret of my tendency to interpret the paganism of the children of nature in a primarily ethical sense. And I am greatly strengthened by this astonishingly radical and decisive rejection, on Goethe's part, of a humane and literary education. Almost I might have dared interpret that gruff "*Narrenpossen!*" as the revolt of Germanic folkishness against the humanistic culture itself. I have every warrant for asserting that Goethe would have fought like Tolstoy the folly of offering watered scholarship to the people for education—a folly by which one waters the people's sense and spirit, debases and insults, instead of, as one fondly imagines, elevating them! Goethe, who in the *Wahlverwandt-schaften* advances—surreptitiously, *"weil die Menge gleich verhöhnet"*—the reactionary and esoteric doctrine: "Bring up the boys to be servants and the girls to be mothers, then all will be well": was he the man to advocate the breeding of "advanced, that is to say irritable and sickly liberals"? And was there not perhaps prophetic vision at work in the severity and the limitations of his educational principles? Did his sense of time, like the Russian's give "Latin and rhetoric" a limit of some hundred years of life? Strange events in our Europe today incline one to regard his maxims in a prophetic light.

The great Revolution in Russia brought to the light of day—that light which is so good at illuminating the *surface* of things—the western Marxism which had put its impress upon Tolstoy's country. But it must not blind us to the spectacle of the Bolshevist Revolution as the end of an epoch: the epoch of Peter the Great, the western, liberalizing, European epoch in the history of Russia, which now, with this Revolution, faces eastward once more. It was to no European idea of progress that the last Czar fell victim. In him Peter the Great was murdered, and his fall opened to his people not the path toward Europe, but the way home to Asia. But is there not also in western Europe, precisely since the time of this crisis— whose prophet Leo Tolstoy was, although Moscow sees it not—is there not also in western Europe a feeling alive that not only for Russia, but for it, for us, for all the world there is at hand the ending of an epoch: the bourgeois, humanistic, liberal epoch, which was born at the Renaissance and came to power with the French Revolution, and whose last convulsive twitchings and manifestations of life we are now beholding? The question is put today whether this Mediterranean, classic, humanistic tradition is commensurate with humanity and thus coeval with it, or whether it is only the intellectual expression and apanage of the bourgeois liberal epoch and destined to perish with its passing. . . .

Beautiful is resolution. But the really fruitful, the productive, and hence the artistic principle is that which we call reserve. In the sphere of music we love it as the painful pleasure of the prolonged note, the teasing melancholy of the not-yet, the inward hesitation of the soul, which bears within itself fulfilment, resolution, and harmony, but denies it for a space, withholds and delays, scruples exquisitely yet a little longer to make the final surrender. In the intellectual sphere we love it as irony: that irony which glances at both sides, which plays slyly and irresponsibly—yet not without benevolence—among opposites, and is in no great haste to take sides and come to decisions; guided as it is by the surmise that in great matters, in matters of humanity, every decision may prove premature; that the real goal to reach is not decision, but harmony, accord. And harmony, in a matter of eternal contraries, may lie in infinity; yet that playful reserve called irony carries it within itself, as the sustained note carries the resolution. In the foregoing pages I have tried it, this "infinite" irony; and my readers may judge upon which extreme it more enjoyed playing, at which side of the eternal contradiction it took keener aim—and draw their conclusions accordingly; only not too far-reaching ones!

Irony is the pathos of the middle . . . It is not, in general, the German way to be hasty in deciding the aristocratic problem—if I may, in this phrase, sum up the whole complex of contrasted values dealt with in the present essay. We are a people of the middle, of the world-bourgeoisie; there is a fittingness in our geographical position and in our *mores*. I have been told that in Hebrew the words for knowing and insight have the same stem as the word for between.

That German writer who has most urgently pondered upon the problem of aristocracy was, philologically speaking, greatly daring when he invented a derivation for the name of the German people: from *Tiusche-Volk*; that is, *Täusche-Volk*. But, for all that, the idea is full of esprit. A people settled in the bourgeois world-middle must needs be the *täuschende*, protean folk: a race that practises sly and ironic reserve toward both sides, that moves between extremes, easily, with non-commital benevolence; with the morality, no, the piety of that elusive "betweenness" of theirs, their faith in knowledge and insight, in cosmopolitan culture.

Fruitful dilemma of the middle, thou art freedom and reserve in one! Let them tell us, as they have told us, that this free-handed policy of ours has brought us, in actual practice, to grief. Practice is doubtful, this disaster even more so. More than probably it came upon us for our own best good; more than probably we were striving to bring it about in a deeper sense than any in which man ever strives to encompass his happiness. Again, devotion in the face of failure is no more noble than humility in the face of success; and nothing but defeatism could shake our faith in the rightness and sanctity of a spiritual attitude whose craving for freedom and ironic reserve is justified, not as an end and aim, but as a final synthesis and harmony, the pure idea of man himself.

That mutual character of the sentimental longing—of the sons of spirit for nature, of the sons of nature for spirit (for, as we found, it is not spirit alone that is sentimental)—argues a higher unity as humanity's goal; which she, in very truth the standard-bearer of all aspiration, endows with her own name, with *humanitas*. That instinct of self-preservation, full of reserve as it is, felt by the German people in their central position as a world-bourgeoisie, is genuine nationalism. For that is the name we give to a people's craving for freedom, to the pains they take with themselves, to their effort after self-knowledge and self-fulfilment. So too the artist is loyally and devotedly convinced that his only thought is to wrest his own work and his very own dream out of the block of stone; and yet, in some solemn and moving hour, may learn that the spirit which possessed him had a purer source, that from the stone he carved there is emerging a loftier image than he knew.

Folk, and humanity. It was a seer out of the east, one of those who, like Goethe, Nietzsche, and Whitman, have looked long into the slowly mounting dawn of a new religious sense—it was Dmitri Merezhkovsky who has said that the animal contains the beast-man and the beast-god. The essence of the beast-god is as yet scarcely comprehended by man, yet it is only the union of the beast-god with the god-man that will some day bring about the redemption of the race of mankind. This "some day," this idea of a redemption, which is no longer Christian and yet not pagan either, carries in itself the solution of the problem of aristocracy, as well as justifying, yes, sanctifying, all ironic reserve on the subject of ultimate values.

We have dealt with confidence with great natures, great creative artists, children of God, in whom the beast-god was strong, as also their sense of self, their feeling for repose, for woman, for the people; we have revelled in the intellectual power of those world-spirits who tempered and humanized their confessed egotism with a strain of the didactic impulse. More hesitantly we have trenched upon the god-man sphere of those others, their emotional opposites, the men of deeds, the sons of spirit, the saintly and sickly. The true saying of that Russian that the essence of the beast-god is as yet scarcely apprehended by man might strengthen our faith in the ironic doctrine that there is more of grace among those who at bottom "can love nobody but themselves." But well we know that there is no deciding the question which of these two lofty types is called to contribute more and better to the highly cherished idea of a perfected humanity.

VIKTOR SHKLOVSKY

Parallels in Tolstoy

In order to make of an object an ar-
tistic fact, one must pry it loose of the facts of life. To do this it is necessary
to "shake up" the thing the way Ivan the Terrible used to "shake up" his
henchmen. It is necessary to tear it out of the context of habitual associations, to turn it like a log in a fire. The artist is always the instigator of
a revolt of things. With poets, things mutiny, shuck off their old names;
in assuming new ones they take on a new aspect. The poet uses images—
tropes, similes. He calls fire a red flower, he attaches new epithets to old
nouns. He will even, like Baudelaire, say that the carrion raised its legs
like a woman inviting obscene caresses. In this way the poet effects a
"semantic shift." He snatches a notion from the semantic plane at which
it is usually found, and with the aid of a word (trope) he transfers it to a
new semantic plane. We are struck by the novelty resulting from placing
the object in a new ambience. A new word fits the object like a new dress.
This is one way of converting an object into something palpable, something
capable of becoming the material of art. Another method is to create a
"staircase-like construction": an object is bifurcated through the medium
of reflections and juxtapositions. This strategy is nearly universal. Many
stylistic devices are based on it, notably parallelism. . . .

In Leo Tolstoy's works, which are as formal as musical compositions,
he employed the device of "making it strange" (not calling things by their
usual names) as well as provided examples of a "staircase-like construction."

I have had occasion to write a good deal about "making it strange"
in Tolstoy. One variant of this device consists in bearing down, focusing

Translated by Victor Erlich. From *Twentieth-Century Russian Literary Criticism*. Copyright
© 1975 by Yale University Press.

on a certain detail in a picture, and distorting proportions thereby. Thus, in a battle scene, Tolstoy elaborates the motif of a moist, chewing mouth. By drawing attention to such details, a singular displacement is achieved. In his excellent book on Tolstoy, Konstantin Leontiev failed to grasp this device. But the most common strategy in Tolstoy is one of refusing to recognize an object, of describing it as if it were seen for the first time. Thus a stage setting is called a "piece of painted cardboard" (*War and Peace*), the sacramental wafer a "bun." An assertion is therefore made that Christians eat their God.

This Tolstoyan device can, I believe, be traced back to French literature, possibly to Voltaire's *L'Ingénu* or to the description of life at the French court offered by Chateaubriand's savage. Be that as it may, Tolstoy "made strange" the works of Wagner, describing them as seen from the vantage point of a shrewd peasant, that is, one who like the French "savage" lacks habitual associations. Incidentally, the same device of describing a city as seen by a rustic was employed in the ancient Greek novel (see Veselovsky).

The other device, that of "staircase-like construction," has many interesting uses. I will not attempt to give even the most summary sketch of how Tolstoy employed this device in the process of creating his own singular poetics and will content myself with a few examples. The young Tolstoy used parallelism rather naïvely. Thus, in order to elaborate the theme of dying, to deploy it, he found it necessary to juxtapose three motifs—the death of a gentlewoman, the death of a serf, the death of a tree. I am speaking here about the story "Three Deaths." The various parts of the tale are linked together by a definite "motivation": the serf is coach-man to the gentlewoman, the tree is cut down to make a coffin for the serf.

In "Kholstomer" the parallel between horse and man is drawn: "the dead body of Serpukhovsky, after having walked and eaten and drunk on this earth, was put away into the ground much later. Neither his skin, nor his bones [nor his meat] were of any use to anyone." The connection made here rests on the fact that Serpukhovsky was at one time the horse's master. In "Two Hussars" the parallelism, announced in the very title of the story, pervades the incidents—love affairs, card games, friendships, and so on.

The connection between the two terms of the parallel is provided by the kinship of the protagonists.

When one compares Tolstoy's craft to that of Maupassant, one find that the French master tends to omit the second term of the parallel. In a Maupassant short story this element—be it the traditional short-story pattern or the conventional, French bourgeois outlook—is often implicit. In many of his stories Maupassant describes a peasant's death; he does so with great simplicity, yet he "makes it strange": the standard literary portrayal of a city dweller's death functions here, by implication, as a source of contrast, even though such a description does not actually appear in the story.

In this regard Tolstoy is, if one will, cruder than Maupassant; he needs an explicit parallel, for example, the contrast between kitchen and drawing room in "The Fruits of Enlightenment." This may be explained by the greater availability of the French literary tradition. The French reader feels a violation of the canon more keenly; he identifies the terms of the parallel more readily than our reader, whose conception of the norm is rather hazy.

Let me say, in passing, that when I speak of a literary tradition, I do not have in mind one author's borrowing from another. I see the writer's tradition as his dependence on an extant set of literary norms just as an inventor's tradition is the sum total of the currently available technical resources.

The juxtapositions of various protagonists or of two groups of protagonists are among the more complex instances of parallelism in Tolstoy's novels. In *War and Peace*, for example, one can clearly discern the following juxtapositions: Napoleon vs. Kutuzov and Pierre Bezukhov vs. Andrei Bolkonsky, with Nikolai Rostov serving as an external point of reference for both parties. In *Anna Karenina* the Anna–Vronsky group is set off against the Lëvin–Kitty group. Their coexistence is "motivated" by kinship. This is the usual motivation in Tolstoy, and, perhaps, among novelists in general. Tolstoy himself wrote [in a letter] that he had made the "old" Bolkonsky father to a brilliant young man (Andrei), "since it is awkward to treat a character not related to someone else in the novel." Another method favored by English novelists whereby one and the same protagonist participates in various configurations was hardly ever used by Tolstoy; as a matter of fact he used it only in the Petrushka–Napoleon episode, where it was employed for the purpose of "making it strange."

The actual link between the juxtaposed groups in *Anna Karenina* is so tenuous that the connection can only be conceived as having been motivated by artistic necessity.

Yet Tolstoy did use kinship in a highly interesting way—not to "motivate" a parallel but to create a "staircase-like construction." In the Rostov family we encounter two brothers and one sister. They seem to represent an unfolding of a single type. Tolstoy at times compares them to one another, as in the section preceding the death of Petia. Nikolai Rostov is a simplified, "crude" version of Natasha. By the same token, Stiva Oblonsky reveals one side of Anna Karenina's inner makeup. The words "a wee bit," which she says with Stiva's intonation, are a throwback to the childhood home they shared. Stiva is a step below his sister. Here the connection between characters does not really stem from kinship. As we have seen, Tolstoy was not averse to making relatives of independently conceived characters. Kinship was needed in order to achieve a staircase-like construction. That literary conventions governing portrayal of relatives do not require characterological affinity is best shown by the traditional device of juxtaposing a noble brother with a wicked one.

Here everything, as always in art, is motivation of the artifice.

PHILIP RAHV

The Green Twig and the
Black Trunk

T he critic's euphoria in the Tolstoyan
weather. Tolstoy and literature. The green twig and the black trunk. The art of
Tolstoy is of such irresistible simplicity and truth, is at once so intense and
so transparent in all of its effects, that the need is seldom felt to analyze
the means by which it becomes what it is, that is to say, its method or
sum of techniques. In the bracing Tolstoyan air, the critic, however ad-
dicted to analysis, cannot help doubting his own task, sensing that there
is something presumptuous and even unnatural, which requires an almost
artificial deliberateness of intention, in the attempt to dissect an art so
wonderfully integrated that, coming under its sway, we grasp it as a whole
long before we are able to summon sufficient consciousness to examine the
arrangement and interaction of its component parts.

Tolstoy is the exact opposite of those writers, typical of the modern
age, whose works are to be understood only in terms of their creative
strategies and design. The most self-observant of men, whose books are
scarcely conceivable apart from the ceaseless introspection of which they
are the embodiment, Tolstoy was the least self-conscious in his use of the
literary medium. That is chiefly because in him the cleavage between art
and life is of a minimal nature. In a Tolstoyan novel it is never the division
but always the unity of art and life which makes for illumination. This
novel, bristling with significant choices and crucial acts, teeming with

dramatic motives, is not articulated through a plot as we commonly know it in fiction; one might say that in a sense there are no plots in Tolstoy but simply the unquestioned and unalterable process of life itself; such is the astonishing immediacy with which he possesses his characters that he can dispense with manipulative techniques, as he dispenses with the bel-letristic devices of exaggeration, distortion, and dissimulation. The fable, that specifically literary contrivance, or anything else which is merely in-vented or made up to suit the occasion, is very rarely found in his work. Nor is style an element of compositon of which he is especially aware; he has no interest in language as such; he is the enemy of rhetoric and every kind of artifice and virtuosity. The conception of writing as of something calculated and constructed—a conception, first formulated explicitly in startlingly modern terms by Edgar Allan Poe, upon which literary culture has become more and more dependent—is entirely foreign to Tolstoy.

All that is of a piece, of course, with his unique attitude toward literature, that is, for a writer of modern times. For Tolstoy continually dissociated himself from literature whether considered matter-of-factly, as a profession like any other, or ideally as an autonomous way of life, a complete fate in the sense in which the French writers of Flaubert's gen-eration conceived ot it. In his youth a soldier who saw war at first hand, the proprietor and manager of Yasnaya Polyana, a husband and father not as other men are husbands and fathers but in what might be described as programmatic and even militant fashion, and subsequently a religious phi-losopher and the head of a sect, he was a writer through all the years—a writer, but never a *littérateur*, the very idea repelled him. The *littérateur* performs a function imposed by the social division of labor, and inevitably he pays the price of his specialization by accepting and even applauding his own one-sidedness and conceit, his noncommitted state as witness and observer, and the necessity under which he labors of preying upon life for the themes that it yields. It is with pride that Tolstoy exempted Lermontov and himself from the class of "men of letters" while commiserating with Turgenev and Goncharov for being so much of it; and in his *Reminiscences of Tolstoy* Gorky remarks that he spoke of literature but rarely and little, "as if it were something alien to him."

To account for that attitude by tracing it back to Tolstoy's aristo-cratic status, as if he disdained to identify himself with a plebian profession, is to take much too simple a view of his personality. The point is, rather, that from the very first Tolstoy instinctively recognized the essential in-sufficiency and makeshift character of the narrowly aesthetic outlook, of the purely artistic appropriation of the world. His personality was built on too broad a frame to fit into an aesthetic mold, and he denied that art was anything more than the ornament and charm of life. He came of age at a time when the social group to which he belonged had not yet been thoroughly exposed to the ravages of the division of labor, when men of his stamp could still resist the dubious consolations it brings in its train. Endowed with enormous energies, possessed of boundless egotism and of an equally boundless power of conscience, he was capable, in Leo Shestov's phrase, of destroying and creating worlds, and before he was quite twenty-seven years old he had the audacity to declare his ambition, writing it all solemnly down in his diary, of becoming the founder of "a new religion corresponding with the present state of mankind; the religion of Christ but purged of dogmas and mysticism—a practical religion, not promising future bliss but giving bliss on earth." No wonder, then, that while approaching the task of mastering the literary medium with the utmost seriousness, and prizing that mastery as a beautiful accomplishment, he could not but dismiss the pieties of art as trivial compared with the question he faced from the very beginning, the question he so heroically sought to answer even in his most elemental creations, in which he seems to us to move through the natural world with splendid and miraculous ease, more fully at home there than any other literary artist. Yet even in those creations the very same question appears now in a manifest and now in a latent fashion, always the same question: How to live, what to do?

In 1880, when Turgenev visited Yasnaya Polyana after a long estrangement, he wrote a letter bewailing Tolstoy's apparent desertion of art. "I, for instance, am considered an artist," he said, "but what am I compared with him? In contemporary European literature he has no equal . . . But what is one to do with him. He has plunged headlong into another sphere: he has surrounded himself with Bibles and Gospels in all languages, and has written a whole heap of papers. He has a trunk full of these mystical ethics and of various pseudo-interpretations. He read me some of it, which I simply do not understand . . . I told him, 'That is not the real thing'; but he replied: 'It is just the real thing' . . . Very probably he will give nothing more to literature, or if he reappears it will be with that trunk." Turgenev was wrong. Tolstoy gave a great deal more to literature, and it is out of that same trunk, so offensive in the eyes of the accomplished man of letters, that he brought forth such masterpieces as *The Death of Ivan Ilyich* and *Master and Man*, plays like *The Power of Darkness*, also many popular tales which, stripped of all ornament, have an essential force and grace of their own, and together with much that is abstract and overrationalized, not a few expository works, like *What Then Must We Do?*, which belong with the most powerful revolutionary writings of the modern age. For it is not for nothing that Tolstoy was always rummaging in that black trunk. At the bottom of it, underneath a heap of old papers, there lay a little mana-object, a little green twig which he carried with him through the years, a twig of which he was told at the age of five by his brother Nicholas—that it was buried by the road at the edge of a certain ravine and that on it was inscribed the secret by means of which "all men would cease suffering misfortunes, leave off quarreling and beging angry, and becoming continuously happy." The legend of the green twig was part of a game played by the Tolstoy children, called the Ant-Brothers, which consisted of crawling under chairs screened off by shawls and cuddling together in the dark. Tolstoy asked to be buried on the very spot at the edge of the ravine at Yasnaya Polyana which he loved because of its association with the imaginary green twig and the ideal of human brotherhood. And when he was an old man he wrote that "the idea of ant-brothers lovingly clinging to one another, though not under two arm-chairs curtained by shawls but of all mankind under the wide dome of heaven, has remained unaltered in me. As I then believed that there existed a little green twig whereon was written the message which would destroy all evil in men and give them universal welfare, so I now believe that such truth exists and will be revealed to men and will give them all it promises." It is clear that the change in Tolstoy by which Turgenev was so appalled was entirely natural, was presupposed by all the conditions of his development and of his creative consciousness. In the total Tolstoyan perspective the black trunk of his old age represents exactly the same thing as the green twig of his childhood.

Even the crude heresies he expounded in *What Is Art?* lose much of their offensiveness in that perspective. In itself when examined without reference to the author's compelling grasp of the central and most fearful problems of human existence, the argument of that book strikes us as a willful inflation of the idea of moral utility at the expense of the values of the imagination. But actually the fault of the argument is not that it is wholly implausible—as a matter of fact, it is of long and reputable lineage in the history of culture—as that it is advanced recklessly and with a logic at once narrow and excessive; the Tolstoyan insight is here vitiated in the same way as the insight into sexual relations is vitiated in *The Kreutzer Sonata.* Still, both works, the onslaught on modern love and marriage as well as the onslaught on the fetishism of art to which the modern sensibility has succumbed, are significantly expressive of Tolstoy's spiritual crisis—a crisis badly understood by many people, who take it as a phenomenon disruptive of his creative power despite the fact that, in the last analysis, it is impossible to speak of two Tolstoys, the creative and the noncreative, for there is no real discontinuity in his career. Though there is a contradiction between the artist and the moralist in him, his personality retains its basic unity, transcending all contradictions. Boris Eichenbaum, one of the very best of Tolstoy's Russian critics, has observed that the spiritual crisis did not operate to disrupt his art because it was a crisis internally not externally determined, the prerequisite of a new act of cognition through which he sought to rearm his genius and to ascertain the possibility of new creative beginnings. Thus *My Confession*, with which Tolstoy's later period opens and which appeared immediately after *Anna Karenina*, is unmistakably a work of the imagination and at the same time a mighty feat of consciousness.

Six years after writing *What Is Art?* Tolstoy finished *Hadji Murad* (1904), one of the finest *nouvelles* in the Russian language and a model of narrative skill and objective artistry. Is not the song of the nightingales, that song of life and death which bursts into ecstasy at dawn on the day when Hadji Murad attempts to regain his freedom, the very same song which rises in that marvelous sensual scene in *Family Happiness*, a scene bathed in sunlight, when Masha, surprising Sergey Mikhaylych in the cherry orchard, enjoys for the first time the full savor of her youthful love? *Hadji Murad* was written not less than forty-five years after *Family Happiness*. It can be said of Tolstoy the man that he was a rationalist who was usually at odds with human beings; nor did he especially love them. As a novelist, however, he was not merely exceptionally aware of them but was capable of investing them with a heroic sympathy that broke the barriers to their inner being. In the portrait of Hadji Murad we at once sense the author's love of the warrior chieftan who is fated, by his tribal code and indeed the whole weight of the past, to be crushed like a lone thistle flower in a plowed field. The twin images that recur through the story—that of the nightingales' song of love and death and that of the crimson thistle plant tenaciously clinging to its bit of soil—serve both as a musical motif drawing together the narrative parts and as a symbol, wonderful in its aptness and simplicity, of the inviolable rhythm of nature and human destiny. Nature and human destiny!—that their rhythm is eternally one is the very essence of Tolstoy's vision of life. His religious conversion forced him to modify his central idea or intuition, and it is wholly appropriate that in *Hadji Murad*, a late work written many years after his renunciation of the objective art of his great novels, he should have reverted to the vision of his major creative period. To himself Tolstoy might have explained away the lapse by claiming that this work of his old age conformed to his notion of "good universal art," which he of course placed in a category below that of religious art; still it is worth noting that he refrained from publishing *Hadji Murad* and that it appeared in print only after his death.

And in *The Devil*—a moral tale, the product, like *The Kreutzer Sonata*, of Tolstoy's most sectarian period and extremest assertion of dogmatic asceticism—what we remember best is not Eugene Irtenev's torments of conscience, his efforts to subdue his passion, but precisely the description of his carnal meetings in the sun-drenched woods with Stephanida, the fresh and strong peasant girl with full breasts and bright black eyes. The truth is that in the struggle between the old moralist and the old magician in Tolstoy both gave as good as they got.

The rationalist and anti-Romantic in Tolstoy. Sources in the eighteenth century. Divergence from the intelligentsia. Creative method.

Tolstoy has been described as the least neurotic of all the great Russians, and by the same token he can be said to be more committed than any of them to the rational understanding and ordering of life and to the throwing off of romantic illusions. Unlike Dostoevsky, he owes nothing either to the so-called natural school of Gogol or to the Romantic movement in Western literature. The school of Gogol is a school of morbidity, whereas Tolstoy is above all an artist of the normal—the normal, however, so intensified that it acquires a poetical truth and an emotional fullness which we are astounded to discover in the ordinary situations of life. Analysis is always at the center of the Tolstoyan creation. It is the sort of analysis, however, which has little in common with the analytical modes of such novelists as Dostoevsky and Proust, for example, both characteristically modern though in entirely different ways. While in their work analysis is precipitated mainly by deviations from the norm, from the broad standard of human conduct, in Tolstoy the analysis remains in line with that standard, is in fact inconceivable apart from it. Dostoevsky's "underground" man, who is a bundle of plebeian resentments, is unimaginable in a Tolstoyan novel. Even in Tolstoy's treatment of death there is nothing actually morbid—certainly not in the description of the death of Prince Andrey in *War and Peace* and of Nikolay Levin in *Anna Karenina*. As for *The Death of Ivan Ilyich*, that story would be utterly pointless if we were to see Ivan Ilyich as a special type and what happened to him as anything out of the ordinary. Ivan Ilyich is Everyman, and the state of absolute solitude into which he falls as his life ebbs away is the existential norm, the inescapable realization of mortality. Nothing could be more mistaken than the idea that Tolstoy's concern with death is an abnormal trait. On the contrary, if anything it is a supernormal trait, for the intensity of his concern with death is proportionate to the intensity of his concern with life. Of Tolstoy it can be said that he truly lived his life, and for that very reason he was so tormented by the thought of dying. It was a literal thought, physical through and through, a vital manifestation of the simplicity with which he grasped man's life in the world. This simplicity is of a metaphysical nature, and in it, as one Russian critic has remarked, you find the essence of Tolstoy's world-view, the energizing and generalizing formula that served him as the means unifying the diverse motives of his intellectual and literary experience. It is due to this metaphysical simplicity that he was unable to come to terms with any system of dogmatic theology and that in the end, despite all his efforts to retain it, he was compelled to exclude even the idea of God from his own system of rationalized religion. Thus all notions of immortality seemed absurd to Tolstoy, and his scheme of salvation was entirely calculated to make men happy here and now. It is reported of Thoreau that when he lay dying his answer to all talk of the hereafter was "one world at a time." That is the sort of answer with which Tolstoy's mentality is wholly in accord.

The way in which his rationalism enters his art is shown in his analysis of character, an analysis which leaves nothing undefined, nothing unexplained. That systematization of ambiguity which marks the modern novel is organically alien to Tolstoy. Given the framework in which his characters move we are told everything that we need to know or want to know about them. The tangled intimate life, the underside of their consciousness, their author is not concerned with: he sets them up in the known world and sees them through their predicaments, however irksome and baffling, without ever depriving them of the rationality which supports their existence. For just as in Tolstoy's religiosity there is no element of mysticism, so in his creative art there is no element of mystery.

Unlike most of his contemporaries, Tolstoy did not pass through the school of Romanticism, and perhaps that is the reason he never hesitated to strike out the dark areas in the place in which he outlined his leading figures. He has few links with the literary culture evolved in Russia after 1820; the fact is that he has more in common with his literary grandfathers than with his literary fathers. Insofar as he has any literary affiliations at all they go back to the eighteenth century, to Rousseau, to Sterne, to the French classical writers, and in Russia to the period of Karamzin, Zhukovsky, Novikov, and Radichev. He has their robustness and skepticism. His quarrels with Turgenev, his inability to get on with the liberal and radical writers grouped around the *Contemporary*, a Petersburg periodical edited by the poet Nekrasov in which Tolstoy's first stories were published, are explained not so much by personal factors, such as his intractability of temper, as by the extreme differences between the conditions of his development and those of the Russian intelligentsia, whose rise coincides with the appearance of the plebeian on the literary scene. Tolstoy's family background was archaistic, not in the sense of provincial backwardness, but in the sense of the deliberate and even stylized attempt made by his family—more particularly his father—to preserve at Yasnaya Polyana the patriarchal traditions of the Russian nobility of the eighteenth century. It was a conscious and militant archaism directed against the "new" civilization of Petersburg, with its state-bureaucracy and merchant princes. The young Tolstoy was scornful of the "theories" and "convictions" held by the writers he met in Petersburg in the 1850s; instead of putting his trust in "theories" and "convictions" he relied on those Franklinesque rules and precepts of conduct with which he filled his diaries—rules and precepts he deduced from his idea of unalterable "moral instincts." In Nekrasov's circle he was regarded as a "wild man," a "troglodyte"; and in the early 1860s, when he set out on his second European tour, Nekrasov and his friends hoped that he would return in a mood of agreement with their notions of education and historical progress. Nothing came of it, of course, for he returned armed with more of those "simplifications" that cut under their assumptions. But if the Westernizers found no comfort in Tolstoy, neither did the Slavophils. The latters' ideology, with its forced and artificial doctrine of superiority to the West, was also aligned with plebeian social tasks; at bottom it represented the discomfiture of a small and weak plebeian class in a semifeudal society, a discomfiture idealized through national messianism. It was an obscurantist ideology incompatible with Tolstoy's belief in self-improvement and in the possibility of human perfection. Moreover, in Tolstoy's approach to Western culture there was no distress, no anger, no hostility. He was never put off by it, for he considered European culture to be a natural sphere the products of which he could appropriate at will, and in any order he pleased, without in the least committing himself to its inner logic. He felt no more committed by his use of Western ideas than the French-speaking gentry in *War and Peace* feel obligated to import the social institutions of France along with its language. Thus Tolstoy was able to sort out Western tendencies to suit himself, as in *War and Peace*, where he is to some extent indebted for his conception of Napoleon to certain French publicists of the 1850s and sixties, who in their endeavor to deflate the pretensions of Napoleon III went so far in their polemics as also to blot out the image of his illustrious ancestor. Again, in that novel he is partly indebted for his so-called organic idea of war to Proudhon's book *La Guerre et la Paix*, which came out in a Russian translation in 1864. (Tolstoy had met Proudhon in Brussels in March 1861.) And the arbitrary way in which he helped himself to the ideas of Western thinkers is shown by the fact that he entirely ignored Proudhon's enthusiastic affirmation of Napoleon's historical role. The West was the realm of the city, a realm so strange to Tolstoy that he could regard it as neutral territory. The city was essentially unreal to him; he believed in the existence solely of the landowners and of the peasants. The contrast between Dostoevsky and Tolstoy, which Merezhkovsky and after him Thomas Mann have presented in terms of the abstract typology of the "man of spirit" as against the "man of nature," is more relevantly analyzed in terms of the contradiction between city and country, between the alienated intellectual proletariat of the city and the unalienated patriciate-peasantry of the country.

Much has been written concerning the influence of Rousseau on Tolstoy, but here again it is necessary to keep in mind that in Western literature we perceive the Rousseauist ideas through the colored screen of Romanticism while in Tolstoy Rousseau survives through his rationalism no less than through his sensibility. In point of fact, the Rousseauist cult of nature is operative in Tolstoy in a manner that leads toward realism, as is seen in his Caucasian tales, for instance. If these tales now seem romantic to us, it is largely because of the picturesque material of which they are composed. A narrative like *The Cossacks* is actually turned in a tendencious way against the tradition of "Caucasian romanticism" in Russian literature—the tradition of Pushkin, Lermontov, and Marlinsky. Olenin, the protagonist of *The Cossacks*, is so little of a Romantic hero that he is incapable of dominating even his own story; the impression of his personality is dissipated as the attention shifts to the Cossack led Lukashka, to Daddy Eroshka, and to the girl Marianka. Think what Chateaubriand would have made of a heroine like Marianka. In Tolstoy, however, she is portrayed in an authentically natural style, with all the calm strength, unawareness of subjective values, and indifference of a primitive human being. Though she is a "child of nature" and therefore an object of poetical associations, she is seen much too soberly to arouse those high-flown sentiments which "nature" inspires in Romantic poets like Novalis or even the Goethe of *Werther*. Where the Romantics convert nature into a solace for the trials of civilization, into a theater of lyrical idleness and noble pleasures, Tolstoy identifies nature with work, independence, self-possession.

Compared with Pierre, Prince Andrey, or Levin, Olenin is a weak hero, but he is important in that in his reflections he sums up everything which went into the making of the early Tolstoy and which was in later years given a religious twist and offered as a doctrine of world-salvation. The primacy which the issue of happiness assumes in Olenin's thoughts is the key to his Tolstoyan nature. "Happiness is this," he said to himself, "happiness lies in living for others. That is evident. The desire for happiness is innate in every man; therefore it is legitimate. When trying to satisfy it selfishly—that is, by seeking for oneself riches, fame, comforts, or love— it may happen that circumstances arise which make it impossible to satisfy these desires. It follows that it is these desires which are illegitimate, but not the need for happiness. But what desires can always be satisfied despite external circumstances? What are they? Love, self-sacrifice." In these few sentences we get the quintessence of the Tolstoyan mentality: the belief that ultimate truth can be arrived at through common-sense reasoning, the utilitarian justification of the values of love and self-sacrifice and their release from all other-worldly sanctions, the striving for the simplification of existence which takes the form of a return to a life closer to nature—a return, however, involving a self-consciousness and a constant recourse to reason that augurs ill for the success of any such experiment.

Tolstoy's art is so frequently spoken of as "organic" that one is likely to overlook the rationalistic structure on which it is based. This structure consists of successive layers of concrete details, physical and psychological, driven into place and held together by a generalization or dogma. Thus in *The Cossacks* the generalization is the idea of the return to nature; in *Two Hussars* it is the superiority of the older Turbin to the younger, that is to say, of the more naive times of the past to the "modern" period. (The original title of the story was *Father and Son.*) The binding dogma in *Family Happiness* is the instability and deceptiveness of love as compared with a sound family life and the rearing of children in insuring the happiness of a married couple. Yet the didacticism of such ideas seldom interferes with our enjoyment of the Tolstoyan fiction. For the wonderful thing about it is its tissue of detail, the tenacious way in which it holds together, as if it were a glutinous substance, and its incomparable rightness and truthfulness.

Parallelism of construction is another leading characteristic of the Tolstoyan method. In *War and Peace,* in the chronicle of the lives of the Bolkonsky and Rostov families, this parallelism is not devised dramatically, as a deliberate contrast, but in other narratives it is driven toward a stark comparison, as between Anna and Vronsky on the one hand and Kitty and Levin on the other in *Anna Karenina,* or between two generations in *Two*

Hussars, or between Lukashka and Olenin in *The Cossacks.* One writer on Tolstoy put it very well when he said that in the Tolstoyan novel all ideas and phenomena exist in pairs. Comparison is inherent in his method.

His early *nouvelles* can certainly be read and appreciated without reference to their historical context, to the ideological differences between him and his contemporaries which set him off to confound them with more proofs of his disdain for their "progressive" opinions. Still, the origin of *Family Happiness* in the quarrels of the period is worth recalling. At that time (in the 1850s) public opinion was much exercised over the question of free love and the emancipation of women; George Sand was a novelist widely read in intellectual circles, and of course most advanced people agreed with George Sand's libertarian solution of the question. Not so Tolstoy, who opposed all such tendencies, for he regarded marriage and family life as the foundations of society. Thus *Family Happiness,* with its denigration of love and of equal rights for women, was conceived, quite apart from its personal genesis in Tolstoy's affair with Valerya Arsenev, as a polemical rejoinder to George Sand, then adored by virtually all the Petersburg writers, including Dostoevsky.

The faith in family life is integral of Tolstoy. It has the deepest psychological roots in his private history, and socially it exemplifies his championship of patriarchal relations. It is a necessary part of his archaistic outlook, which in later life was transformed into a special kind of radicalism, genuinely revolutionary in some of its aspects and thoroughly archaistic in others. *War and Peace* is as much a chronicle of certain families as a historical novel. The historical sense is not really native to Tolstoy. His interest in the period of 1812 is peculiarly his own, derived from his interest in the story of his own family. He began work on *Anna Karenina* after failing in the attempt to write another historical novel, a sequel to *War and Peace.* And *Anna Karenina* is of course the novel in which his inordinate concern with marriage and family life receives its fullest expression.

The existential center of the Tolstoyan art. Tolstoy as the last of the unalienated artists.

So much has been made here of the rationalism of Tolstoy that it becomes necessary to explain how his art is saved from the ill effects of it. Art and reason are not naturally congruous with one another, and many a work of the imagination has miscarried because of an excess of logic. "There may be a system of logic; a system of being there can never be," said Kierkegaard. And art is above all a recreation of individual being; the system-maker must perforce abstract from the real world while the artist, if he is true to his medium, recoils from the process of abstraction because it is precisely the irreducible quality of life, its multiple divulgements in all their unique-ness and singularity, which provoke his imagination.

Now there is only one novel of Tolstoy's that might be described as a casualty of his rationalism, and that is *Resurrection*. The greater part of his fiction is existentially centered in a concrete inwardness and subjec-tivity by which it gains its quality of genius. In this sense it becomes possible to say that Tolstoy is much more a novelist of life and death than he is of good and evil—good and evil are not categories of existence but of moral analysis. And the binding dogmas or ideas of Tolstoy's fiction are not in contradiction with its existential sense; on the contrary, their interaction is a triumph of creative tact and proof of the essential wholeness of Tolstoy's nature. The Tolstoyan characters grasp their lives through their total per-sonalities, not merely through their intellects. Their experience is full of moments of shock, of radical choice and decision, when they confront themselves in the terrible and inevitable aloneness of their being. To men-tion but one of innumerable instances of such spiritual confrontation, there is the moment in *Anna Karenina* when Anna's husband begins to suspect her relation to Vronsky. That is the moment when the accepted and taken-for-granted falls to pieces, when the carefully built-up credibility of the world is torn apart by a revelation of its underlying irrationality. For ac-cording to Alexey Alexandrovitch's ideas one ought to have confidence in one's wife because jealousy was insulting to oneself as well as to her. He had never really asked himself why his wife deserved such confidence and why he believed that she would always love him. But now, though he still felt that jealousy was a bad and shameful state, "he also felt that he was standing face to face with something illogical and irrational, and did not know what was to be done. Alexey Alexandrovitch was standing face to face with life, with the possibility of his wife's loving someone other than himself, and this seemed to him very irrational and incomprehensible be-cause it was life itself. All his life Alexey Alexandrovitch had lived and worked in official spheres, having to do with the reflection of life. And every time he stumbled against life itself he had shrunk away from it. Now he experienced a feeling akin to that of a man who, while calmly crossing a precipice by a bridge, should suddenly discover that the bridge is broken, and that there is a chasm below. That chasm was life itself, the bridge that artificial life in which Alexey Alexandrovitch had lived. For the first time the question presented itself to him of the possibility of his wife's loving someone else, and he was horrified at it."

It is exactly this "standing face to face with life," and the realization that there are things in it that are irreducible and incomprehensible, which drew Tolstoy toward the theme of death. Again and again he returned to this theme, out of a fear of death which is really the highest form of courage. Most people put death out of their minds because they cannot bear to think of it. Gorky reports that Tolstoy once said to him that "if a man has learned to think, no matter what he may think about, he is always thinking of his own death. All philosophers were like that. And what truths can there be, if there is death?" That is a statement of despair and nihilism the paradox of which is that it springs from the depths of Tolstoy's existential feeling of life; and this is because the despair and nihilism spring not from the renunciation but from the affirmation of life; Tolstoy never gave up the search for an all-embracing truth, for a rational justification of man's existence on the earth.

The fact is that Tolstoy was at bottom so sure in his mastery of life and so firm in his inner feeling of security that he could afford to deal intimately with death. Consider the difference in this respect between him and Franz Kafka, another novelist of the existential mode. In Kafka the theme of death is absent, not because of strength but rather because of neurotic weakness. He was ridden by a conviction, as he himself defined it, of "complete helplessness," and baffled by the seeming impossibility of solving even the most elementary problems of living, he could not look beyond life into the face of death. He wrote: "Without ancestors, without marriage, without progeny, with an unbridled desire for ancestors, marriage, and progeny. All stretch out their hands towards me: ancestors, marriage, and progeny, but from a point far too remote from me." That is the complaint of an utterly alienated man, without a past and without a future. Tolstoy, on the other hand, was attached with the strongest bonds to the patrician-peasant life of Yasnaya Polyana, he was in possession of the world and of his own humanity. His secret is that he is the last of the unalienated artists. Hence it is necessary to insist on the differences not so much between him and other artists generally as between him and the modern breed of alienated artists. It is thanks to this unalienated condition that he is capable of moving us powerfully when describing the simplest, the most ordinary and therefore in their own way also the gravest occasions of life—occasions that the alienated artist can approach only from a distance, through flat naturalistic techniques, or through immense subtleties of analysis, or through the transportation of his subject onto the plan of myth and fantasy.

But, of course, even Tolstoy, being a man of the nineteenth century, could not finally escape the blight of alienation. In his lifetime Russian society disintegrated; he witnessed the passing of the old society of status and its replacement by a cruelly impersonal system of bourgeois relations. Tolstoy resisted the catastrophic ruin of the traditional order by straining all the powers of his reason to discover a way out. His so-called conversion is the most dramatic and desperate episode in his stubborn and protracted struggle against alienation. His attack on civilization is essentially an attack on the conditions that make for alienation. The doctrine of Christian anarchism, developed after his conversion, reflects, as Lenin put it, "the accumulated hate, the ripened aspiration for a better life, the desire to throw off the past—and also the immaturity, the dreamy contemplativeness, the political inexperience, and the revolutionary flabbiness of the villages." Still, the point of that doctrine lies not in its religious content, which is very small indeed, but rather in its formulation of a social ideal and of a utopian social program.

GEORGE STEINER

Tolstoy and Homer

Hugo von Hofmannsthal once re-
marked that he could not read a page of Tolstoy's *Cossacks* without being
reminded of Homer. His experience has been shared by readers not only
of *The Cossacks* but of Tolstoy's works as a whole. According to Gorky,
Tolstoy himself said of *War and Peace:* "Without false modesty, it is like
the *Iliad*," and he made precisely the same observation with regard to
Childhood, Boyhood and Youth. Moreover, Homer and the Homeric atmosphere appear to have played a fascinating role in Tolstoy's image of his own
personality and creative stature. His brother-in-law, S. A. Bers, tells in
his *Reminiscences* of a feast which took place on Tolstoy's estate in Samara:

> a steeplechase of fifty versts. Prizes were got ready, a bull, a horse, a rifle,
> a watch, a dressing-gown and the like. A level stretch was chosen, a huge
> course four miles long was made and marked out, and posts were put up
> on it. Roast sheep, and even a horse, were prepared for the entertainment.
> On the appointed day, some thousands of people assembled, Ural Cos-
> sacks, Russian peasants, Bashkirs and Khirgizes, with their dwellings,
> koumiss-kettles, and even their flocks. . . . On a cone-shaped rise, called
> in the local dialect "Shishka" (the Wen), carpets and felt were spread,
> and on these the Bashkirs seated themselves in a ring, with their legs
> tucked under them. . . . The feast lasted for two days and was merry, but
> at the same time dignified and decorous. . . .

It is a fantastic scene; the millennia dividing the plains of Troy from
nineteenth-century Russia are bridged and Book XXIII of the *Iliad* springs
to life. In Richmond Lattimore's version:

> But Achilleus
> held the people there, and made them sit down in a wide assembly,
> and brought prizes for games out of his ships, cauldrons and tripods,
> and horses and mules and the powerful high heads of cattle
> and fair-girdled women and grey iron.

Like Agamemnon, Tolstoy thrones upon the hillock; the steppe is dotted with tents and fires; Bashkirs and Khirgizes, like Achaens, race the four-mile course and take their prizes from the hands of the bearded king. But there is nothing here of archaeology, of contrived reconstruction. The Homeric element was native to Tolstoy; it was rooted in his own genius. Read his polemics against Shakespeare and you will find that his sense of kinship with the poet, or poets, of the *Iliad* and *Odyssey* was palpable and immediate. Tolstoy spoke of Homer as equal of equal; between them the ages had counted for little.

What was it that struck Tolstoy as peculiarly Homeric in his collection of early memories? Both the setting, I think, and the kind of life he recalled to mind. Take the account of "The Hunt" in the volume on *Childhood:*

> Harvesting was in full swing. The limitless, brilliantly yellow field was bounded only on one side by the tall, bluish forest, which then seemed to me a most distant, mysterious place beyond which either the world came to an end or uninhabited countries began. The whole field was full of sheaves and peasants. . . . The little roan papa rode went with a light, playful step, sometimes bending his head to his chest, pulling at the reins, and brushing off with his thick tail the gadflies and gnats that settled greedily on him. Two borzois with tense tails raised sickle-wise, and lifting their feet high, leapt gracefully over the tall stubble, behind the horse's feet. Milka ran in front, and with head lifted awaited the quarry. The peasants' voices, the tramp of horses and creaking of carts, the merry whistle of quail, the hum of insects hovering in the air in steady swarms, the odour of wormwood, straw, and horses' sweat, the thousands of different colours and shadows with which the burning sun flooded the light yellow stubble, the dark blue of the forest, the light lilac clouds, and the white cobwebs that floated in the air or stretched across the stubble—all this I saw, heard, and felt.

There is nothing here that would have been incongruous on the plains of Argos. It is from our own modern setting that the scene is oddly remote. It is a patriarchal world of huntsmen and peasants; the bond between master and hounds and the earth runs native and true. The description itself combines a sense of forward motion with an impression of repose; the total effect, as in the friezes of the Parthenon, is one of dynamic equilibrium.

And beyond the familiar horizon, as beyond the Pillars of Hercules, lie the mysterious seas and the untrodden forests.

The world of Tolstoy's recollections, no less than that of Homer, is charged with sensuous energies. Touch and sight and smell fill it at every moment with rich intensity:

> In the passage a samovár, into which Mítka, the postilion, flushed red as a lobster, is blowing, is already on the boil. It is damp and misty outside, as if steam were rising from the odorous manure heap; the sun lights with its bright gay beams the eastern part of the sky and the thatched roofs, shiny with dew, of the roomy pent-houses that surround the yard. Under these one can see our horses tethered to the mangers and hear their steady chewing. A shaggy mongrel that had had a nap before dawn on a dry heap of manure, stretches itself lazily, and wagging its tail, starts at a jog-trot for the opposite side of the yard. An active peasant-woman opens some creaking gates and drives the dreamy cows into the street, where the tramping, the lowing and the bleating of the herd is already audible. . . .

So it was when "rosy-fingered Dawn" came to Ithaca twenty-seven hundred years ago. So it should be, proclaims Tolstoy, if man is to endure in communion with the earth. Even the storm, with its animate fury, belongs to the rhythm of things:

> The lightning flashes become wider and paler, and the rolling of the thunder is now less startling amid the regular patter of the rain. . . .

> . . . an aspen grove with hazel and wild cherry undergrowth stands motionless as if in an excess of joy, and slowly sheds bright raindrops from its clean-washed branches on to last year's leaves. On all sides crested skylarks circle with glad songs and swoop swiftly down. . . . The delicious scent of the wood after the spring storm, the odour of the birches, of the violets, the rotting leaves, the mushrooms, and the wild cherry, is so enthralling that I cannot stay in the brichka. . . .

Schiller wrote in his essay *Ueber naive und sentimentalische Dichtung* that certain poets "are Nature" while others only "seek her." In that sense, Tolstoy is Nature; between him and the natural world language stood not as a mirror or a magnifying glass, but as a window through which all light passes and yet is gathered and given permanence.

It is impossible to concentrate within a single formula or demonstration the affinities between the Homeric and the Tolstoyan points of view. So much is pertinent: the archaic and pastoral setting; the poetry of war and agriculature; the primacy of the senses and of physical gesture; the luminous, all-reconciling background of the cycle of the year; the

recognition that energy and aliveness are, of themselves, holy; the acceptance of a chain of being extending from brute matter to the stars and along
which men have their apportioned places; deepest of all, an essential sanity,
a determination to follow what Coleridge called "the high road of life,"
rather than those dark obliquities in which the genius of a Dostoevsky was
most thoroughly at home.

In both the Homeric epics and the novels of Tolstoy the relationship
between author and characters is paradoxical. Maritain gives a Thomistic
analogue for it in his study of *Creative Intuition in Art and Poetry*. He speaks
"of the relationship between the transcendent creative eternity of God and
the free creatures who are both acting in liberty and firmly embraced by
his purpose." The creator is at once omniscient and everywhere present,
but at the same time he is detached, impassive, and relentlessly objective
in his vision. The Homeric Zeus presides over the battle from his mountain
fastness, holding the scales of destiny but not intervening. Or, rather,
intervening solely to restore equilibrium, to safeguard the mutability of
man's life against miraculous aid or the excessive achievements of heroism.
As in the detachment of the god, so there is in the clear-sightedness of
Homer and Tolstoy both cruelty and compassion.

They saw with those blank, ardent, unswerving eyes which look
upon us through the helmet-slits of archaic Greek statues. Their vision was
terribly sober. Schiller marvelled at Homer's impassiveness, at his ability
to communicate the utmost of grief and terror in perfect evenness of tone.
He believed that this quality—this "naïveté"—belonged to an earlier age
and would be unrecapturable in the sophisticated and analytic temper of
modern literature. From it Homer derived his most poignant effects. Take,
for example, Achilles' slaying of Lykaon in Book XXI of the *Iliad*:

> "So, friend, you die also. Why all this clamour about it? Patroklos also
> is dead, who was better by far than you are. Do you not see what
> a man I am, how huge, how splended and born of a great father,
> and the mother who bore me immortal?
> Yet even I have also my death and my strong destiny, and there shall be
> a dawn or an afternoon or a noontime when some man in the
> fighting will take the life from me also either with a spearcast or
> an arrow flown from the bowstring."
> So he spoke, and in the other the knees and the inward heart went slack.
> He let go of the spear and sat back, spreading wide both hands;
> but Achilleus drawing his sharp sword struck him beside the neck
> at the collar-bone, and the double-edged sword plunged full length
> inside. He dropped to the ground, face downward, and lay at
> length, and the black blood flowed, and the ground was soaked
> with it.

The calm of the narrative is nearly inhuman; but in consequence the horror speaks naked and moves us unutterably. Moreover, Homer never sacrifices the steadiness of his vision to the needs of pathos. Priam and Achilles have met and given vent to their great griefs. But then they bethink themselves of meat and wine. For, as Achilles says of Niobe:

> She remembered to eat when she was worn out with weeping.

Again, it is the dry fidelity to the facts, the poet's refusal to be outwardly moved, which communicate the bitterness of his soul.

In this respect, no one in the western tradition is more akin to Homer than is Tolstoy. As Romain Rolland noted in his journal for 1887, "in the art of Tolstoy a given scene is not perceived from two points of view, but from only one: things are as they are, not otherwise." In *Childhood*, Tolstoy tells of the death of his mother: "I was in great distress at that moment but involuntarily noticed every detail," including the fact that the nurse was "very fair, young, and remarkably handsome." When his mother dies, the boy experiences "a kind of enjoyment," at knowing himself to be unhappy. That night he sleeps "soundly and calmly," as is always the case after great distress. The following day he be comes aware of the smell of decomposition:

> It was only then that I understood what the strong, oppressive smell was that mingling with the incense filled the whole room; and the thought that the face that but a few days before had been so full of beauty and tenderness, the face of her I loved more than anything on earth, could evoke horror, seemed to reveal the bitter truth to me for the first time, and filled my soul with despair.

"Keep your eyes steadfastly to the light," says Tolstoy, "this is how things are."

But in the unflinching clarity of the Homeric and Tolstoyan attitude there is far more than resignation. There is joy, the joy that burns in the "ancient glittering eyes" of the sages in Yeats's *Lapis Lazuli*. For they loved and revered the "humanness" of man; they delighted in the life of the body coolly perceived but ardently narrated. Moreover, it was their instinct to close the gap between spirit and gesture, to relate the hand to the sword, the keel to the brine, and the wheel-rim to the singing cobblestones. Both the Homer of the *Iliad* and Tolstoy saw action whole; the air vibrates around their personages and the force of their being electrifies insensate nature. Achilles' horses weep at his impending doom and the oak flowers to persuade Bolkonsky that his heart will live again. This consonance between man and the surrounding world extends even to the cups in which Nestor looks for wisdom when the sun is down and to the birch-leaves that glitter like a sudden riot of jewels after the storm has swept over Levin's estate. The barriers between mind and object, the ambiguities which metaphysicians discern in the very notion of reality and perception, impeded neither Homer nor Tolstoy. Life flooded in upon them like the sea.

And they rejoiced at it. When Simone Weil called the *Iliad* "The Poem of Force" and saw in it a commentary on the tragic futility of war, she was only partially right. The *Iliad* is far removed from the despairing nihilism of Euripides' *Trojan Women*. In the Homeric poem, war is valorous and ultimately ennobling. And even in the midst of carnage, life surges high. Around the burial mound of Patroklus the Greek chieftains wrestle, race, and throw the javelin in celebration of their strength and aliveness. Achilles knows that he is foredoomed, but "bright-cheeked Briseis" comes to him each night. War and mortality cry havoc in the Homeric and Tolstoyan worlds, but the centre holds: it is the affirmation that life is, of itself, a thing of beauty, that the works and days of men are worth recording, and that no catastrophe—not even the burning of Troy or of Moscow—is ultimate. For beyond the charred towers and beyond the battle rolls the wine-dark sea, and when Austerlitz is forgotten the harvest shall, in Pope's image, once again "embrown the slope."

This entire cosmology is gathered into Bosola's reminder to the Duchess of Malfi when she curses nature in agonized rebellion: "Look you, the stars shine still." These are terrible words, full of detachment and the harsh reckoning that the physical world contemplates our afflictions with impassiveness. But go beyond their cruel impact and they convey an assurance that life and star-light endure beyond the momentary chaos.

The Homer of the *Iliad* and Tolstoy are akin in yet another respect. Their image of reality is anthropomorphic; man is the measure and pivot of experience. Moreover, the atmosphere in which the personages of the *Iliad* and of Tolstoyan fiction are shown to us is profoundly humanistic and even secular. What matters is the kingdom of *this* world, here and now. In a sense, that is a paradox; on the plains of Troy mortal and divine affairs are incessantly confounded. But the very descent of the gods among men and their brazen involvement in all-too-human passions give the work its ironic overtones. Musset invoked this paradoxical attitude in his account of archaic Greece in the opening lines of *Rolla*:

> Où tout était divin, jusqu'aux douleurs humaines;
> Où le monde adorait ce qu'il tue aujourd'hui;
> Où quatre mille dieux n'avaient pas un athée. . . .

Precisely; with four thousand deities warring in men's quarrels, dallying with mortal women, and behaving in a manner apt to scandalize even liberal codes of morality, there was no need for atheism. Atheism arises in contrariety to the conception of a living and credible God; it is not a response to a partially comic mythology. In the *Iliad* divinity is quintessentially human. The gods are mortals magnified, and often magnified in a satiric vein. When wounded they howl louder than men, when they are enamoured their lusts are more consuming, when they flee before human spears their speed exceeds that of earthly chariots. But morally and intellectually the deities of the *Iliad* resemble giant brutes or malevolent children endowed with an excess of power. The actions of gods and goddesses in the Trojan War enhance the stature of man, for when odds are equal mortal heroes more than hold their own and when the scales are against them a Hector and an Achilles demonstrate that mortality has its own splendours. In lowering the gods to human values, the "first" Homer achieved not only an effect of comedy, though such an effect obviously contributes to the freshness and "fairy-tale" quality of the poem. Rather, he emphasized the excellence and dignity of heroic man. And this, above all, was his theme.

The pantheon in the *Odyssey* plays a subtler and more awesome role, and the *Aeneid* is an epic penetrated with a feeling for religious values and religious practice. But the *Iliad*, while accepting the mythology of the supernatural, treats it ironically and humanizes its material. The true centre of belief lies not on Olympus but in the recognition of *Moira*, of unyielding destiny which maintains through its apparently blind decimations an ultimate principle of justice and equilibrium. The religiosity of Agamemnon and Hector consists in an acceptance of fate, in a belief that certain impulses towards hospitality are sacred, in reverence for sanctified hours or hallowed places, and in a vague but potent realization that there are daemonic forces in the motion of the stars or the obstinacies of the wind. But beyond that, reality is immanent in the world of man and of his senses. I know of no better word to express the non-transcendence and ultimate physicality of the *Iliad*. No poem runs more strongly counter to the belief that "we are such stuff as dreams are made on."

And this is where it touches significantly on the art of Tolstoy. His also is an immanent realism, a world rooted in the veracity of our senses. From it God is strangely absent. . . . There lies behind the literary techniques of the *Iliad* and of Tolstoy a comparable belief in the centrality of the human personage and in the enduring beauty of the natural world. In the case of *War and Peace* the analogy is even more decisive; where the *Iliad* evokes the laws of *Moira*, Tolstoy expounds his philosophy of history. In both works the chaotic individuality of battle stands for the larger randomness in men's lives. And if we consider *War and Peace* as being, in a genuine sense, a heroic epic it is because in it, as in the *Iliad*, war is portrayed in its glitter and joyous ferocity as well as in its pathos. No measure of Tolstoyan pacifism can negate the ecstasy which young Rostov experiences as he charges down on the French stragglers. Finally, there is the fact that *War and Peace* tells of two nations, or rather of two worlds, engaged in mortal combat. This alone has led many of its readers, and led Tolstoy himself, to compare it with the *Iliad*.

But neither the martial theme nor the portrayal of national destinies should blind us to the fact that the philosophy of the novel is anti-heroic. There are moments in the book in which Tolstoy is emphatically preaching that war is wanton carnage and the result of vainglory and stupidity in high places. There are also times at which Tolstoy is concerned soley with seeking to discover "the real truth" in opposition to the alleged truths of official historians and mythographers. Neither the latent pacifism nor this concern with the evidence of history can be compared to the Homeric attitude.

War and Peace is most genuinely akin to the *Iliad* where its philosophy is least engaged, where, in Isaiah Berlin's terms, the fox is least busy trying to be a hedgehog. Actually, Tolstoy is closest to Homer in less manifold works, in *The Cossacks*, the *Tales from the Caucasus*, the sketches of the Crimean War and in the dread sobriety of *The Death of Ivan Ilych*.

But it cannot be emphasized too strongly that the affinity between the poet of the *Iliad* and the Russian novelist was one of temper and vision; there is no question here (or only in the minute instance) of a Tolstoyan imitation of Homer. Rather, it is that when Tolstoy turned to the Homeric epics in the original Greek, in his early forties, he must have felt wondrously at home.

ISAIAH BERLIN

Tolstoy and Enlightenment

'Two things are always said about Tolstoy,' wrote the celebrated Russian critic Mikhailovsky, in a largely forgotten essay published in the 'eighties, 'that he is an outstandingly good writer of fiction and a bad thinker. This has become an axiom needing no demonstration'. This almost universal verdict has reigned, virtually unchallenged, for something like a hundred years; and Mikhailovsky's attempt to question it remained relatively isolated. Tolstoy dismissed his left-wing ally as a routine radical hack, and expressed surprise that anyone should take interest in him. This was characteristic but unjust. The essay, which its author called 'The Right Hand and the Left Hand of Leo Tolstoy', is a brilliant and convincing defence of Tolstoy on both intellectual and moral grounds, directed mainly against those who saw in the novelist's ethical doctrines, and in particular in his glorification of the peasants and of natural instinct and his constant disparagement of scientific culture, merely a perverse and sophisticated obscurantism which discredited the liberal cause, and played into the hands of priests and reactionaries. Mikhailovsky rejected this view, and in the course of his long and careful attempt to sift the enlightened grain from the reactionary chaff in Tolstoy's opinions, reached the conclusion that there was an unresolved and unavowed conflict in the great novelist's conceptions both of human nature and of the problems facing Russian and Western civilization. Mikhailovsky maintained that, so far from being a 'bad thinker', Tolstoy was no less acute, clear-eyed and convincing in his analysis of ideas than of motive, character and action. In his zeal for his paradoxical thesis—paradoxical certainly at the time at which he wrote it—Mikhailovsky sometimes goes too far. My own remarks are no more than an extended gloss on his thesis; for in substance it seems to me to be correct, or at any rate more right than wrong. Tolstoy's opinions are always subjective and can be (as for example in his writings on Shakespeare or Dante or Wagner) wildly perverse. But the questions which in his more didactic essays he tries to answer nearly always turn on cardinal questions of principle, and his analysis is always first hand, and cuts far deeper, in the deliberately simplified and naked form in which he usually presents it, than those of more balanced, concrete and 'objective' thinkers. Direct vision often tends to be disturbing: Tolstoy used this gift to the full to destroy both his own peace and that of his readers. It was this habit of asking exaggeratedly simple but fundamental questions, to which he did not himself—at any rate in the 'sixties and 'seventies—claim to possess the answers, that gave Tolstoy the reputation of being a 'nihilist'. Yet he certainly had no wish to destroy for the sake of destruction. He only wanted, more than anything else in the world, to know the truth. How annihilating this passion can be, is shown by others who have chosen to probe below the limits set by the wisdom of their generation: the author of the *Book of Job*, Machiavelli, Pascal, Rousseau. Like them, Tolstoy cannot be fitted into any of the public movements of his own, or indeed any other, age. The only company to which he belongs in the subversive one of questioners to whom no answer has been, or seems likely to be, given—at least no answer which they or those who understand them will begin to accept.

As for Tolstoy's positive ideas—and they varied less during his long life than has sometimes been represented—they are his own but not unique: they have something in common with the French enlightenment of the eighteenth century; something with those of the twentieth; little with those of his own times. He belonged to neither of the great ideological streams which divided educated Russian opinion during his youth. He was not a radical intellectual with his eyes turned to the West, nor a Slavophil, that is to say, a believer in a Christian and nationalist monarchy. His views cut across these categories. Like the radicals, he had always condemned political repression, arbitrary violence, economic exploitation and all that creates and perpetuates inequality among men. But the rest of the 'westernizing' outlook—the overwhelming sense of civic responsibility, the belief in natural science as the door to all truth, in social and political reform, in democracy, material progress, secularism—this celebrated amalgam, the heart of the ideology of the intelligentsia—Tolstoy rejected early in life. He believed in individual liberty and indeed in progress too, but in a queer sense of his own. He looked with contempt on liberals and socialists, and with even greater hatred on the right-wing parties of his time. His closest affinity, as has often been remarked, is with Rousseau; he liked and admired Rousseau's views more than those of any other modern writer. Like Rousseau, he rejected the doctrine of original sin, and believed that man was born innocent and had been ruined by his own bad institutions; especially by what passed for education among civilized men. Like Rousseau again, he put the blame for this process of decadence largely on the intellectuals and the institutions which they support—in particular the self-appointed *élites* of experts, sophisticated *côteries*, remote from common humanity, self-estranged from natural life. These men are damned because they have all but lost the most precious of all human possessions, the capacity with which all men are born—to see the truth, the immutable, eternal truth, which only charlatans and sophists represent as varying in different circumstances and times and places—the truth which is visible fully only to the innocent eye of those whose hearts have not been corrupted—children, peasants, those not blinded by vanity and pride, the simple, the good. Education, as the West understands it ruins innocence. That is why children resist it bitterly and instinctively: that is why it has to be rammed down their throats, and, like all coercion and violence, maims the victim and at times destroys him beyond redress. Men crave for truth by nature; therefore true education must be of such a kind that children and unsophisticated, ignorant people will absorb it readily and eagerly. But to understand this, and to discover how to apply this knowledge, the educated must put away their intellectual arrogance and make a new beginning. They must purge their minds of theories, of false, quasi-scientific analogies between the world of men and the world of animals, or of men and inanimate things. Only then will they be able to re-establish a personal relationship with the uneducated—a relationship which only humanity and love can achieve. In modern times only Rousseau, and perhaps Dickens, seem to him to have seen this. Certainly the people's condition will never be improved until not only the Czarist bureaucracy, but the 'progressists', as Tolstoy called them, the vain and doctrinaire intelligentsia, are 'prised off the people's necks'—the common people's, and the children's too. So long as fanatical theorists bedevil education, little is to be hoped for. Even the old-fashioned village priest—so Tolstoy maintains in one of his early tracts—was less harmful: he knew little and was clumsy, idle and stupid; but he treated his pupils as God's creatures, not as scientists treat specimens in a laboratory; he did what he could; he was often corrupt, ill tempered, ignorant, unjust, but these were human—'natural'—vices, and therefore their effects, unlike those of machine-made modern instruction, inflicted no permanent injury.

With these opinions it is not surprising to find that Tolstoy was personally happier among the Slavophil reactionaries. He rejected their ideas, but at least they seemed to him to have some contact with reality—the land, the peasants, traditional ways of life. At least they believed in the primacy of spiritual values, and in the futility of trying to change men by changing the superficial sides of their life by means of political or constitutional reforms. But the Slavophils also believed in the Orthodox Church, in the unique historical destiny of the Russian people, in the sanctity of history as a divinely ordained process and therefore as the justification of many anomalies because they were native and ancient, and thus instruments in the divine tactic; they lived by a Christian faith in the mystical body—at once community and church—of the generations of the faithful, past, present and yet unborn. Intellectually, Tolstoy utterly repudiated all this; temperamentally he responded to it all too strongly. As a writer he truly understood only the nobility and the peasants: and the former better than the latter. He shared many of the instinctive beliefs of his country neighbours: like them he had a natural aversion from all forms of middle-class liberalism: the *bourgeoisie* scarcely appears in his novels: his attitude to parliamentary democracy, the rights of women, universal suffrage, was not very different from that of Cobbett or Carlyle or Proudhon or D. H. Lawrence. He shared deeply the Slavophil suspicion of all scientific and theoretical generalizations as such, and this created a bridge which made personal relations with the Moscow Slavophils congenial to him. But his intellect was not at one with his instinctive convictions. As a thinker he had profound affinities with the eighteenth-century *philosophes*. Like them, he looked upon the patriarchal Russian State and Church, idealized by the Slavophils (and the implication that common ideals united the educated ruling minority and the uneducated masses) as organized, hypocritical conspiracies. Like the moralists of the Enlightenment, he looked for true values not in history, nor the sacred missions of nations or cultures or churches, but in the individual's own personal experience. Like them, too, he believed in eternal (and not in historically evolving) ends of life, and rejected with both hands the romantic notion of race or nation or culture as creative agencies, still more the Hegelian conception of history as the self-realization of self-perfecting reason incarnated in men, or movements, or institutions (ideas which had deeply influenced the Slavophils); all his life he looked on this as cloudy metaphysical nonsense.

Tolstoy's cold, clear, uncompromising realism is quite explicit in the notes, diaries and letters of his early life. The reminiscences of those who knew him as a boy or as a student in the University of Kazan, reinforce this impression. His character was deeply conservative, with a streak of caprice and irrationality; but his mind remained calm, logical and unswerving; he followed the argument easily and fearlessly to whatever extreme it led and then embraced it—a typically Russian, and sometimes fatal, combination of qualities. What did not satisfy his critical sense, he rejected, he left the University of Kazan because he decided that the professors were incompetent and dealt with trivial issues. Like Helvétius and his friends in the mid-eighteenth century, Tolstoy denounced theology, history, the teaching of dead languages and literatures—the entire classical curriculum—as an accumulation of data and rules that no reasonable man could wish to know. History particularly irritated him as a systematic attempt to answer trivial or non-existent questions, with all the real issues carefully left out. 'History is like a deaf man answering questions which nobody has put to him,' he announced to a startled fellow student while they were both locked in the University detention room for some minor act of insubordination. The first extended statement of his full 'ideological' position belongs to the 'sixties. The occasion for it was his decision to compose a treatise on education. All his intellectual strength and all his prejudice went into this attempt.

II

In 1860 Tolstoy, then thirty-two years old, found himself in one of his periodic moral crises. He had acquired some fame as a writer: *Sebastopol, Childhood, Adolescence and Youth* and two or three shorter tales had been praised by the critics. He was on terms of friendship with some of the most gifted of an exceptionally talented generation of writers in his country— Turgenev, Nekrassov, Goncharov, Panaev, Pisemsky, Fet. His writing struck everyone by its freshness, sharpness, marvellous descriptive power and the precision and originality of its images. His style was at times criticized as awkward and even barbarous; but he was the most promising of the younger prose writers; he had a future; and yet his literary friends felt reservations about him. He paid visits to the literary *salons*, both right and left wing, but he seemed at ease in none of them. He was bold, imaginative and independent; but he was not a man of letters, not fundamentally concerned with problems of literature and writing, still less of writers; he had wandered in from another, less intellectual, more aristocratic and more primitive world. He was a well-born dilettante; but that was nothing new: the poetry of Pushkin and his contemporaries—unequalled in the history of Russian literature—had been created by amateurs of genius. It was not his origin but his unconcealed indifference to the literary life as such—to the habits and problems of professional writers, editors, publicists—that made his friends among the men of letters feel uneasy in his presence. This worldly, clever young officer could be exceedingly agreeable; his love of writing was genuine and very deep; but he was too contemptuous, too formidable and reserved, he did not dream of opening his heart in a *milieu* dedicated to intimate, unending self-revelation. He was inscrutable, disdainful, disconcerting, a little frightening. It was true that he no longer lived the life of an aristocratic officer. The wild nights on which the young radicals looked with hatred or contempt as characteristic of the dissipated lives of the reactionary *jeunesse dorée* no longer amused him. He had married, he had settled down, he was in love with his wife, he became for a time a model (if at times exasperating) husband. But he did not trouble to conceal the fact that he had infinitely more respect for all forms of real life—whether of the free Cossacks in the Caucasus, or of the rich young Guards officers in Moscow with their racehorses and balls and gypsies— than for the world of books, reviews, critics, professors, political discussions, and talk about ideals, or philosophy and literary values. Moreover, he was opinionated, quarrelsome, and at times unexpectedly savage; with the result that his literary friends treated him with nervous respect, and, in the end, drew away from him; or perhaps he abandoned them. Apart from the poet Fet, who was an eccentric and deeply conservative country squire himself, Tolstoy had scarcely any intimates among the writers of his own generation. His breach with Turgenev is well known. He was even remoter from other *littérateurs*. There were times when he was fond of Vassili Botkin; he liked Nekrassov better than his poetry; but then Nekrassov was an editor of genius and had admired and encouraged him from his earliest beginnings.

The sense of the contrast between life and literature haunted Tolstoy all his life, and made him doubt his own vocation as a writer. Like other young men of birth and fortune, he was conscience stricken by the appalling condition of the peasants. Mere reflection or denunciation seemed to him a form of evasion. He must act, he must start at home. Like the eighteenth-century radicals, he was convinced that men were born equal, and were made unequal by the way in which they were brought up. He established a school for the boys of his own village; and, dissatisfied with the educational theories then in vogue in Russia, decided to go abroad to study Western methods in theory and in practice. He derived a great deal from his visits to England, France, Switzerland, Belgium, Germany—including the title of his greatest novel. But his conversations with the most advanced Western authorities on education, and his observation of their methods, had convinced him that they were at best worthless, at worst harmful, to the children upon whom they were practised. He did not stay long in England and paid little attention to its 'antiquated' schools. In France he found that learning was almost entirely mechanical— by rote; prepared questions, lists of dates, for example, were answered competently, because they had been learnt by heart. But the same children, when asked for the same facts from some unexpected angle, often produced absurd replies, which showed that their knowledge meant nothing to them. The schoolboy who replied that the murderer of Henry IV of France was Julius Caesar seemed to him typical: the boy neither understood nor took an interest in the facts he had stored up: all that was gained, at most, was a mechanical memory. But, the true home of theory was Germany. The pages which Tolstoy devotes to describing teaching and teachers in Germany rival and anticipate the celebrated pages in *War and Peace* in which he makes savage fun of admired experts in another field—the German strategists employed by the Russian Army—whom he represents as grotesque and pompous dolts.

In *Yasnaya Polyana*, the journal called after his estate, which he had had privately printed in 1859–61, Tolstoy speaks of his educational visits to various schools in the West and, by way of example gives a hair-raising (and exceedingly entertaining) account of the latest methods of elementary teaching used by a specialist trained in one of the most advanced of the German teachers' seminaries. He describes the pedantic, immensely self-satisfied schoolmaster, as he enters the room and notes with approval that the children are seated at their desks, crushed and obedient, in total silence, as prescribed by German rules of behaviour. 'He casts a look round the class and is quite clear in his mind about what they ought to understand; he knows it all already, he knows what the children's souls are made of and a good many other things that the seminary has taught him.' The schoolmaster enters, armed with the latest and most progressive pedagogic volume, called *Das Fischbuch*. It contains pictures of a fish.

'What is this, dear children?' 'A fish,' replies the brightest. 'No, no. Think. Think!' And he will not rest until some child says that what they see is not a fish, but a book. That is better. 'And what do books contain?' 'Letters,' says the bravest boy. 'No, no', says the schoolmaster sadly. 'You really *must* think of what you are saying.' By this time the children are beginning to be hopelessly demoralized: they have no notion of what they are meant to say. They have a confused and perfectly correct feeling that the schoolmaster wants them to say something unintelligible— that the fish is not a fish; they feel that whatever it is that he wants them to say is something that they will never think of. Their thoughts begin to stray. They wonder (this is very Tolstoyan) why the master is wearing spectacles, why he is looking through them instead of taking them off, and so on. The master urges them to concentrate; he harries and tortures them until he manages to make them say that what they see is not a fish, but a picture, and then, after more torture, that the picture represents a fish. If that is what he wants them to say, would it not be easier, Tolstoy asks, to make them learn this piece of profound wisdom by heart, instead of tormenting them with the idiotic Fishbook method, which so far from causing them to think 'creatively', merely stupefies them? The genuinely intelligent children know that their answers are always wrong; they cannot tell why, they only know that this is so; while the stupid, who occasionally provide the right answers, do not understand why they are praised. All that the German pedagogue is doing is to feed dead human material—or rather living human beings—into a grotesque mechanical contraption invented by fanatical fools who think that this is a way of applying scientific method to the education of men. Tolstoy assures us that his account (of which I have quoted only a short fragment) is not a parody, but a faithful reproduction of what he saw and heard in the advanced schools of Germany and in 'those schools in England which have been fortunate enough to acquire these wonderful modern methods'.

Disillusioned and indignant, Tolstoy returned to his Russian estate and began to teach the village children himself. He built schools; continued to study and reject and denounce current doctrines of education; published periodicals and pamphlets; invented new methods of learning geography, zoology, physics; composed an entire manual of arithmetic of his own; inveighed against all methods of coercion, especially those which consisted of forcing children against their will to memorize facts and dates and figures. In short, he behaved like an energetic, opinionated, somewhat eccentric eighteenth-century landowner, who had become a convert to the doctrines of Rousseau or the abbé Mably. His accounts of his theories and experiments fill two stout volumes in the pre-revolutionary editions of his collected works. They are still fascinating, if only because they contain some of the best descriptions of village life, and especially of children, both comical and lyrical, that even he had ever composed. He wrote them in the 'sixties and 'seventies, when he was at the height of his creative powers. The reader tends to lose sight of Tolstoy's overriding didactic purpose before the unrivalled insight into the twisting, criss-crossing pattern of the thoughts and feelings of individual village children, and the marvellous concreteness and imagination of the descriptions of their talk and their behaviour and of physical nature round them—of trees, meadows, sky, light and darkness and winter in a village in Central Russia. Yet side by side with this expression of a direct vision of human experience there run the clear, firm dogmas of a fanatically doctrinaire eighteenth-century rationalist—doctrines not fused with the life that he describes, but superimposed upon it, like windows with rigorously symmetrical patterns drawn upon them, unrelated to the world on which they open, and yet achieving a kind of illusory artistic and intellectual unity with it, owing to the unbounded vitality and constructive genius of the writing itself. It is one of the most extraordinary performances in the history of literature.

The enemy is always the same: experts, professionals, men who claim special authority over other men. Universities and professors are a frequent target for attack. There are intimations of this already in the section entitled *Youth* of his earlier autobiographical novel. There is something eighteenth century, reminiscent both of Voltaire and of Bentham, about Tolstoy's devastating accounts of the dull and incompetent professors and the desperately bored and obsequious students in Russia in his youth. The tone is unusual in the nineteenth century: dry, ironical, didactic, mordant, at once withering and entertaining; the whole based on the contrast between the harmonious simplicity of nature and the self-destructive complications created by the malice or stupidity of men—men from whom the author feels himself detached, whom he affects not to understand and mocks at from a distance. We are at the earliest beginnings of a theme which grew obsessive in Tolstoy's later life, that the solution to all our perplexities stares us in the face—that the answer is about us everywhere, like the light of day, if only we would not close our eyes or look everywhere but at what is there, before our very eyes, the clear, simple irresistible truth.

Like Rousseau and Kant and the believers in Natural law, Tolstoy was convinced that men have certain basic material and spiritual needs in all places, at all times. If these needs are fulfilled, they lead harmonious lives, which is the goal of their nature. Moral, aesthetic and other spiritual values are objective and eternal, and man's inner harmony depends upon his correct relationship to these. Moreover, Tolstoy constantly defended the proposition that human beings are more harmonious in childhood than under the corrupting influence of education in later life; and also something that he believed much more deeply and expressed in everything he wrote or said—that simple people, peasants, Cossacks, and the like have a more 'natural' and correct attitude than civilized men towards these basic values and that they are free and independent in a sense in which civilized men are not. For (he insists on this over and over again) peasant communities are in a position to supply their own material and spiritual needs out of their own resources, provided that they are not robbed or enslaved by oppressors and exploiters; whereas civilized men need for their survival the forced labour of others—serfs, slaves, the exploited masses, ironically called 'dependents' because their masters depend on *them*. The masters are parasitic upon others: they are degraded not merely by the fact that to enslave and exploit others is a denial of such objective values as justice, equality, human dignity, love—values which men crave to realize because they must, because they are men—but for the further and, to him, even more important reason, that to live on robbed or borrowed goods and so fail to be self-subsistent, falsifies 'natural' feelings and perceptions, corrodes men morally, and makes them both wicked and miserable. The human ideal is a society of free and equal men, who live and think by the light of what is true and right, and so are not in conflict with each other or themselves. This is a form—a very simple one—of the classical doctrine of Natural law, whether in its theological or secular, liberal-anarchist form. To it Tolstoy adhered all his life, as much in his 'secular' period as after his 'conversion'. His early stories express this vividly. The Cossacks Lukashka or Uncle Yeroshka in *The Cossacks* are morally superior as well as happier and aesthetically more harmonious beings than Olenin. Olenin knows this; indeed that is the heart of the situation. Pierre in *War and Peace* and Levin in *Anna Karenina* sense this in simple peasants and soldiers; so does Nekhlyudov in *The Morning of a Landowner*. This conviction fills Tolstoy's mind to a greater and greater degree, until it overshadows all other issues in his later works; *Resurrection* and *The Death of Ivan Ilyich* are not intelligible without it.

Tolstoy's critical thought constantly revolves round this central conflict—nature and artifice, truth and invention. When in the 'nineties he laid down conditions of excellence in art (in the course of an introduction to a Russian translation of some of Maupassant's stories), he demanded of all writers, in the first place, the possession of sufficient talent; in the second, that the subject itself must be morally important; and finally, that they must truly love and hate what they describe—'commit' themselves—retain the direct moral vision of childhood, and not maim their natures by practising self-imposed, self-lacerating and always illusory objectivity and detachment. Talent is not given equally to all men; but everyone can, if he tries, discover what is good and what is bad, what is important and what is trivial. Only false—'made up'—theories blind men and writers to this, and so distort their lives and creative activity. He applies his criteria quite literally. Thus Nekrassov, according to Tolstoy, treated subjects of profound importance, and possessed superb skill as a writer; but he failed because his attitude towards his suffering peasants and crushed idealists remained chilly and unreal. Dostoevsky's subjects, Tolstoy concedes, lack nothing in seriousness, and his concern is profound and genuine; but the first condition is not fulfilled: he is diffuse and repetitive, he does not know how to tell the truth clearly, and then to stop—one can, after the first hundred pages or so, predict all the rest. Turgenev writes well and stands in a real, morally adequate, relationship to his subjects; but he fails fearfully on the second count: the level is too superficial—the issues are too trivial—and for this no degree of integrity or skill can compensate. For, Tolstoy insists again and again, content determines form, never form content; and if the topic is too small, nothing will save the work of the artist. To hold the opposite of this—to believe in the primacy of form—is to sacrifice truth: to end by producing works that are contrived. There is no harsher word in Tolstoy's entire critical vocabulary than 'made up'—indicating that the writer did not truly experience or imagine, but merely 'composed', 'contrived', 'made up' that which he is purporting to describe. So, too, Tolstoy maintained that Maupassant, whose gifts he admired greatly (and perhaps overestimated), betrayed his genius precisely owing to false and vulgar theories of this kind; yet he was judged, none the less, to be a good writer to the degree to which, like Balaam, although he might have meant to curse the good, he could not help discerning it: and this perception inevitably attracted his love to it and forced him against his own will towards the truth. Talent is vision, vision reveals the truth, truth is eternal and objective. To see the truth about nature or about conduct, to see it directly and vividly as only a man of genius (or a simple human being or a child) can see it, and then, in cold blood, to deny or tamper with the vision, no matter with what motive, is always monstrous, unnatural, a symptom of a deeply, perhaps fatally, diseased condition.

III

Truth, for Tolstoy, is always discoverable, to follow it is to be good, inwardly sound, harmonious. Yet it is clear that our society is not harmonious or composed of internally harmonious individuals. The interests of the educated minority—what he calls 'the professors, the barons, and the bankers'—are opposed to those of the majority—the peasants, the poor. Each side is indifferent to, or mocks, the values of the other. Even those who, like Olenin, Pierre, Nekhlyudov, Levin, realize the spuriousness of the values of the professors, barons and bankers, and the moral decay in which their false education has involved them, even those who are truly contrite, cannot, despite Slavophil pretensions, go native and 'merge' with the mass of the common people. Are they too corrupt ever to recover their innocence? Is their case hopeless? Can it be that civilized men have acquired (or discovered) certain true values of their own, which barbarians and children may know nothing of, but which they—the civilized—cannot lose or forget, even if, by some impossible means, they could transform themselves into peasants or the free and happy Cossacks of the Don and the Terek? This is one of the central and most tormenting problems in Tolstoy's life, to which he goes back again and again, and to which he returns conflicting answers.

Tolstoy knows that he himself clearly belongs to the minority of barons, bankers, professors. He knows the symptoms of his condition only too well. He cannot, for example, deny his passionate love for the music of Mozart or Chopin or the poetry of Pushkin or Tyutchev—the ripest fruits of civilization. He needs—he cannot do without—the printed word and all the elaborate paraphernalia of the culture in which such lives are lived and such works of art are created. But what is the use of Pushkin to village boys, when his words are not intelligible to them? What real benefits has the invention of printing brought the peasants? We are told, Tolstoy observes, that books educate societies ('that is, make them more corrupt'), that it was the written word that has promoted the emancipation of the serfs in Russia. Tolstoy denies this: the government would have done the same without books or pamphlets. Pushkin's *Boris Godunov* pleases him, Tolstoy, deeply, but to the peasants means nothing. The triumphs of civilization? The telegraph informs him about his sister's health, or about the political prospects of King Otto I of Greece; but what benefit do the masses gain from it? Yet it is they who pay and have always paid for it all, and they know this well. When peasants in the 'cholera riots' kill doctors because they regard them as poisoners, what they do is no doubt wrong, yet these murders are no accident: the instinct which tells the peasants who their oppressors are is sound, and the doctors belong to that class. When Wanda Landowska played to the villagers of Yasnaya Polyana, the great majority of them remained unresponsive. Yet can it be doubted that it is these simple people who lead the least broken lives, immeasurably superior to the warped and tormented lives of the rich and educated? The common people, Tolstoy asserts in his early educational tracts, are self-subsistent not only materially but spiritually—folksong, ballads, the *Iliad*, the Bible, spring from the people itself, and are therefore intelligible to all men everywhere, as Tyutchev's magnificent poem *Silentium*, or *Don Giovanni*, or the Ninth Symphony are not. If there is an ideal of human life, it lies not in the future but in the past. Once upon a time there was the Garden of Eden, and in it dwelt the uncorrupted human soul—as the Bible and Rousseau conceived it—and then came the Fall, corruption, suffering, falsehood. It is mere blindness (Tolstoy says over and over again) to believe, as liberals or socialists—'the progressives'—believe, that the golden age is still to come, that history is the story of improvement, that advances in natural science or material skills coincide with real moral progress. The truth is the reverse of this.

The child is closer to the ideal harmony than the man, and the simple peasant than the torn, 'alienated', morally and spiritually unanchored, self-destructive parasites who form the civilized élite. From this doctrine springs Tolstoy's notable anti-individualism; and in particular his diagnosis of the individual's will as the source of misdirection and perversion of 'natural' human tendencies, and hence the conviction (derived largely from Schopenhauer's doctrine of the will as the source of frustration) that to plan, organize, rely on science, try to create ordered patterns of life in accordance with rational theories, is to swim against the stream of nature, to close one's eyes to the saving truth within us, to torture facts to fit artificial schemes, and torture human beings to fit social and economic systems against which their natures cry out. From the same source, too, comes the obverse of this moral: Tolstoy's faith in the intuitively grasped direction of things as being not merely inevitable but objectively—providentially—good; and therefore belief in the need to submit to it: his quietism.

This is one aspect of his teaching, the most familiar, the central idea of the Tolstoyan movement. It runs through all his mature works, imaginative, critical, didactic, from *The Cossacks* and *Family Happiness*, to his last religious tracts; this is the doctrine which both liberals and Marxists duly condemned. It is in this mood that Tolstoy (like Marx whom he neither respected nor understood) maintains that to imagine that heroic personalities determine events is a piece of colossal megalomania and self-deception. His narrative is designed to show the insignificance of Napoleon or Alexander, or of aristocratic and bureaucratic society in *Anna Karenina*, or of the judges and official persons in *Resurrection*; or again, the emptiness and intellectual impotence of historians and philosophers who try to explain events by employing concepts like 'power' attributed to great men, or 'influence' ascribed to writers, orators, preachers—words, abstractions, which, in his view, explain nothing, being themselves more obscure than the facts for which they purport to account. He maintains that we do not begin to understand, and therefore cannot explain or analyse, what it is to wield authority or strength, to influence, to dominate. Explanations that do not explain, are, for Tolstoy, a symptom of the destructive and self-inflated intellect, the faculty that kills innocence and leads to false notions and the ruin of human life.

That is one strain, inspired by Rousseau and present in that early romanticism which inspired primitivism in art and in life, not in Russia alone. Tolstoy imagines that this state can be achieved by observing the lives of simple people and by the study of the Gospels.

His other strain (interwoven with the first) is the direct opposite of this. Mikhailovsky in his essay on Tolstoy says, justly enough, that Olenin cannot, charmed as he is by the Caucasus and the Cossack idyll, transform himself into a Lukashka, return to the childlike harmony, which in his case has long been broken. Levin knows that if he tried to become a peasant this could only be a grotesque farce, which the peasants would be the first to perceive and deride; he and Pierre and Nicolai Rostov know obscurely that in some sense they have something to give that the peasants have not. In the famous essay entitled *What Is Art?* Tolstoy unexpectedly tells the educated reader that the peasant 'needs what your life of ten generations uncrushed by hard labour has given you. You had the leisure to search, to think, to suffer—then give him that for whose sake you suffered; he is in need of it . . . do not bury in the earth the talent given you by history . . .' Leisure, then, need not be merely destructive. Progress can occur; we can learn from what happened in the past, as those who lived in that past could not. It is true that we live in an unjust order. But this itself creates direct moral obligations. Those who are members of the civilized *élite*, cut off as they tragically are from the mass of the people, have the duty to attempt to rebuild broken humanity, to stop exploiting other men, to give them what they most need—education, knowledge, material help, a capacity for living better lives. Levin in *Anna Karenina*, as Mikhailovsky remarks, takes up where Nicolai Rostov in *War and Peace* leaves off; they are not quietists, yet what they do is right. The emancipation of the peasants, in Tolstoy's view, although it did not go far enough, was nevertheless a powerful act of will—good will—on the part of the government, and now it is necessary to teach peasants to read and write and grasp the rules of arithmetic, which the peasants cannot do for themselves; to equip them for the use of freedom. I may be unable to merge myself with the mass of peasants; but I can at least use the fruit of the unjustly obtained leisure of myself and my ancestors—my education, knowledge, skills—for the benefit of those whose labour made it possible. This is the talent which I may not bury. I must work to promote a just society in accordance with those objective standards which all men, except the hopelessly corrupt, see and accept, whether they live by them or not. The simple see them more clearly, the sophisticated more dimly, but all men can see them if they try; indeed, to be able to see them is part of what it is to be a man. When injustice is perpetrated, I have an obligation to speak out and act against it; nor may artists, any more than other men, sit with folded hands. What makes good writers good is first and foremost, ability to see truth—social and individual, material and spiritual—and so present it that it cannot be escaped. Tolstoy holds that Maupassant, for example, is doing exactly this, despite all his aesthetic fallacies. Maupassant may, because he is a corrupt human being, take the side of the bad against the good, write about a worthless Paris seducer with greater sympathy than he feels for his victims. But provided that he tells the truth at a level that is sufficiently profound (and men of talent cannot avoid doing this) he will face the reader with fundamental moral questions—even though this may not be his intention—questions which the reader can neither escape nor answer without severe and painful self-examination. This, for Tolstoy, opens the path to regeneration, and is the proper function of Art. Vocation, talent, artistic conscience—all these are obedient to an inescapable inner need: to satisfy it is the artist's purpose and duty. Nothing therefore, is more false than the view of the artist as a purveyor or a craftsman whose sole function is to create a beautiful thing, as the aesthetes—Flaubert, or Renan, or Maupassant (or Mr. Evelyn Waugh) maintain. There is only one true human goal, and it is equally binding on all men—landowners, doctors, barons, professors, bankers, peasants: to tell the truth and act according to it, that is, to do good and persuade others to do so. That God exists, or that the *Iliad* is beautiful, or that men have a right to be free and to be equal, are all eternal and absolute truths. Therefore, we must persuade men to read the *Iliad* and not pornographic French novels, and to work for an equal society, not a theocratic or political hierarchy. Coercion is evil; this is self-evident and men have always known it to be true; therefore they must work for a society in which there will be no wars, no prisons, no executions, in any circumstances, for any reason—for a society in which there is the highest attainable degree of individual freedom. By his own route Tolstoy arrived at a programme of Christian anarchism which had much in common with that of the 'realist' school of painters and composers—Mussorgsky, Repin, Stassov—and with that of their political allies, the Russian Populists, although he rejected their belief in natural science and their doctrinaire socialism and faith in the methods of terrorism. For what he now appeared to be advocating was a programme of action, not of quietism; this programme underlay the educational reforms that Tolstoy attempted to carry out. *L'éducation peut tout* said Helvétius a hundred years before, and Tolstoy in effect agreed. Ignorance is responsible for misery, inequality, wars. He writes with indignation about the prevalent 'inequality of education', and in particular 'the disproportion of the educated and uneducated, or more exactly the savage and the literate'.

If it were not for ignorance, human beings could not be exploited or coerced. 'One man cannot compel others—only a dominant majority can do that, united in its lack of education. It only looks as if Napoleon III concluded the peace of Villafranca, suppresses newspapers or wants to conquer Savoy, actually all this is done by the Félixes and Victors who cannot read newspapers.' This is the seed of the doctrine that henceforth determines all his thoughts—that the real agents of history are the masses—the collection of obscure individuals, the Félixes and Victors, although responsibility for them is mistakenly attributed to leaders and great men. If the Félixes and Victors refused to march, there would be no wars; if they were educated and could read newspapers—and if these newspapers contained truth instead of falsehood—they would not march. This is eighteenth-century rationalist doctrine in its clearest form. For Tolstoy, at this stage, all social movements can be analysed into the specific behaviour of specific individuals. Peoples, governments, nations, armies, are only collective nouns, not genuine entities—to attribute to them the characteristics of human beings, to speak of them as literally active or powerful, as authors of this achievement or that feature—is not misleading only if it is remembered that they can (and not in principle only) be analysed into their constituent elements. This positivist conviction Tolstoy holds in a stronger form than Marx or Comte—as strongly as the most extreme empiricists of our own time: like them, he denounces as myth, as metaphysical obfuscation, anything that implies that collective behaviour is not analysable into the behaviour of the individuals who compose the collective; and to this he adds the corollary that the real activity of a man is the 'inner' activity of his spirit, and not the 'outer' activity as expressed in social or political life. And he quotes the activist and revolutionary Herzen towards whom his attitude was at all times highly ambivalent in support of this position. It is hardly necessary to add that the whole of *War and Peace* and much of *Anna Karenina* and *Resurrection* is an incarnation of this central idea. All the results of advancing civilization—the telegraph, steamers, theatres, academies, literature, etc.—are useless so long as only one per cent of the people are receiving education. 'All this (i.e. universities, etc.) is useful, but useful as a dinner in the English Club might be useful if all of it were eaten by the manager and the cook. These things are created by all the seventy million Russians, but are of use only to thousands.' Who shall determine what is the right kind of education? When in doubt Tolstoy returns to Rousseau. 'The will of the people is the sole factor by which our (educational) activity should be guided.'

'If we offer the people certain kinds of knowledge . . . and find that they have a bad influence on it, I conclude not that the people is bad because it doesn't absorb this knowledge, nor that the people, unlike ourselves, is not adult enough to do so . . . but that this kind of knowledge is bad, abnormal, and that with the help of the people we must work out new sorts of knowledge more suitable for us all—that is both for the educated and for the common people . . .' 'Someone might ask: Why should we assume that the arts and sciences of our own educated class are false? Why should you infer their falsity from the mere fact that the people does not take to it? This question is answered very easily: because there are thousands of us, but millions of them.'

This democratic programme is Tolstoy's answer to the hated 'liberals' and 'progressives' and the specialists and civilized *élites* to whom they look for salvation. Faithful to Rousseau (and if he had but known it), to Kant, he strove to discover, collect, expound eternal truths; awaken the spontaneous interest, the imagination, love, curiosity, of children or simple folk; above all liberate their 'natural' moral, emotional and intellectual powers, which he did not doubt, as Rousseau did not doubt, would achieve harmony within men and between them, provided that we took care to eliminate whatever might cramp, maim, and kill them.

IV

This programme—that of making possible the free self-development of all human faculties—rests on one vast assumption: that there exists at least one path of development which ensures that these faculties will neither conflict with each other, nor develop disproportionately—a sure path to the complete harmony in which everything fits and is at peace; with the corollary that we can find it—that knowledge of man's nature gained from observation or introspection or moral intuition, or from the study of the lives and writings of the best and wisest men of all ages or of the simple hearts of the 'millions' and not of the 'thousands', will show it to us. This is not the place for considering how far this doctrine is compatible with ancient religious teachings or modern psychology. The point I wish to stress is that it is, above all, a programme of action, a call for universal education and re-education, a declaration of war against current social values, against the tyranny of states, societies, churches, against brutality, injustice, ignorance, stupidity, hypocrisy, weakness, above all, against vanity and moral blindness. A man who has fought a good fight in this war will thereby expiate the sin of having been a hedonist and an exploiter, and the son and beneficiary of robbers and oppressors.

This is what Tolstoy believed, preached and practised. His 'conversion' altered his view of what was good and what was evil. It did not weaken his faith in the need for action. His belief in the principles themselves henceforth never wavered. The enemy entered by another door: Tolstoy's sense of reality was too inexorable to keep out a terrible doubt how these principles—no matter how true themselves—should be applied. Even though *I* believe some things to be beautiful or good, and others to be ugly and evil, what right have *I* to bring up others in the light of my convictions, when I know that, do what I might, I cannot help liking Chopin and Maupassant, while these far better beings—peasants or children—do not? Have I, who stand at the end of a long period of decadence—of generations of civilized, unnatural living—have *I* the right to touch *their* souls?

To seek to influence someone, however mysterious the process, is to engage in a dark, morally suspect enterprise. This is obvious in the case of the crude manipulation of one man by another. But in principle it holds equally of education. All educators seek to shape the minds and lives of human beings in the direction of a given goal, or in the light of a specific ideal model. But if we—the sophisticated members of a deeply corrupt society—are ourselves unhappy, inharmonious, gone astray, what can we be doing but trying to change children who are born healthy into our own sick semblance, to make of them cripples like ourselves? We are what we have become; we cannot help our love of Pushkin's verses, of Chopin's music; we discover that children and peasants find them unintelligible or tedious. What do we do? We persist, we 'educate' them, until they too, appear to enjoy these works, or, at least, grasp why we enjoy them. What have we done? We find the works of Mozart and Chopin beautiful only because Mozart and Chopin were themselves children of our degenerate culture, and therefore their words speak to our diseased minds; but what right have we to infect others, to make them as corrupt as ourselves? ('The works of Pushkin, Gogol, Turgenev, Derzhavin . . . are not needed by the people and will bring it no benefit.') We see the blemishes of other systems. We see all too clearly how the human personality is destroyed by Protestant insistence on blind obedience, by Catholic belief in social emulation, by the appeal to material self-interest and the value of social rank and position on which Russian education, according to Tolstoy, is based. Is it not, then, either monstrous arrogance or a perverse inconsistency to behave as if our own system of education—something recommended by Pestalozzi, or by the inventors of the Lancaster method, or by some other expert, systems that reflect their inventors' civilized and consequently perverted, personalities— as if such ideas were necessarily superior, or even less destructive than what we condemn so readily and justly in the superficial French or the stupid and pompous Germans?

How is this to be avoided? Tolstoy repeats the lessons of Rousseau's *Emile*. Nature, only nature will save us. We must seek to find what is 'natural', spontaneous, uncorrupt, sound, in harmony with itself and other objects in the world, and then to clear paths for development on these lines; not seek to alter, to force into a mould. We must listen to the dictates of our stifled original nature—not look on it as mere raw material on which to impose our unique individual personalities and powerful wills. To defy, to be Promethean, to create goals and build worlds in rivalry with what our moral sense knows to be eternal truths, given once and for all to all men, truths, knowledge of which alone renders them men and not beasts— that is the monstrous sin of pride, committed by all reformers, all revolutionaries, all men judged by the world to be great and effective. It is committed in just as large a measure by those in authority—by legislators, bureaucrats, judges, country squires who, out of liberal convictions or simply caprice or boredom, dictate, bully and interfere with the lives of peasants. Do not teach: learn; that is the central notion of Tolstoy's essay, written nearly a hundred years ago, 'Should we teach the peasants' children how to write, or should they teach us?' and it goes through all the notes on education, published in the 'sixties and 'seventies and written with his customary freshness, attention to detail and unapproachable power of direct perception. In one of these he gives examples of stories written by the children in his village, and speaks of the awe which he felt, face to face with the act of pure creation in which, he assures us, he played no part himself; these stories would only be spoilt by his 'corrections'; they seem to him far deeper than anything by Goethe. He speaks of how deeply ashamed they made him feel of his own superficiality, vanity, stupidity, narrowness, lack of moral and aesthetic sense. If, he tells us, one can help children and peasants at all, it is only by making it easier for them to advance freely along their own instinctive path; to direct is to spoil; men are good and only need freedom to realize their goodness.

'We speak,' writes Tolstoy in the 'seventies, 'of bringing a man up to be a scoundrel, a hypocrite, a good man: of the Spartans as bringing up brave men, of French education as producing one-sided and self-satisfied persons, and so on.' But this is speaking of, and using, human beings as so much raw material for us to model, this is what 'to bring up' to be like this or like that, means. We are evidently ready to alter the direction spontaneously followed by the souls and wills of others, to deny them independence—in favour of what? Of our own corrupt, false, or, at best, uncertain values? 'Education', Tolstoy says elsewhere, 'is the action of one person on another with a view to causing the other to acquire certain moral habits'; but this always involves some degree of moral tyranny. And in a wild moment of panic, he adds 'Is not the ultimate motive of the educator *envy*—envy of the purity of the child; desire to make the child more like himself, that is to say, more corrupt?' he goes on to add, 'What has the entire history of education been?' he answers: 'All philosophers of education, from Plato to Kant, professed to want one thing: to free education from the chains of the evil past—from its ignorance and its errors—to find out what men truly need, and adjust the new schools to that.' They struck off one yoke only to put another in its place. Certain scholastic philosophers insisted on Greek, because that was the language of Aristotle who knew the truth. Luther, Tolstoy continues, denied the authority of the Fathers and insisted on inculcating the original Hebrew, because he *knew* that that was the language in which God had revealed eternal truths to men. Bacon looked to empirical knowledge of nature, and his theories contradicted those of Aristotle, Rousseau proclaimed his faith in life—life as he conceived it—and not in theories. But about one thing they were all agreed: that one must liberate the young from the blind despotism of the old; and each immediately substituted his own fanatical, enslaving dogma in its place. If I am sure that I know the truth and that all else is error, does that alone entitle me to superintend the education of another? Is such certainty enough? Whether or not it disagrees with the certainties of others? Have I the right to put a wall round the pupil, exclude all external influences, and try to mould him as I please, in my own, or somebody else's, image? The answer to this question, Tolstoy passionately says to the 'progressives', 'must be "yes" or "no" . . . , if it is "yes", then the church schools and the Jews' schools have as much right to exist as our universities'. He declares that he sees no moral difference, at least in principle, between the compulsory Latin of the traditional establishments and the compulsory materialism with which the radical professors indoctrinate their captive audiences. There might indeed, be something to be said for the things that the liberals delight in denouncing: education at home, for example; for it is surely natural that parents should wish their children to resemble them. Again there is a case for a religious upbringing, since it is natural that believers should want to save all other human beings from what they are certain must be eternal damnation. Similarly the Government is entitled to train men, for society cannot survive without some sort of government, and governments cannot exist without some qualified specialists to serve them. But what is the moral basis of 'liberal education' in schools and universities, staffed by men who do not even claim to be sure that what they teach is true? Empiricism? The lessons of history? The only lesson that history teaches us is that all previous educational systems have proved to be despotisms founded on falsehoods, and later roundly condemned. Why should the twenty-first century not look back on us in the nineteenth with the same scorn and amusement as that with which we now look on mediaeval schools and universities? If the history of education is the history merely of tyranny and error, why should we, and what right have we, to carry on this abominable farce? And if we are told that it has always been so, that it is nothing new, that we cannot help it and must do our best— is this not like saying that murders have always taken place, so that we might as well go on murdering even though we have now discovered what it is that makes men murder? In these circumstances, we should be villains if we did not say at least this much: that since, unlike the Pope or Luther or modern positivists, we do not ourselves claim to base our education (or other forms of interference with human beings) on knowledge of absolute truth, we must at least stop torturing others in the name of something that we do not know. All we can know for certain is what men actually want. Let us at least have the courage of our admitted ignorance, of our doubts and uncertainties. At least, we can try to discover what others—children or adults—require, by taking off the spectacles of tradition, prejudice, dogma, and making it possible for ourselves to know men as they truly are, by listening to them carefully and sympathetically, and understanding them and their lives and their needs, one by one, individually. Let us at least try to provide them with what they ask for, and leave them as free as possible. Give them *Bildung* (for which Tolstoy produces an equivalent Russian word—pointing out with pride that it has none in French or English), that is to say, seek to influence them by precept and by the example of your own lives; but not apply 'education' to them, which is essentially a method of coercion and destroys what is most natural and sacred in man— the capacity for knowing and acting for oneself in accordance with what one thinks to be true and good—the power and the right of self-direction.

But he cannot let the matter rest there, as many a liberal has tried to do. For the question immediately arises; how are we to contrive to leave the schoolboy and the student free? By being morally neutral? By imparting only factual knowledge, not ethical, or aesthetic, or social or religious doctrine? By placing the 'facts' before the pupil, and letting him form his own conclusions, without seeking to influence him in any direction, for fear that we might infect him with our own diseased outlooks? But is it really possible for such neutral communications to occur between men? Is not every human communication a conscious or unconscious impression of one temperament, attitude to life, scale of values, upon another? Are men ever so thoroughly insulated from each other that the careful avoidance of more than the minimum degree of social intercourse will leave them un-sullied, absolutely free to see truth and falsehood, good and evil, beauty and ugliness, with their own, and only their own eyes? But this is an absurd conception of individuals as creatures who can be kept pure from all social influence, and seemed absurd in the world even of Tolstoy's middle years, even, that is, without the new knowledge of human beings that we have acquired today as the result of the labours of psychologists, sociologists, philosophers. We live in a degenerate society; only the pure, Tolstoy says, can rescue us. But who, he reasonably asks, will educate the educators? Who is so pure as to know how, let alone be able, to heal our world or anyone in it?

Between these poles—on one side the facts, nature, what there is; on the other duty, justice, what there should be; on one side innocence, on the other education; between the claims of spontaneity and those of obligation, of the injustice of coercing others, and of the injustice of leaving them to their own ways, Tolstoy wavered and struggled all his life. And not only he, but all those populists and socialists, the doctors, engineers, agricultural experts, painters and composers and idealistic students in Russia who 'went to the people' and could not decide whether they had gone to teach or to learn, whether the 'good of the people' for which they were ready to sacrifice their lives, was what 'the people' in fact desired, or something that the reformers and they alone knew to be good for it—something which the 'people' should desire—would desire if only they were as educated and wise as their champions—but, in fact, in their benighted state, often spurned and violently resisted. These contradictions, and his unswerving recognition of his failure to reconcile or modify them, are, in a sense, what gives its special meaning both to Tolstoy's life and to the morally agonized, didactic pages of his art. He furiously rejected the com-promises and alibis of his liberal contemporaries as mere feebleness and evasion. Yet he believed that a final solution to the problem of how to apply the principles of Jesus must exist, even though neither he nor any one else had wholly discovered it. He rejected the very possibility that some of the tendencies and goals of which he speaks might be literally both valid and incompatible. Historicism versus moral responsibility; quietism versus the duty to resist evil; teleology or a causal order against the play of chance and irrational force; on the one hand, spiritual harmony, simplicity, the mass of the people, and on the other, the irresistible attraction of the culture of minorities and their sciences, and arts, the conflict between corruption of the civilized portion of society and its direct duty to raise the masses of the people to its own level; the dynamism and falsifying influence of passionate, simple, one-sided faith, as against the clear-sighted sense of the complex facts and inevitable weakness in action which flows from enlightened scepticism—all these strains are given full play in the thought of Tolstoy. His adhesion to them appears as a series of inconsistencies in his system, because the conflicts may, after all, exist in fact and lead to collisions in real life. Tolstoy is incapable of suppressing, or falsifying, or explaining away or 'transcending' by reference to dialectical or other 'deeper' levels of thought, any truth when it presents itself to him, no matter what this entails, where it leads, how much it destroys of what he most pasionately longs to believe. Everyone knows that Tolstoy placed truth highest of all the virtues. Others have made such declarations and have celebrated her no less memorably. But Tolstoy is among the few who have truly earned that rare right: for he sacrificed all he had upon her altar—happiness, friendship, love, peace, moral and intellectual certainty, and, in the end, his life. And all she gave him in return was doubt, insecurity, self-contempt, insoluble contradictions. In this sense (although he would have repudiated this most violently) he is a martyr and a hero in the central tradition of the European enlightenment. This seems a paradox: but then his entire life is in this sense a great paradox, inasmuch as it bears constant witness to a proposition to the denial of which his last years were dedicated—that the truth is seldom wholly simple or clear, or as obvious as it may sometimes seem to the eye of the ordinary, sensible man.

R. P. BLACKMUR

The Dialectic of Incarnation: Tolstoy's "Anna Karenina"

If there is one notion which repre-
sents what Tolstoy is up to in his novels—emphatically in *Anna Karenina*
and *War and Peace*—it is this. He exposes his created men and women to
the "terrible ambiguity of an immediate experience" (Jung's phrase in his
Psychology and Religion), and then, by the mimetic power of his imagination,
expresses their reactions and responses to that experience. Some reactions
are merely protective and make false responses; some reactions are so deep
as to amount to a change in the phase of being and make honest responses.
The reactions are mechanical or instinctive, the responses personal or
spiritual. But both the reactions and the responses have to do with that
force greater than ourselves, outside ourselves, and working on ourselves,
which whether we call it God or Nature is the force of life, what is shaped
or misshaped, construed or misconstrued, in the process of living. Both
each individual life and also that life in fellowship which we call society
are so to speak partial incarnations of that force; but neither is ever complete; thus the great human struggle, for the individual or for the society,
is so to react and so to respond to "the terrible ambiguity of an immediate
experience" as to approach the conditions of rebirth, the change of heart,
or even the fresh start. Tragedy comes about from the failure to apprehend
the character or the direction of that force, either by an exaggeration of
the self alone or of the self in society. That is why in Tolstoy the peasants,

From *Eleven Essays in the European Novel.* Copyright © 1964 by R. P. Blackmur. Harcourt,
Brace and World.

the simple family people, and the good-natured wastrels furnish the background and the foils for the tragedy, for these move according to the momentum of things, and although they are by no means complete incarnations of the force behind the momentum are yet in an equal, rough relation to it. The others, the tragic figures, move rather, by their own mighty effort, in relation, reaction, response to that force, some with its momentum, some against it; some falsifying it in themselves, some falsifying it in society, but each a special incarnation of it; some cutting their losses; some consolidating their gains; some balancing, some teetering, in a permanent labor of rebirth. There is thus at work in the novels of Tolstoy a kind of dialectic of incarnation: the bodying forth in aesthetic form by contrasted human spirits of "the terrible ambiguity of an immediate experience" through their reactions and responses to it. It is this dialectic which gives buoyancy and sanity to Tolstoy's novels.

Let us see how this happens in *Anna Karenina*—how it happens not only in the name and tale of the heroine but also and in relation to the tale of Levin; and how these gain some of their significance through being told against the background of Stiva and Dolly Oblonsky's unhappy marriage. That unhappy marriage is the image of society in momentum, that momentum which only requires the right face to be put upon it to be tolerable, which is true neither for the illicit affair of Anna and Vronsky nor for the profoundly lawful affair of Levin and Kitty. Stiva and Dolly are too near the actual manner of things, are too wholly undifferentiated from the course of society and of individuals, ever to feel the need or the pang of rebirth. All they want is for things to be as they are. Stiva, as the old nurse tells him when Dolly has caught him in an affair with a governess, Stiva has only to do his part; and Dolly has only, now and always, to return to her part. Anna and Levin are very different. Each, in a separate and opposed way, can be satisfied with nothing less than a full incarnation, a rebirth into the force which at crisis they feel moves them. Anna craves to transmute what moves her from underneath—*all* that can be meant by libido, not sex alone—into personal, individual, independent love; she will be stronger than society because she is the strength of society, but only so in her death at the hands of society. Levin craves to transmute himself upwards, through society, into an individual example of the love of God; he, too, will be stronger than society because he finds the will of God enacted in the natural order of things of which society is a part, but he will only do so as long as God is with him in his life. What separates both Anna and Levin from the ruck of rebels is that they make their rebellions, and construct their idylls, through a direct confrontation and apprehension of immediate experience. There is nothing arbitrary about their intentions, only their decisions; there is nothing exclusive or obsessed about their perceptions, only their actions. They think and know in the same world as Stiva and Dolly, and indeed they had to or they could never have been in love with such eminently natural creatures as Vronsky and Kitty. They live in the going concern of society, and they are aside from it only to represent it the better.

This is the world, the society, which is for the most part understood through its manners; and that is how Tolstoy begins his novel, by showing his people through the motion of their manners, first those of Stiva and Dolly, then those of the others. By the end of the first Part of the novel, we know very well the manner of life of each person and could extend it to suit any further accident of life: we know the probable critical point in the temperament of each which rises or descends to some old or new form of action or inaction, and we know it by the kind of manners each exhibits and by how far into the being of each the manners seem to penetrate: into all that is on the surface of Stiva, into all there is anywhere for Dolly, into a layer of permanent irritation for Levin, into a layer of perpetual possibility for Anna, into the radiant sweep of things not yet her own for Kitty, and into the animal vitality of things for Vronsky (who is at the beginning, and always, less a man than a sensual force inhabiting a man). For all this the comedy of Stiva's manners and Dolly's manners coming to terms with each other, not *they* but their manners, stands. Stiva deals with the ambiguities, Dolly with the intolerable things of marriage by manners. Stiva brings the huge pear of his own zest, but he can also weep. Dolly has a temper, but she can also weep. For both, tears are a kind of manners; and thus a reconciliation is effected. We see in this couple how it is that manners dictate the roles by which we escape acknowledging reality.

We begin with the same *kind* of manners Jane Austen mastered, the manners that pass for things otherwise only potentially present. But in Tolstoy we know at once that the manners are *of* something whose potency is pressing into the actual situation, something yet to be revealed in the words of the book, or at any rate to be carried into the open of our consciousness by them. Manners are a flowing stream; they are on the surface of what is swept along, hardly more by themselves but a wayward intimation of what is swept. In Jane Austen, even in *Emma*, the shape— the very water-shapes—of the stream of manners is itself pretty much the subject. In Tolstoy the stream will gradually take on the subject, will become united with it, as a brook takes on the brown of wood-earth and peat: as the Mississippi pushes its mud-color burden twenty miles to sea. Indeed the process begins in *Anna Karenina*, in the first half-dozen pages with the old nurse's remark to Stiva: Go, do your part. She tells us real things are at stake in this play of manners, things to be dealt with even the more because they are not acknowledged. And so it is with each personage as he turns up, except perhaps for Vronsky. There are hints of something pushing through.

For Dolly, there are the children, a noise in the hall and a clatter in the nursery, the *unattended* children; and they hint that Dolly's manners, temper and all, are only a part—of what? For Stiva, there is the moment of extreme aloofness after dinner in the restaurant, that aloofness among intimates for which he knew what to do: to make conversation with some *aide-de-camp*, or some actress, with someone not at the center but approaching the center; and so we are aware that the aloofness is from something. For Anna, there is, as an exercise in manners, her *first taking note* of her hypocrisy in dealing with her husband. For Kitty there are such things, still in the play of manners, as her recognition in Anna of something uncanny and her excitement at the utterance, not the substance, of Levin's declaration of love for her. Only for Vronsky there is nothing, as if his manners were so vital or his life so lacking that they were equal to his need.

But for Levin, the other half of Vronsky, there is enough to make up for all the rest. He is, in his unmannerliness, in his steady breach of the expected manner, an effort at declaring what the manners are about; but he is only one effort, one declaration, which can by no means minimize or defeat the others should they come to make their declarations. Levin's very breaches of manners are organized into manners themselves, as organized as the fools and the plain-spoken men in Shakespeare. He is a foil, a contrast, a light to Anna, Stiva, Karenin, Kitty, and Vronsky; and he is a successful foil by the accident of the condition of his temperament, by what he misses or ignores of what they all see. Stiva was right: Levin had no idea of girls as girls; he had no idea how good a fresh roll might smell and taste even after dinner—and indeed there is something vulgar in Levin when he sees a wife as a dinner, vulgar in the bad sense. But he is vulgar in the good sense when, thinking of Kitty, he tells Stiva it is not love but the force outside him which has taken possession of him. It is as if he had found a concrete parallel to the perception which had come to him in reading a sentence from Tyndall: "The connection between all the forces of nature is felt instinctively." Better still is his deep human illumination of the relativity of morals when under the impact of his rejection by Kitty in presumed favor of Vronsky, he comes to a new and compassionate judgment of that intellectual wastrel and revolutionary libertine his brother Nikolay. He thinks of him, and sees how the good force is corrupted. No doubt it is in this passage that we see through Levin's vision of his brother the death and life that are to come in the book. The shift from scorn to compassion, under the pressure of his own brooked love, seems a true act of imitation—of mimesis—which Aristotle tells us is a fundamental delight to man's mind, no matter whether the object of imitation is ugly or beautiful or monstrous.

But this is perhaps to get ahead of the story, when what we want is to become part of the momentum of the story to which the manners of the characters point. The instances of perception isolated above are all pretty mechanical; they do not yet occur organically, by the psychic drive of what has already been formed; they merely illustrate how the characters are being gotten hold of by the story: by the little or big things manners cannot quite either cover up or handle. Mainly, so far, it is a story told of how the people do cover up and do handle. We are on our most familiar living ground. For manners are the medium in which the struggle between the institutions of society and the needs of individuals is conducted. Viable dramatic manners exist so long as the struggle has not become to one-sided, so long as no total credit is given either to one side or the other. When in imagination or dogma the institutions are seen to triumph the manners become hollow, cold, and cruel. When the needs of the individual triumph the manners tend to disappear, so that life *together* becomes impossible. In either case we get a monstrous egoism, incapable either of choice or comparison, an exercise in moral suicide and sterile fancy.

No such case is reached in this novel. Far from breaking down in either direction, we find, even at the worst, at Anna's death or at Levin's access of life, everywhere but at the last retreat of Vronsky to a death in which he does not believe, that the great part of human behavior is viable in manners. It is through manners that the needs and possibilities of each person are seen in shifting conflict with the available or relevant institutions, including the twilight institutions—the illicit, amorphous institutions—which stand at the edges of the institutions of broad day. Stiva, Anna, and Vronsky depend on the twilight institutions of marriage and general social conduct which encroach on the edges of the broad day institutions upon which Dolly, Kitty, and Levin depend. Karenin, at Petersburg, belongs to something else again; he has composed his dissatisfactions in a manner which contains its own rebelliousness: his jeering, desiccated conformity. But it is only the public aspect of the struggle which is between the broad day and the twilight. In actuality the struggle is conducted in the medium of manners between individuals trying from their different needs to shape institutions into some tolerable relation to their own partial apprehensions of reality. Here again it is Levin who has the first illumination; he knows there can be no victory and that there must be a balance. Himself a disbeliever in institutions, and therefore the more apprehensive of their force, he resents the maimed and maiming complaints of his brother Nicolay against the need of institutions: the forever need of make-shift. But best of all are the brother and sister Oblonsky, Stiva and Anna of the voided marriages: the one whose manners will last him forever, the other whose manners will be less and less good to her where they lead her, until at last she creates a fatal manner of her own. Stiva rises always into good nature. Anna is herself a form of nature. Both have something more than sincerity and both, because of the twilight of their actions, have something less than honesty. Think of Stiva at waking reaching for his dressing gown and finding, because he is not in his wife's bedroom, uncertainty instead. Think of Anna, away from home and because of that looking down the stairs at Vronsky and seeing possibility.

What Stiva finds, what Anna sees, is the momentum their manners had been about; and if we look at the gap between Part One and Part Two we see that the momentum is what carries us across the gap. Everybody has been left in an unfinished situation (Anna, Vronsky, Levin, the Oblonskys) or in a "finished" situation (Kitty) which must change. Thus there is both anticipation (uncertain but selected) and expectation (certain but unknown) but we cannot know which is which and cannot determine what is authentic until it has transpired. The business of the novel is how to find out and body forth what has already happened. We know only that for each of these people and for all of them together there must be more of the same thing, with the difference that they will know it better.

The emergence of this sort of knowledge depends on plot, but not upon the mechanical plot, not upon the plot of the "well-made" novel, or at least not primarily, but upon the organic, self-perpetuating, self-reproducing plot (reproducing whether by cycle, by scission, by parallel) which, as Aristotle says, is the soul of action. Surely it is not too much to say that the soul of action is momentum, and that, therefore, plot is the articulation of momentum. Only, in our stage of culture, we do not know ahead of time, we have only means of tentative guessing, what is the significance of plot conceived as the soul of action. We are not in the position of putting these people into relation with some received or religious or predicted concept of significance—as Sophocles, Vergil, Dante were. We are working the other way round: we have to find out in the process of the experience itself. We are about the great business of the novel, to create out of manners and action motive, and out of the conflict of the created motive with the momentum to find the significance: an image of the theoretic form of the soul.

To accomplish this art of psychology, this art of the psyche, this driving form and drifting form (as the stars drift) is perhaps the characteristic task of the novel in a society like that of the nineteenth century: a society without a fixed order of belief, without a fixed field of knowledge, without a fixed hierarchy; a society where experience must be explored for its significance as well as its content, and where experience may be created as well as referred. This is the society where all existing orders are held to be corruptions of basic order; or, to put it differently, where, in terms of the confronted and awakened imagination, the creation of order has itself become a great adventure. This is what Anna and Levin have, great personal adventures in the creation of order; an order is the desperate requirement each has for the experience each bodies forth.

Let us look at a few examples in the Second Part of the relation between manners and momentum and of the force under the momentum breaking through. There is the gradual spread of the scandal of Anna and Vronsky from rumor to declaration to conflagration. At first Anna *uses* the manners of the fashionable set to promote her relations with Vronsky, then she *breaches* manners to soldify them, and at last—with her husband, with society, with Vronsky—she throws manners away, and the force which has been there all along takes over although she does not as yet wholly know it. When asked at Betsy's party what she thinks of repairing the mistakes of love after marriage, she answers: " 'I think,' said Anna, playing with the glove she had taken off, 'I think . . . of so many men, so many minds, certainly so many hearts, so many kinds of love.' " After that party her husband, home to read, finds himself uneasy at the situation there tacitly (by manners) acknowledged between Anna and Vronsky. They have breached the formal role of the husband of a pretty wife, and he must speak to her in order to correct their estimate of the situation. As he thinks and walks the floor we see there is something more. When one set of manners impeaches another set—when the twilight assaults the broad day—an ambiguity appears. He who had always worked with reflections of life, and had shrunk away from life itself as something irrational and incomprehensible, now found himself "standing face to face with life." He had walked a bridge over the chasm of life and now the bridge was broken. Thus he is forced outside his official manners, is forced to think of Anna's *own* life for the first time. The plans he makes are all official, to communicate a firm decision and to exact obedience. But when Anna appears, glowing, a conflagration on the dark night, he found he was assaulting an impenetrable barrier and was reduced to begging. She had closed the door into herself, and he knew it would remain closed. As for Anna, his assault found her armored with an impenetrable falsehood and was strengthened, Tolstoy says, by an *unseen force*. His very speaking confirmed the new force and focussed it on Vronsky. In attempting to deceive him she makes the mistake of being natural, candid, light-hearted, qualities which in the circumstance are effects of the unseen force. In the new life between Karenin and Anna, Anna could lie awake feeling the brilliance of her own eyes, but Karenin found himself powerless because the spirit of evil and deceit which possessed her possessed him too. He could only implore and jeer.

When Anna and Vronsky perfect their new life in adultery they find they have murdered the first stage of their love. "Shame at their spiritual nakedness crushed her and infected him." Without the aid, rather the enmity, of decorum, manners, institutions, they cannot cope with the now visible force that binds *and* splits them. Being what they are—that is, being by Tolstoy condemned to full and direct experience—they cannot let the force pass. Vronsky tries to cover up with kisses. Anna tries, and puts off trying, to join together the shame, rapture, and horror of "stepping into a new life." She tries for and cannot find an order in thought. But in her dreams, when she was not protecting herself from her thoughts, she sees the hideous nakedness of her position. She dreams of two husbands, two Alexeys, two happinesses, and the dream weighed like a nightmare because it dramatized the impossibility of the only solution. As for Vronsky there is what happened when he went to see his mare, Frou Frou, the day before the race. The mare's excitement infected Vronsky. "He felt that his heart was throbbing, and that he, too, like the mare, longed to move, to bite; it was both dreadful and delicious." Swift never did this better; and Tolstoy does it without bitterness, though the scene is one which contains most of the occasions for human bitterness. What Vronsky wanted was Anna like the horse. But like the horse, Anna must be used in reckless pastime, or not at all. Take away the pastime, and the recklessness becomes un-controllable and all the beautiful anarchy in the animal—all the unknown order under orders known—is lost. So, as with Anna, Vronsky failed to keep pace with Frou Frou and broke her back.

While Anna and Vronsky are bodying forth reality, Kitty is being cured of one reality by immersion in another. She is away, taking the waters. Tolstoy gives the tale of her cure lightly and ironically, but it is nevertheless accomplished by very hazardous means, and furnishes interesting analogies to what happened to Vronsky, Anna, Karenin, and in a way, also, to Levin who is immersing himself in the idyll of the simple life on his estate. Almost Kitty becomes a "pietist," a professional doer of good, a conspicuous instrument of false charity: a filler-up of the void of life with the "manners" of sincerity, virtue, and faith in the phase where life is left out. One hardly knows whether it is Mme. Stahl or Mlle. Varenka who better represents the negation of vitality. Both are unconscious charlatans of charity: the one for occupation, the other for duty. Kitty is taken in by both, and being a creature of vital impulse, herself tries the role of charlatan of charity from her heart. She has reached a moment of conversion, but not to recognition of life or God, rather to puerile substitutes for them, when she is rescued by the sick man Petrov's hysterical "love" for her combined with the return of her father full of health and humor and buoyancy. Petrov's "love" she recognizes, though she does not put it into words: "one of those things which one knows but which one can never speak of even to oneself so terrible and shameful would it be to be mistaken." Through her father, through the contagion of life he spreads, she sees Mme. Stahl's short legs and hears the feeble laughter of Varenka. And in the little crisis of these recognitions, she is converted *back* to life.

The figure of Varenka remains only as a threat, the threat of something the opposite of reality. This is the threat of public life, of life in public: the threat of turning the heart into an institution: the situation so desired by Karenin, in which one no longer feels what one ignores; when without conscious hypocrisy or deceit one ignores both the nature and the springs of human action, when all natural piety is transformed into the artifact of piety. There is no sympathy in it, much less mimesis, only empty histrionics: the vanities of spiritual ill-health mistaken for the pangs of vocation.

In all this Tolstoy never leaves us in the dark. It is only Kitty, the little Princess, who is led astray into thinking here is a career, or a new life, with these creatures who take no part in the momentum which sweeps them along. It takes only the lyric stagger of her "lover" Petrov, repeated to show it was doubly meant, a stagger for disease and a stagger for love, and the genuine momentum of her father the old Prince to pull her back into the stream. If we the readers remember in what language Tolstoy introduced Varenka we should ourselves never have been deceived. A creature without youth, nineteen *or* thirty, "she was like a fine flower, already past its bloom and without fragrance, though the petals were still unwithered." She is one of those who have nothing to suppress, no matter what the situation.

It may be, of course, that Tolstoy wrote all this to express his instinctive hatred of professional bad health: the bad health that keeps on living and makes of the open air a morass. These people also however make a parallel to the true purpose of the book: they cover up the encroaching reality of death much as Dolly and Karenin cover up what is for them the vanishing reality of life. The difference is that the sick and the charlatans succeed: they are equal to what they admit of their condition, and so take power over the living (nobody can so dominate a situation as the confirmed invalid); while Dolly and Karenin are never equal to their situation and still struggle with it, however pitifully or pretentiously, and lose power over others as over themselves with each successive act. The difference may be small from another perspective, but from Tolstoy's perspective it is radical. That is why the figure of Nikolay Levin passes, a small harsh whirlwind, across the scene: the very whirlwind of a man preparing and building into the reality of his death: tall, with stooping figure, huge hands, a coat too short for him, with black, simple, and yet terrible eyes: this figure shouting at the doctor and threatening him with his stick.

Tolstoy has many skills in the dialectic of incarnation. Here is one where the incarnation is of raw force itself, but it must be thought of in its setting. Consider how he surrounds the affair of Anna and Vronsky—the seduction, pregnancy and declaration—on the one side with the true idyll of Levin in the spring and on the other side the false idyll of Kitty at the watering place. It is across Vronsky and Anna that Kitty and Levin reach. At the very center lies Frou Frou, the mare, with her broken back, struggling up on her forelegs, then falling: all because Vronsky could not keep pace with her. Vronsky kicked her with his heel in the stomach. "She did not stir, but thrusting her nose into the ground, she simply stared at her master with her speaking eyes."

Vronsky's unpardonable act was no accident; neither was it done by intention. It was rather that, at a moment of high arbitrary human skill, at a moment of death-risk and momentary glory, the center of all eyes and the heart of an almost universal act of mimetic participation—at that moment something like fate broke the rhythm. Yet Vronsky was right: "for the first time in his life he knew the bitterest sort of misfortune, misfortune beyond remedy, and caused by his own fault." What is beyond remedy is beyond judgment: is its own justice; and if it is nevertheless caused by Vronsky's own fault, it is because the fault is universal. It is the fault that inheres in Kitty and Levin, in Dolly and Stiva, Anna and Vronsky alike: the fault of not keeping pace. This does not seem hard to understand in its general symbolic reach, that it may happen or that it may not that a breach of pace may be fatal. It is a harsher act of imagination to grasp the actuality of the absolute intimacy *and* the absolute inadequacy—the deliciousness *and* the dread—in human relationship; precisely what must be grasped if that phase has been reached.

But what is even more terrifying about Tolstoy's honesty—or let us say what is more astonishing about his genius—is that he could have broken the back of a mare in the midst of the crisis in the passion of Anna and Vronsky without either adding or diminishing *human* significance but rather deepening the reality. It is as if in this image he had gotten into the conditions of life from which the conditions we know of emerge: into conditions purer and conditions more intolerable: into an order which includes all human disorders.

These are affairs, as Tolstoy like Dante knew, of which the sane mind makes no report except in symbol, however they may remain thereafter the very growth of the mind. So it was with Vronsky. His friend Yashvin the rake understood it best, "overtook him with his cap, and led him home, and half an hour later Vronsky had regained his self-possession." The death of Frou Frou had become a part of him, no longer separately recognized.

Like the death of Frou Frou, so it is with the passions that inhabit our heroes. The passion of the force will pass but not the force, and if the passion has not wrecked the hero (as it does Karenin) the force will be stronger after the passion has passed than before. That is why the notion of purification is attached to the passion of tragic action. Society, nature, and the individual in society and nature, have three common arrangements to take care of the situation when genuine passion has passed. There is the arrangement for outlets in the demi-monde or twilight world. There is the arrangement for the cultivation of passion for its own sake, which suits those afraid of being *otherwise* occupied. And there is the arrangement that when the passion passes those who have been joined in it will find themselves insuperably bound—unless a fresh passion of the force supervene. Both for Anna and for Levin, with their different aspirations, none of these arrangements is enough. Or rather, for Levin none of them will do at all, and for Anna they will all do in their turns. But both need the identification of force with love, the one outside society and nature, the other through society and nature. Anna needs to become herself standing for everybody, Levin needs to become everybody in order to find himself represented. That is why both Anna and Levin are subject to fearful jealousies. Their rebirth into new life is never complete and the identification of force with love is never complete. Thus the force remains free, capable of assuming all possible forms. That is why Anna dreads in Vronsky and Levin in Kitty and positive enactment of what is at constant potential in themselves. Their jealousy is that they crave each other's possibilities, and hence each is bound to muster out of the force that moves them a new burst of passion in the hope that this time the new birth will take place but in the hidden certainty that it will not.

Vronsky, even more than Anna, as their love becomes more of a scandal, is deprived of the social phases of "force" and is required to envisage it as if naked, and an enemy. The worm of ambition in him which had been covered in the first stages of love is now uncovered by the scandal of love. He understands perfectly what his friend the successful general means when he says, "Women are the chief stumbling-block in a man's career. It's hard to love a woman and do anything." He understands but he answers softly that the general has never loved, and he understands even better when the general returns it, "We make an immense thing of love, but they are always *terre à terre.*" It is what he understands, and keeps out of sight, that gives him a hard expression when Anna tells him she is pregnant. He is thinking of all that is lost, and of the duel that must come. Anna does not understand that and gives up all hope that his love will be enough for her, though in the same breath of her mind she tells him that it will be. She sees he has already been thinking and will not tell her all he thought. She is, she tells him, proud, proud, proud—but she cannot say what she is proud of; and Vronsky if he had spoken must have said the same thing. They get at so differently what lies between them that they wholly misunderstand each other, but never for a second do they fail to grasp the force that compels the misunderstanding.

As for what happens to Karenin there is no better image than the lawyer whom he consults about a divorce: he plucks four moths out of the air, as if he were the law engorging the individual. Unlike Anna and Vronsky, who are deprived of them, Karenin is more and more taken over by the brutality of the social phases of "force." He makes one final effort to reverse himself—as do Anna and Vronsky—when Anna, in childbirth, thinks herself dying. Then all three reverse and renounce their roles, and do so in deep analogy to Levin and Kitty at the true death of Levin's brother Nikolay where they gain great access to their true roles. It is the image of death—the attractive and repulsive force of death—which takes over each of them. There is someting in the rhythm of death which for Vronsky, Anna, and Karenin elicits a supreme failing effort to keep pace, as there is for Levin in his brother's death. For each, it is as far as they can go in their opposed directions.

Indeed it is Anna's literally incomplete death-scene which is the death in which rebirth takes place. She makes a histrionic mimesis of death because of the two women within her. Thinking, in her last spasm of social guilt, to kill one, actually she kills the other. No, not by thinking does she do this, unless it is something outside the mind that thinks. Rather she, the whole of her, takes advantage of the vision of death to find out what can be seen through it. Her mistake is only initial. The rebirth is accompanied by an exorcism, which she sees and feels but which, so great is the force of the world, she does not at once recognize for what it is. She has become single; it seems to be by renunciation; actually it is by an access of devotion—for she is not a woman gifted with renunciation, and her first practice of it shows as irritation and inability, as something to overcome and something to perfect. Had Vronsky not come, had he not rushed in, and stroked her cropped hair, calling her a pretty boy, she might never have found out in actuality what her new singleness was. Instead of positive desperation she would have ended in self-contemptuous despair. There would have been nothing to break down, only the collapse of a dry shell. As it is, she begins at once, against the world-and-his-wife and contemptuous of both, the long course of building her own desperation, the positive desperation of her own cause, to the point where her own strength but not that of her cause should be exhausted.

That is the nature of her tragedy, that her own strength cannot be equal to her cause. The independence of the individual is never equal to the cause of independence. And the flaw is as it should be, both in her and in the nature of things, and not at all less guilty for that (or if you like, less innocent): a flaw in any case, a human need, which as it finds its mode of action and creates its motive becomes less and less the kind of flaw that asks for the forgiveness of understanding and is more and more revealed as a single, eminent aspect of the general nature of things which brings the mind to compassion.

How otherwise—how if it is not this train that has been set going—can we look at the irony of the pure, lawful, and successful love affair of Levin and Kitty as anything but cheap and puerile "moralism"?—that is, not irony at all. Levin in new life, Levin on wings, has also singled his life, has made an act of devotion, to which he will necessarily turn out inadequate, not so much because of inadequate strength but because the cause itself (in the form of his original impulse) will desert him. The very, brutal force of the world-and-his-wife, which will bring ruin to Anna and Vronsky because they contest it, is the force Levin leans on—his cause—and it is a force hardly less reliable taken as a cause than as the enemy.

No institution and no individual may ever be more than a partial incarnation of the underlying or superior force; nor can any set of individuals and institutions taken together. It is only Stiva or the peasant with the pretty daughter-in-law whom Levin had seen pitching hay who can use or abuse this force indifferently: with the kind of faith that makes no enquiries and would not know a vision if it saw one. For Stiva, there is always a way out, not death. For the peasant girl—she is herself a way out, and death is a matter not yet experienced. These are the creatures not subject to individual rebirth, they are the nearest thing to permanence: momentum or recurrence.

But the shoe of Anna's rebirth pinches sharpest, under the impact of symbolic death, on Karenin and Vronsky: the one wih his head in the hollow of Anna's elbow, the other with his face in his hands: the one suffering total and permanent spiritual change, the other suffering total humiliation followed by recovery through violence: the one inwardly transcending his society, the other rejecting his society and both to be ever afterwards victimized by it—though one, Karenin, is put in contempt by society, and the other, Vronsky, is made a hero so to speak outside society. Karenin can never get back into society and is in a misunderstood position above it. Vronsky can never leave society behind him: it goes with him: he is a kind of pet public outcast. They have passed, by humiliation and self-contempt, through their relations to Anna's symbolic death, to the roles most nearly opposite to those in which we first saw them.

That is, to each of them comes a deep reversal of role through a direct, but miscomprehended, experience of the force of life in the phase of sex under the image of an incomplete death. We shall see the deaths completed diversely. Meanwhile we see Anna, Vronsky, Karenin, and Levin tied in the hard knot of individual goodness, and each, in that goodness, in a different relation to the manners and momentum of society. I mean, by goodness, that each has been reborn into a man or woman for once, and at last, proper to his or her own nature. Each has *virtu*, and to the point of excess. But—such is the power of Tolstoy's imagination—without loss of humanity. Each, seen beside the self, is more the self than ever. Levin, seen in society, is no more representative of it than the other three, who are seen against it.

It is for this goodness that they pay the cost. The good, said Aristotle, is that which all things aim at, and when an aim has been taken everything flies that way—whether the target was indeed the good or not. We see Levin in doubt and delight about everything, desiring not to desire, as we see Vronsky equally in doubt, but so full of *ennui* that he desires desire. We see that Anna's problem is to maintain the state of crisis in love, to be always a young girl in love, and that Vronsky's problem is to find substitutes, caprices of action, to prevent *ennui* from absorbing crisis. In Vronsky's house all were guests, in Levin's all were part of the household; and so on. Tolstoy gives us hundreds of comparisons and analogies of the two honeymoons. But perhaps the most instructive is the comparison of Veslovsky at Levin's and at Vronsky's. This young man with unseemly eyes, fat thighs, and hand-kissing habits was very much a gentleman of the bedchamber: altogether in place at Vronsky's, very much a part of the general pretense at occupation. Vronsky ignores in him what had genuinely put Levin in a rage, and Anna was amused at him where Kitty was ashamed. Kitty and Levin made a fight for life within the fold, Anna and Vronsky fight in abuse of the fold; and a little in the background Dolly surrenders to life within a broken fold.

Each of them is inadequate to him or herself as a solitary actor; and perhaps this is nowhere shown so clearly as in the image of Dolly making her solitary visit to Anna sitting in the coach, afraid to look in her glass, daydreaming herself a perfect paramour. Again we see it in Dolly in her darned gown listening with aversion and distrust to Anna talk of birth-control. She knows suddenly that in the very numbers of her children is her safety: not in perspective, future or past, but in numbers, in everyday life. Dolly is the monitor of all that is living: she has paid the cost of goodness without ever having had it, and in so very deep a way that no fresh start—neither rebellion now new effort along old lines—could ever get it for her. She is neither good nor evil; neither hopeless nor desperate. She believes in high principles, and that they must not be forgotten, but in every act of her being she knows the necessity, if she is to survive, of the alternate assertion and abuse of these principles. The compassionate gesture of her visit to Anna is symbolic of all this; and it is the kind of peak of meaningfulness she can reach at any time with no need for crisis. So we begin to see what she is doing in this novel: she is to be recognized, not understood. But we should never have believed her, or in her, had we seen her in such a moment at the beginning; nor would she have believed in herself. She would have been a bad Varenka, a hypocrite unendurable. It was right that she had to be brought round by Anna, just as it is right now that her presence should remind Anna of all the life she was smothering. But best of all is to think of Dolly with the road dust in the creases about her eyes, imagining at the end of her daydream of illicit love, what the expression on Stiva's face would be, when, like Anna to Karenin, she flaunted her infidelity in his face.

This image of Dolly may have come to Tolstoy as an afterthought, as a debt to his novel he had not known he was incurring and which he had therefore all the more obligation to pay. He had thought of Rachel, but not of Leah. But with the other image in this part of the book—the death of Nikolay—it is the other way round. This is the death that lived in Tolstoy all his life, for which he made three great images of which this is the first and greatest—the others are "Ivan Ilych" and *The Living Corpse*. Death is the inevitable thing from which there is no freedom by recognition but only by enactment. Where Anna (as Dolly saw) has learned a new gesture, to half close her eyes on what is threatening her and cannot be dealt with, Tolstoy himself has to force a steady gaze on death physical, spiritual, and dramatic (poetic, dialectic, rhetorical). He has to mime death. He has to show in fact that death, as well as good, is what all things aim at; that death is the moving *and* the fixed background of life. He knows and must show that it is a commonplace truth and illusion that men die well. The whole commonplace is there in the physical—the terribly physical—death of Nikolay: and in the longing for death that surrounds it.

This death—the most innocent and most mature in all fiction—though it has nothing to do directly with the plot is yet a center of attractive force presiding over its whole course. Everything else is drawn to it, across a gap. It is this attractive force that begins to complete the actions of each of our persons, those actions which were focussed in the partial deaths endured by Anna and Levin in the middle portion of the book, and which were initiated by the death of Frou Frou at the first crisis in the action: it is the solitary and menacing incarnation of all these. And it should be well noted that in this death everything is as near the physical as possible without affront to the spiritual and the dramatic. The turbulence is all of something watched by Kitty or felt by Levin. It is death as raw force, a concrete, focal, particular epiphany of the raw force of death. It is the after part of every forethought.

Surely that is what is somehow in Levin's mind when, in making his one call on Anna in her Coventry, he sees her face as stone and more beautiful than ever, the very Medusa-face of life (Henry James's phrase) to which for a moment he succumbs. Altogether these nine or ten pages of Levin's vision of Anna are a high example of what may be meant in the novel by full drama. As in the modern stage drama, a great deal depends on what has gone before, now summarized and brought to a fresh and conclusive action against a background which may and will come forward when the action is done: when the violent inner light of conflagration in Anna is changed to the lightning that momentarily obsures the stars for

Levin. That is what the dramatic action is for, to pull the whole background forward. It is the background in which they are all implicated, and in which the action is a series of parallels and series of analogies which show all our principal persons in deeply but narrowly different responses to the same force: each lawful, each valid, complementing each other like ice and water, or night and day, converging like slush or twilight, like midnight and noon. Each is brought to a clarity, of which the meaning is seen, not alone in relation to the other persons, but also with respect to the sweep of things: the sweep which moves with the strange intimate noise which Shakespeare calls the endless jar of right and wrong in which justice resides. It is against this that Anna's face was stone and more beautiful than ever.

There is a nakedness in this sort of experience for Anna which ends in death, and an unarmored defencelessness for Levin which begins in birth. It leaves both of them without the protection or clothes of the intellect. And there is a harshness in the compassion required of total response to each—the compassion of peace with a sword—which is possible only to a saint or a great artist. Such response touches what is under our behavior, and what comes into our behavior, which whether we shun it or salute it, remakes, while the contact lasts, our sense of relation with ordinary life. We cannot live at crisis, at the turning point, but must make out of it either a birth or a death in the face of ordinary life. This is what happens to morality in art. It is an image of passing one way or the other; which may explain what Eliot had in mind when he observed that as morals are only a preliminary concern to the saint so they are only a secondary concern to the artist. That is the condition, between the preliminary and the secondary, of harsh compassion that made Tolstoy reject his novels, including this one, along with Shakespeare. He rejected the uncopeable truth, because he wanted to remake the world piecemeal in terms of morality as a central authority. In the novels he wanted only the mimesis of morality as a central experience, both in the world and in the crisis of individuals who were somehow, because of the crisis, removed from it.

The novels wanted to show the tacit, potential crisis which gave the ordinary world meaning, and which in turn put individuals to the test. It is in contest and concert with the ordinary world that crisis is reached and given worth; and it is into the ordinary world that things break through and are bodied forth, visibly in crisis, actually all along. The last two parts of *Anna Karenina* put into parallel and analogy such recognitions as these. Under pressure of the action even the parallels seem to become analogies, to be in proportional relation to each other: as in the stream of consciousness—the articulate hysteria—in which Anna's last hours are recorded,

which is both parallel and analogous to Levin's final conversion in company
with the beetle under the dusty shade of the poplars at noon.

For a major parallel which is also analogy, let us look at the whole
structure in the next to last part of the book. We begin with Kitty's delayed
confinement and from it see Levin moved through Moscow's "society,"
intellect, and club life, to reach that other form of delayed or arrested
vitality which is Anna, and in which he is for a moment absorbed. Then
through quarrel and jealousy we are moved sharply to the scream of birth
for Kitty and the plunge to death for Anna: the birth which for Anna
meant death not herself, which to Kitty meant new life not herself, and
which to Levin were one and the same. Between the two sets of movements
there is a chapter in which an independent evil spirit grew up in Anna
because there was a delay in her affairs, just as there was an independent
new life in Kitty in the delay of *her* affairs. The one ends in senseless rage,
the other in senseless joy. In either case it is the uncopeable power not
themselves which moves them, and to each it shows with the terrible
ambiguity of an immediate experience.

Surely it is not providential that before returning to Anna and her
death, Tolstoy carries us to Petersburg, the city of government and decorum
and manners, and gives us, so we may make our own irony, images of what
happens when people insist on coping with their own troubles in terms of
the unilluminated ordinary world. We see all this in Stiva pursuing his
double errand, to get himself a better job and to get Anna her divorce. To
get the job he has to descend into humiliation. To prevent himself from
giving the divorce, Karenin, with Lidia aiding, has to descend to a false
appeal to a false force pretending to govern a false society: he descends to
the clairvoyance of a charlatan, to an "induced" change of heart. By betrayal
of his own traditions, Stiva gets his job; so does Karenin refuse the divorce.
Anna is not a matter of genuine consideration. In this analogy, Tolstoy
presents all that is left, in these people, of the true force: he sees that Stiva
and Karenin have become all manners and no men.

Nor is it providential, it is the very essence of the prepared drama,
that we return from Stiva in Petersburg to find Anna in Moscow, herself
clutching at manners—in the form of quarrels, jealousies, formal emotions—in the one place where manners cannot act but can only cover up
ugly action—the place where people are outside society, but where, since
so little else is left except the raw emotion of the self, appearances must
be kept up. It is their manners, failing, that keep Anna and Vronsky from
joining their emotions. They neither do their part nor keep pace. It is
when her manners wholly fail that Anna brims over, sees herself clear, and

comes on that unintermediated force which makes her suffer, and it is in desperate pursuit of some manners into which she can deliver that suffering that she finds her death: precisely as she thought she had done so long ago in her false death. Her tragedy is that she has destroyed too much of the medium, too many of the possibilities, of actual life, to leave life tolerable, and she has done this partly by dissociating manners from the actual world and partly by losing her sense of the sweep of things. Thus her last turning point, her last effort at incarnation, was death.

With no less of the force in him that drove Anna, Levin turned the other way. He too had been at the point of death and for months at a time, but through the death of his brother and the delivery of his wife found himself alive instead. It could have been the other way; Levin and Anna were aimed equally at life or at death. Human life cannot stand the intensity of Anna, but works toward it; human life requires the diminution of intensity into faith and of faith into momentum which is Levin. The one is very near the other. Only Anna's face was stone and more beautiful than ever. Yet it is in the likeness not the difference that the genuineness and the dialectic of Tolstoy's incarnation lies.

BARBARA HARDY

Form and Freedom:
Tolstoy's "Anna Karenina"

I n Part II, Chapter XV, [of *Anna Karenina*], Levin and Oblonsky go shooting. We are made to feel both the sense of Kitty's presence, which for a long time they do not mention, and its unrelatedness to the pleasure and activity. After the splendid shooting Levin at last asks Oblonsky if Kitty is married. He feels "so strong and calm that he thought the answer, whatever it might be, could not agitate him." He is shocked by the news Kitty is ill, and Tolstoy marks the personal absorption by telling us that Laska, the dog, looks at the sky and thinks that the interruption will make them miss the woodcock. They do not miss; they both shoot and Levin says exultantly that the bird "belongs to both," then remembers that "there was something unpleasant! . . . Yes, of course, Kitty is ill! But what can I do? I am very sorry . . ." and breaks off to praise Laska, "Found? good dog!" and takes the warm bird from the dog's mouth. This is almost the opposite of James's presentation of phenomena in terms of obsession. The scene is free because Tolstoy is saying that men's griefs are complex, are not always wholly absorbing, that work or play can be exhilarating even at such a time. Because the phenomena are so vividly present—the creak of growing grass, the exhilaration of the hunt—the scene is free from symbol. The sharing of the bird might, in a novel by Stevenson or James, be made indicative of the common family interest, but even this rejected interpretation sounds ludicrous here.

From *The Appropriate Form: An Essay on the Novel.* Copyright © 1970 by Barbara Hardy. Northwestern University Press.

Such vivid realism and complexity appear in different ways in the two following chapters, where Oblonsky makes the bad bargain with Ryabinin about the sale of the forest. Levin disapproves strongly, but he is feeling generally depressed and irritated—itself a sign of emotional flux, since his earlier reaction was to feel pleased that Kitty is sick and unhappy. Oblonsky realizes that Levin's jealous humiliation about Vronsky will colour all his reactions, "knowing well that everything would now seem wrong to Levin," and observing that he is "down in the dumps today." But the Ryabinin affair has its own independent status, like the spring and the shoot, and Tolstoy makes it plain, although Levin's irritation is caused mainly by feeling insulted and therefore "angry not with what had upset him but with everything that presented itself," that this is not an irrational feeling about a swindle. Ryabinin's face assumes "a hawklike, rapacious, and cruel expression," and Levin's anger is intimately related to his feeling for land and class and work. The two feelings merge eventually when Levin bursts out in fury at Oblonsky's comment that Vronsky is an aristocrat and therefore an attractive match:

> You talk of his being an aristocrat. But I should like to ask you what is Vronsky's or anyone else's aristocracy that I should be slighted because of it? . . . I consider myself and people like me aristocrats. . . . You consider it mean for me to count the trees in my wood while you give Ryabinin thirty thousand roubles; but you will receive a Government grant and I don't know what other rewards, and I shan't, so I value what is mine by birth and labour.

The fury drives him into the admission that he has proposed to Kitty and been refused. It would be hard to say which subject and which feeling is primary here, as one usually can in a Jamesian novel, and indeed in most novels. Both the love and the land are matters of feeling—the Ryabinin episode is not merely brought in as a springboard to the private admission. The complexity of these scenes is not "economical" and concentrated because Tolstoy is giving each aspect of Levin's life a fully realistic importance. The largeness and looseness of the treatment—not incompatible with a graduated movement to a climax—records a wide range of emotional reaction.

This is not the whole story. The life in this novel does not spring merely from a complex psychology which demands a complex rendering. In the scenes I have just mentioned, the character of Ryabinin flashes upon us briefly and vividly, but is no more fully rendered than many minor characters in Victorian novels. Apart from characters like Ryabinin, who have only a momentary appearance, there is a dense population of secondary characters whose life, from an economical Jamesian standpoint, is extravagantly rendered. There is indeed something basically inappropriate about talking of Tolstoy's "minor" characters. There is never, as far as I remember, any use of the threatrical technique such as we find even in characters like Mrs. Poyser or Bartle Massey, who are given the weight of implied life and the vividness of personality, but largely by means of a sharp definition of idiosyncrasy, linguistic and otherwise. They are not grotesques, as they would be in a Dickens novel, but they stand in relation to Tolstoy's minor characters rather as the Dickensian minor grotesques (Mrs. Micawber or Trabb's boy) stand in relation to them. Tolstoy's creation of this dense population of characters who have no grotesque definition and often no obvious function, whose lives impinge naturally and sporadically on the destinies of the main characters, is an essential part of his admirable freedom or what James calls his "waste."

I can here only briefly touch on this neglected subject of the population of novels. *Robinson Crusoe, Jane Eyre,* and *Wuthering Heights* are all novels with tiny populations, and the restriction seems to be an important aspect or function of their quality of dream with its concentrated selection of inner adventure. In Jane Austen the restriction has other implications, both moral and social. In Henry James the concentration on one or two centres of consciousness makes restriction essential, and in James Joyce economy and total relevance stamps most of his large population with structural symbolism. Even in the crowded life of *Middlemarch* the characters have, somewhere in their complex or lively appearances, a thematic stamp. There are no extras to give us the impression of either the bulkiness or the temporal flow of life. Indeed, George Eliot is occasionally given to creating shadows, like Gwendolen Harleth's half-sisters, whose names most critics would have to look up if they wanted to refer to them.

None of the novelists I have mentioned take pains to adapt the population of the novel to the flow of time. We do have occasional new characters appearing as time goes on, but we hardly ever leave any established characters behind. And vivid appearances tend always to be significant in the action, as well as developing or repeating the main moral preoccupations. In *Anna Karenina,* a novel much more compressed in time than *War and Peace,* some characters appear sporadically, some are left behind, and many have absolutely no influence on the main action. They are tethered to the action by their relations with the major characters but could be dropped without any loss to the moral clarity or even the development of character. What would be lost without such characters as Vronsky's friend, Yashvin, the rake and gambler and man of bad principles who is the only one who can understand Vronsky's passion and take it seriously? There is no obvious thematic contrast or parallel here, as there is with his other friend, Serpukhovsky, who emphasizes Vronsky's lack of professional energy and ambition, just as Sviyazhsky brings out Levin's vagueness and discontent, then his consistency and honesty. There are very many structural connections which give secondary characters in this novel the same kind of thematic function as in most novels. The difference is that the function is not invariably present. Functional characters are not only disguised by vividness, but may often only be "functional" in the way they fill and complete a man's environment. We feel the real and full presence of Vronsky's life or Levin's because they are surrounded by a changing population of friends and acquaintances. Family relations are also shown in this sporadic way. Levin's two brothers have obvious functions of contrast. Nicholas brings him face to face with death, and creates a moral crisis which is not resolved until the end of the novel. Koznyshev is to Levin as Levin is to Nicholas, an apparently more determined and successful man. The family relations are presented with the ebb and flow of life, with contact forced by crisis and visit. Levin's relations with is sister-in-law, Lvova, and her husband, are beautifully and vividly rendered, though the relationship itself is briefly shown and the characters disappear from the novel very quickly.

Another striking difference between Tolstoy's realism and that of other novelists . . . is his lack of contrivance. Just as there are no minor characters in *Anna Karenina*, so there are no coincidences or contrived encounters. There are only a few in *Middlemarch*, but it is relatively easy to move characters in and out and to contrive encounters in a restricted environment. In Tolstoy all the movements and meetings are brought about with utter naturalness. Not only are characters not brought together in contrived significant meetings by the novelist, but many of the meetings have no plot function whatsoever. Indeed, plot itself is another odd term to use of the novel. There is the story of infidelity in Dolly and Oblonsky, the story of the rough course of true love for Kitty and Levin, and the story of passion and death for Karenin, Anna, and Vronsky. But there is no plot in the sense of elaborate scheming and intricate intrigue. I am not referring to the absence of sensational discovery and coincidence and elaborate mystery—though these are plainly absent—but to the author's creation and solution of problems through plot-contrivance.

Nothing hangs by a thread in *Anna Karenina*. We may take for granted the way in which both George Eliot and Henry James hang destiny on threads. Supposing Dorothea had said "Yes" to Casaubon on the morning of his death, before he went out into the garden? Supposing that Strether had not been looking at the river when Chad and Mme de Vionnet came by in their boat? These two examples are of rather different status. It could have totally transformed the novel had Dorothea given her pledge, as she intended, before Casaubon's death, whereas James might have devised a less coincidental "discovery" of "the lie in the affair." But in each case, and in many more, George Eliot and James *contrive* their plot in this way. I am not denigrating their art by pointing this out (though I do, in fact, think the *Middlemarch* episode a weakness in the novel). There are very few novelists who even aim at complete realism, and we certainly tolerate conventions of plot which impose rather greater strain on credulity than either of these examples. But we do not meet with this kind of literary arbitrariness or contrivance in *Anna Karenina*. The plot has little responsibility for destiny. Destiny is the plot.

Not only are there no such crises of chance in the novel, but there are also very few crises of moral decision, comparable to those in George Eliot and Henry James. Their novels are propelled, for the most part, not by the "mechanical" plot contrivances, but by moments of moral decision. There is Dorothea's decision to go back to Rosamond, Gwendolen's decision to marry Grandcourt, Merton Densher's bargain with Kate, and his last ultimatum, Strether's final renunciation. These crises determine the developmental structure of the novels, and they themselves are determined by the moral categories which George Eliot and James set up, and by the generalization which emerges from these categories. Tolstoy is conducting a rather different process of generalization.

In George Eliot and Jenry James, for all the subtlety of their particulars, there is a basic sheep and goats division. George Eliot in *Middlemarch*, for instance, is applying a fundamental moral test—are the people acting from self-interest or from love? The novel raises the question, and it is not possible to answer it crudely, but by the end of the action we can give a fairly satisfactory answer, and never have to reply "Don't know." Casaubon and Rosamond and Bulstrode act from self-interest (and in one case, at least, this is not self-destructive) while Lydgate, Dorothea, and Caleb Garth act from love. Tolstoy is, I suggest, not directly concerned with this moral question which is centrally important in so many Victorian novels. He is more interested in a metaphysical question, in finding a meaning in a life so quickly ended by death. Even though this discovery of meaning frees Levin to love, Tolstoy's categories are not George

Eliot's. His characters are not made to perform in the same kind of moral obstacle race.

They are shown as moving inevitably on their course, without being solicited by clear alternatives. Dorothea can marry or not, and when she does, she makes a grave mistake. So does Lydgate. So does Gwendolen. Maggie can choose to renounce Stephen or not, and when she does most readers accept the ethos of the novel and endorse her action. Secondary characters like Caleb Garth or even a major character like Grandcourt, are—exceptionally—shown without the process of choice and self-determinism, but the main interest of the novel depends on the movement through moral crisis and chosen alternatives. Tolstoy does not organize his action in this way. There is the implication of choice, of course, but it is given no emphasis. Anna could choose to renounce Vronsky, and, later, after Karenin's forgiveness, she could choose to stay with her husband, but we do not see her in conflict. We see her choosing unconsciously, with little debate. Her agony over leaving her son, for instance, does not come to the fore until after she has left him. Tolstoy is a marvellous recorder of this kind of drifting, where the uneventful moment, not the spotlit crisis of choice, determines the future. We see a slow accumulation of events, not a succession of moral crises.

A good example of this comes at the end of Anna's life, in the final quarrel which ends with her suicide. Vronsky comes in to find that she has packed, and they are both agreed about leaving for the country. Then he explains that there must be a day's delay before they leave since he has to see his mother. Anna uses this in order to attack him, and he gives in to her. She attacks again and forces him to go, sends him messages which do not reach him until it is too late, then sets off on her last journey. Tolstoy shows us these recoils and shifts in order to make it plain that the tension between these two people has become destructive—it is now too late for choice. There is no possibility of imagining alternatives, as there is in *Middlemarch*. If Fred Vincy had not listened to Farebrother after his moral lapse, if Farebrother had not spoken, if Lydgate had not gone back to see Rosamond in order to demonstrate his freedom, then the whole course of the novel could so easily have been different. The course of action which the characters reject is often just as "likely," in terms of moral endowment, temperament, and social pressure, as the course they choose. The characters are placed in an action persistently punctuated and determined by decisive choice: the deeds determine destiny in a very literal sense, and the alternative determination makes its possibilities felt. Tolstoy gives us characters whose destinies are less plainly determined by actual choice, and where there is decision it is underplayed or strung out in time. The moment of choice is not isolated.

The dense vivid population, the slow drift of time, the unimportance of plot and moral crisis all combine to make this novel a much larger and looser form than *Middlemarch*. These features may also help to explain why a novel by Tolstoy is for some people difficult to read and for many difficult to remember. There is not the clear diagrammatic pattern of decisive in- cident and decisive moral crisis to create concentrated tension, or to act as a useful, if reductive, pattern in memory. Many of the vivid moments in *Anna Karenina* stand out as isolated in time, sometimes because they are indeed isolated, sometimes because they do not take place in a clearly patterned development. Take, for instance, the small episode, Tchekovian in mood and content, of Koznyshev's proposal to Varenka, which never comes off. This is actually an exception to Tolstoy's usual avoidance of the crisis of decision and the presentation of alternatives. Here is a moment of choice, and two possible alternatives. In the early chapters of Part VI, all of the characters think of the likelihood that the match will come off, and in Chapter iv, we see Koznyshev weighing the pros and cons and coming to a decision. He will propose to Varenka. In the next chapter we actually begin with the words of his declaration of love, in direct speech, but when the inverted commas close we are told that the words are "what Koznyshev said to himself." He begins to talk to Varenka and she mentions her childhood, but then the conversation goes the wrong way, and becomes less personal. Instead of remaining silent Varenka goes back to their talk about finding mushrooms, and "without wishing to" he goes on with the conversation. He repeats again the unspoken words of his intended proposal but does not say them aloud, instead he goes on talking about mushrooms. The banal and misleading conversation is a correlative not only for their inability to speak but also for their tension, but that soon drops, bringing to both the odd sense of relief that the words of the proposal will not be spoken.

Although at first sight this is very like the trembling crisis of decision we get when Lydgate goes back to Rosamond or when Grandcourt comes to propose to Gwendolen, it is in fact very different. Destiny does indeed here hang on a thread, but it is not the thread of social and moral pressures, but a more fragile thread of accidentality and triviality. No character in a novel by George Eliot has destiny determined by a missed cue, and although it might be argued that the importance of the missed cue depends on the lack of passionate urge in both people, we are not given enough evidence for such a view. Tolstoy is showing the importance of tiny threads. The unlikely pressures prove stronger than the obvious ones, and whether we put this down to an accidental lack of *rapport* or a fundamental lack of desire, it is presented as a movingly decisive accident.

As far as the novel is concerned, it is also movingly indecisive. The whole episode could be dropped without loss to the story of Kitty and Levin. It is true that it brings out Kitty's confident match-making. It also forms some contrast with the "bite" of her love and Levin's, when she says to her husband of Varenka and Koznyshev "Won't bite." This local function is a small and subordinate aspect of the power and truth of the episode. What applies to the episode applies also to the characters who play their part in it. Varenka has certain obvious functions in the novel: she converts Kitty to an energetic charity which is both a help in breaking her *ennui* after Vronsky's failure to propose, and a moral false start which she comes to reject as wrong for her. In several ways Varenka acts as a contrast with Kitty: she too has had her tragic love (in the past) and she too expects a proposal and does not get it. We might argue that Kitty's character and situation are influenced and defined by Varenka. But the interest of the proposal which does not come off has, I think, very little to do with this kind of structural function. Varenka is as solidly presented, though in a brief space, as Kitty, and her scene with Koznyshev has an independent vitality. It is one of the moments of "waste" in the novel which has its own incomplete life which adds to the density of the total impression. Levin and Kitty gain in reality from inhabiting a world of individuals, not a world of functional characters. The insistent function is appropriate to the moral exploration of Dickens or George Eliot, and to the dramatic economy of Henry James, but it is not needed in this novel.

I have suggested that this is a "disposable" scene, but what I have said about the lack of developmental pattern in much of the novel applies to scenes which are essential parts of the progress of the main action. Tolstoy shows moral change as momentary and sporadic, not as part of a clear pattern of improvement or deterioration. Karenin rises to great heights of nobility when Anna's daughter is born, and he loves and forgives. Some time later his love and forgiveness have disappeared—partly because of the disappearance of emotional crisis, partly because of the influence of Lydia Ivanovna's possessiveness and religiosity. There is no straightforward line of development. A scene like the forgiveness of Vronsky by Karenin, in which everyone responds most nobly, would be followed, in a novel by Dickens or George Eliot, by a rising intonation of consistent progress. Tolstoy's truthful refusal to categorize is seen most plainly in this instance, where conduct and feeling are shown as determined by the moment, and not as determining the whole of destiny. Karenin behaves plausibly but in a way which is unpurposive, unrelated to what goes before or to what comes after.

These cases could be paralleled by many others—Levin's reaction to his child, his combination of enchantment and disenchantment in the early days of his marriage, Vronsky's feeling that he loves Anna less, followed by his feeling that he has never loved her so much. These are part of the dense emotional complexity of the novel, with which it indeed begins when Oblonsky, the unfaithful husband whose wife has discovered all, wakes up, feeling happy and trying to hold on to his delightful dream about little decanters that were really women, then remembers that he is in a domestic crisis. This is immediately followed by the memory of his wife's discovery of the letter, to which he first reacted by smiling "his usual kindly and therefore silly smile." The psychological subtlety of the novel needs no documentation, and it is there in moments and minor characters as well as in the big scenes and main relationships.

In spite of its largeness and looseness, *Anna Karenina* is an organized novel. It has indeed many of the formal features of those novels with which I have been contrasting its plot and its populations. Its symbolism is never as extensive as that of Dickens and George Eliot, but it does exist. Its structure is less symmetrical than that of a novel by Henry James, but there is the movement of parallelism, contrast, anticipation and echo. Time drifts and is not always organized in crisis or decision, the moment may be vivid but isolated, but there is progress through a story—two stories—with shape and tension.

Like *Vanity Fair*, *Bleak House*, and *Middlemarch*, *Anna Karenina* is another novel of divided action. The movement from one story to another is itself a source of punctuation and emphasis, and the stories are meaningfully connected. It tells the story of three marriages, which can be roughly described as the *modus vivendi* of Dolly and Oblonsky, the tragic relationship of Karenin, Anna, and Vronsky, and the happier marriage of Levin and Kitty. This structural division is not nearly as plain as it is in the English novels I have just mentioned, because of the sheer density and detail and "waste," but it does emerge as a statement of variations, significantly grouped. The characters inhabit a common environment, though the Oblonskys are based in Moscow, the Karenins in Petersburg, and the Levins mainly in the country. But the characters move about, from one city to another, and from city to country. One aspect of the contrast to which I can give no space, but which is obviously organized with care and point, is the value attached to various places, to Petersburg's ethos compared with

Moscow's, to city as against country. And if we looked at a map of these significant places, it would have the conspicuous links of the railway. All this gives a representative impression of a large and varied society, with different conventions and codes and atmospheres, and establishes a firm sense of rooted life against which we come to follow the rootless wanderings of Anna and Vronsky. There are family links, too. Oblonsky and Anna are brother and sister, Dolly and Kitty are sisters, and there is the added link of Oblonsky's friendship with Levin and with Vronsky. The pattern of these three connected actions is much less clearly balanced than the pattern of the four actions in *Middlemarch* which rotate in turn, each coming in for roughly the same proportion of narrative time and interest. *Middlemarch* begins with an introduction to Dorothea which looks as if it is to be the main story, but which takes its place with the other actions, linked by environment and accident. *Anna Karenina* begins with the Oblonsky family, plunging in at the moment of crisis when Dolly discovers her husband's infidelity, but the initial emphasis never repeats itself, and the Oblonsky story is really over before the two main actions begin. Dolly makes her decision, to compromise and pretend and make the best of things. Though she and Oblonsky play an important role throughout the novel, it is essentially a minor role, given its weight by their early prominence, but having no plot tension and occupying little space. For most of the novel we have a divided narrative, moving from the Karenins to the Levins, and each story has a tension which stretches from the very beginning of the novel, when we meet Levin and Anna in deceptively minor roles in the Oblonsky story, to the end, with Anna's suicide and Levin's vision.

This is an unusual construction for the multiple plot, but not I think, a casual one. George Eliot and Thackeray, Dickens and George Eliot, divide their narrative more evenly, whether the division is one of separate actions, closely or loosely connected, or one of separate actions narrated in sharply differing modes, as in Dickens or Trollope, giving us the equivalent in fiction of the main plot and subplot structure of drama. *Anna Karenina's* uneven construction gives a free and wayward air to the novel, but this is not its only effect.

Tolstoy begins by establishing the normal case. The Oblonsky marriage represents the common problem with the common compromise: Oblonsky no longer finds his wife attractive, after several confinements, and both his sensuality and the conditions which give it scope, are established calmly, more or less taken for granted. The same applies to Dolly's acceptance and forgiveness: she knows that Oblonsky's repentance is merely a

light punctuation mark, indicating no real change, and her love for him
and for her children, her training and character, make compromise the
natural thing. She minds very much but can do nothing. There is no need
for further action—the crisis in the Oblonsky family soon ends, and the
future is determined. This is the context in which we meet Anna and Levin
at the beginning of their more dramatic and varied histories, and Anna's
passion and Levin's idealism are sharply dramatized, and stand out as exceptional cases. Anna, unlike Dolly, will not accept the conditions of her
marriage; Levin, unlike Oblonsky, wants a stable love, and unlike Karenin,
wants a loving stability. They are, it is true, more sharply contrasted with
each other than with the Oblonskys, and here again the advantage of the
chosen beginning shows itself. Tolstoy is basing his novel on an antithesis,
the contrast between instability and stability, an unhappy marriage and
love, and a happy married love, but it is not going to be a stark and complete
antithesis. The first case makes it clear, from the beginning, that we are
going to see variations on the theme of love and marriage, and not a rigid
contrast between the Karenins and the Levins. Life is not going to be shown
in terms of a grand polar tension, and the middle way sets up the right
kind of expectations, as well as creating the impression of normalilty. Life
is composed of Oblonskys as well as Annas and Levins, and this has a
significance beyond the theme of marriage. Both Anna and Levin are people
who make great demands of life, and although Anna's demands end in her
nihilistic vision, and Levin's with his discovery of faith, they have much
more in common with each other than with Oblonsky, the *homme moyen
sensuel* whose demands are realistic and easy. Anna and Vronsky and Levin
are all tempted to suicide—the difference between them and Oblonsky is
most easily, if crudely, summed up in this fact. We cannot imagine Oblonsky's passions and ideas bringing him to this edge. His dinners, his work,
his liberalism, his opera-girls, his wife, and his children, are all accom-
modated within his selfish but limited range of demands.

From the beginning of the novel Tolstoy sets up the antithesis, only
to turn it into a parallel. He sets it up very quietly and gradually. The two
actions begin together, with Levin and Vronsky as rivals for Kitty's love,
and are first opposed only in this relationship of personal rivalry. The same
applies to Anna and Kitty. Moreover, the antithesis is undeveloped for a
very long time, until the second volume, when—at roughly the same time—
Anna goes away with Vronsky, and Levin marries Kitty. Until this point
we move from Anna's love-story to Levin or Kitty, leading their separated
lives. Although, looking back, we may be conscious of the contrast between
the self-absorbed passions of Anna and Vronsky, and the out-turned ener-

gies of Levin, this is not only a contrast which the author does not emphasize, but one which is not plain until the final antithetical action really starts.

Here the author does direct our attention to the structural relations between the two couples. We follow the first months of Vronsky's union with Anna, and the first months of Levin's with Kitty. But although the reader expects an antithesis, it is an incomplete one. Both couples are uneasy, tormented with jealousy, and Levin feels himself uprooted and without occupation, just like Vronsky. But in spite of this, there is the basic contrast between Levin's radiant joy and the restlessness of the Vronskys. This ironical offering of contrast and comparison goes on in detail. There is the contrast between the occupations of the two women: Kitty's conduct in Nicholas Levin's sickroom, and Anna's architecturally knowledgeable talks about the new hospital; Kitty's pregnancy and reactions to her child, and Anna's pregnancy, reactions to her daughter, and her subsequent decision to have no more children. Here the third term blurs the antithesis, for it is Dolly's point of view which governs our reaction to Anna, and in the marvellous scenes of Dolly's visit we have Anna's self-chosen sterility beautifully evaluated. Dolly has had her own private fantasy of having *her* Vronsky. Now her shabbiness and unhappiness make her see the glamour of Anna's existence, but she rejects it hastily. But Dolly's condition also justifies Anna—this is what happens if you stay with your husband and accept a woman's lot. Finally, there is the contrast between jealousies: Levin's jealousy of Veslovsky and Vronsky's tolerance, Kitty's dislike of his tone and Anna's "civilized" response. And at the close, Anna's despair and pessimism, generalized in the last railway-ride, and Levin's qualified vision. She puts out the candle, he sees a light. She sees the appropriately peopled world of cheapness, shabbiness, and pretence; he sees the endurance of the peasants. This too is a qualified contrast: his vision is not going to be easy to live with, and it cannot be shared with his wife. The very last page does not set up unqualified triumph after despair—Anna has killed herself, Vronsky goes off on the pointless Turkish expedition, Oblonsky gets the appointment. Levin's vision is set squarely in a realistic context.

Not only is the novel inconspicuously divided, not only does it constantly compare as well as contrast, it cannot be said to insist even on the pattern which does emerge. It is a pattern which we may very well not be strongly aware of until the end, when we may go back and see it embedded in action which strikes us in its particularity rather than its resonance. Levin's reaction to his child does not remind us of Karenin's, both are striking in themselves. It is rather that all the characters are subjected to similar tests, the common tests of fatherhood, profession, and faith, and that the parellelism is often scarcely noticeable. It may be argued that this is true of most nineteenth-century fiction, where the pattern is the means and not the end, and that it is only later fiction, where the figure in the carpet is like a figure in a carpet, conspicuous and even an end in itself, that makes us go back and abstract the muted figures of Victorian novels. There is, I think, as much difference between Tolstoy and George Eliot or Dickens as there is between James Joyce and George Eliot and Dickens. We may not need to observe the structural relations in *Middlemarch* as we do in *Ulysses* or *The Wild Palms* where we cannot read the novel without being aware of reading form as notation, but once we start looking, the relations are persistently present, governing scenes and characters and rhetoric. Sometimes it is very explicit, as with Dickens's extension of the prison symbol in *Little Dorrit*, so that the common symbol or metaphor forces us to see the parallel, and insistently. Sometimes it is less explicit, as in *Middlemarch*, where we can observe the difference between Dorothea and Rosamond without observing the careful contrast in the flowers associated with them, in their clothing, their attitude to jewels, their habits of looking into mirrors or out of windows. It is very likely that we may exaggerate the symbolic emphasis of such parallels, which are reinforcements of value rather than totally responsible vehicles. Tolstoy has relatively few symbolic reinforcements of this kind.

In *Anna Karenina* technical device never distorts character and action, by omission or stereotype, and seldom gives that heightened and poetic halo which cannot be appraised by realistic standards. When George Eliot makes Rosamond and Dorothea use exactly the same words, or when she makes Dorothea and Mrs. Bulstrode perform a similar act of ritual in clothing, there is nothing unrealistic about the symbolism, but the characters and events are being artificially arranged for various purposes of moral and psychological emphasis. When Henry James makes Maggie find the golden bowl, or when Fanny Assingham smashes it, neither the plot contrivance nor the symbolic act is primarily moving as revelations of truths outside the novel, but are symbolic acts which have their meaning within the novel. We say of them that they are acceptable and exciting in that context, not allowing ourselves to judge contrivance or convention by the tests of likeliness so long as these tests are passed elsewhere, by the psychological detail or the moral generalization. When Dickens uses the motif of the wild waves in *Dombey and Son*, we do not apply quite the same test of internal reality, but we may again accept the convention as a poetic heightening, more or less successful in tone and function, which makes its first appearance within the natural context of character, as part of Paul's strained fancy, stimulated by his actual environment, and later becoming an unashamed piece of rhetoric spoken in the author's own voice, and not testable by reference to external truth. Neither the unrealistic contrivance which successfully pretends to be part of the imitation of the action, nor the unrealistic symbol, appears in Tolstoy. Tolstoy is of course contriving and organizing, but his contrivance is very muted.

There are symbols and recurrent metaphors in the novel, but their quality is subdued and literal. Take, for instance, the use of the railway train. This is not only striking in itself, and the nearest thing to a binding symbol in the novel, but it can usefully be compared with Dickens's use of the railway in *Dombey and Son,* where its association with death is powerfully exploited. Both novels deal with the expansion of railways, and there are many discussions in *Anna Karenina* which keep us aware of social function, novelty, and commercial exploitation. There are several significant railway scenes, the first scene when Anna arrives in Moscow, her return journey with Vronsky, the scene of her death, and the last scene when Oblonsky meets Vronsky. There is the railway game which Serezha plays, which has its grim anticipation. The railway carries characters across the map of Russia, and has the same documentary status as the buildings, hospitals, hotels, and farms. Only two or three of these scenes are linked by ironical resonance, and here the comparison with Dickens is interesting, because the railway is a monster for Dombey and for Carker, and never puts in an innocent appearance. Dickens does on occasion use the literal scene for such symbolic resonance, but not here. Tolstoy does use the railway symbolically, but in his own way.

We first meet Anna in Part I, Chapter xvii, at the Petersburg railway station in Moscow, where Oblonsky has come to meet her, and where he meets Vronsky, who has come to meet his mother, also from Petersburg. In the preceding chapter Oblonsky and Vronsky talk about the previous evening at the Shcherbatskys, and Oblonsky's cheerful bland impartiality links Vronksy with Levin, for he offers the same Pushkin quotation: "Fiery steeds by *'something'* brands I can always recognize, Youths in love." This first irony gives place to another, for Vronksy counters Oblonsky's mention of the "lovely woman" he has come to meet with the same kind of banter, "Dear Me!" which is answered, *"Honi soi qui mal y pense."* Throughout the next lines of dialogue Vronsky thinks of Karenin as some one stiff and dull. The train comes in slowly with a few accompanying details of "workmen in sheepskin coats and felt boots crossing the curved railway lines," comment on the extreme cold, "frosty mist" and "frozen air," the description of the engine driver bent and covered with hoar-frost, and, lastly, with no emphasis, "a peasant with a sack over his shoulder." In the next chapter Vronsky sees Anna without knowing who she is, and we have the first impression of her vitality, as she "deliberately tries to extinguish that light in her eyes." Anna and the Countess Vronskya have taken to each other, and been talking about their sons, and the old Countess says to Anna, "But please don't fret about your son, you can't expect never to be parted." Earlier, in the middle of explaining how she has come to travel with Anna, she says to Vronsky "And you I hear . . . *vous filez le parfait amour. Tant mieux, mon cher, tant mieux.*" He replies "coldly"—in contrast to his reply to Oblonsky.

The brief scene is loaded with ironical anticipation, and acts just like a Jamesian scene, as the stage on which later action is to figure. All the roles and relations are to be reversed. By the time we reach the second railway-scene in which Anna appears, she is separated from her son, and the affection the Countess first feels for her has been replaced by hatred and jealousy. They are both separated from their sons, and on this journey Anna is pursuing in Vronsky. On the first occasion Anna has come as peacemaker, to help reconcile the estranged couple, and later it is to be Oblonsky, with his old insouciance, making puns over dissolved marriages, who acts as mediator. All the characters are bound together, either actually or in insistent reference.

There is more than this carefully set stage, which is to be eventually upset. The railway is associated with death: "A watchman, either tipsy or too much muffled up because of the severe frost, had not heard a train that was being shunted, and had been run over." Vronsky's relationship with Anna begins: she only says "Can nothing be done for her?" and Vronsky glances at her, goes off, and gives 200 roubles for the widow. Anna knows what this means, and when her brother asks her why she is so upset—as he has been himself a minute before—she says, "It is a bad omen." Oblonsky's *"Honi soit"* which was said so lightly, becomes a curse.

When we come to her last railway journey we see that Anna has learnt from the details ("cut in half," "a very easy death," "How is it that precautions are not taken?") when she methodically places herself on the line. The ominousness of original scene is not allowed to stay below the surface for the whole of this long novel. Tolstoy takes one tiny detail— the peasant with a bag—and uses him, just as George Eliot uses the dead face in *Daniel Deronda*, to haunt the novel, at very well-spaced intervals. Vronsky and Anna both dream of him. Their dreams coincide in time but

in Vronsky's dream the peasant is a beater at the bear-hunting and Vronsky
cannot see exactly what he is doing. Anna tells him in Part IV, Chapter
iii, that she has "dreamed it a long time ago." The French words are
"incomprehensible" to Vronsky and repeated by Anna, *"Il faut le battre, le
fer: le broyer, le pétrir."* He is there at her death. The watchman and the
peasant are oddly juxtaposed in the dream, since in fact neither Vronsky
nor Anna have seen the first man. The ominousness is just picked up enough
to provide the link of sinister recognition at the end. At the beginning,
love and death are linked. It is a fatal meeting. And, a tiny but typical
touch, we never know why the watchman was killed—he is the instructor,
the first opportunity for the show of love, and the curse, but the refusal to
tell keeps us within the observer's point of view, and insists on his stubborn
opaque reality. The incomplete human detail shows life which is larger
than symbolic function.

I do not think there are many examples of this kind of artifice and
cluster, though there is the image of the candle, and there is the appropriate
journey to death, with Ana's nightmarish distortion of her fellow-travellers.
The symbolism overarches the novel, comes out strongly in these two crises,
but is not part of the habitual mode of narrative. Even in these scenes
there is the usual realistic stability of the women's conversation, Vronsky's
reactions to his friend and then to his mother, Oblonsky's quick easy
sentimental reactions. The scene ends "And Oblonsky began his story,"
but it is Anna's which is really begun here.

The end of Anna's story is carefully related to the beginning—
another reason, perhaps, why we feel so strongly the inevitability and lack
of choice in the action—but it is also carefully related to Levin's story.
Anna has crossed his path though they do not meet except once, late in
the story, and it is Anna who has freed Kitty, and left her for Levin. She
frees Kitty and Levin for their slowly developing love, where for a long
time obstacles from without and within hold up the development, and their
love and hers are, at the end, contrasted. Anna's vision of "anxieties,
deceptions, grief, and evil" and Levin's final vision of faith and purpose
are described in images of light. Throughout the last five chapters leading
to Anna's suicide we have the image of the candle, which appears in actual
form in Part VII, Chapter xxvi:

> She lay in bed with open eyes, looking at the stucco cornice under the
> ceiling by the light of a single burnt-down candle, and at the shadow of
> the screen which fell on it, and she vividly imagined what he would feel
> when she was no more, when she was for him nothing but a memory.
> "How could I say those cruel words to her?" he would say. "How could
> I leave the room without saying anything? But now she is no more! She

has gone from us for ever! She is there . . ." Suddenly the shadow of the screen began to move and spread over the whole of the cornice, the whole ceiling. Other shadows rushed toward it from another side; for an instant they rushed together, but then again they spread with renewed swiftness, flickered, and all was darkness. "Death!" she thought. And such terror came upon her that it was long before she could realize where she was and with trembling hand could find the matches to light another candle in the place of the one that had burnt down and gone out.

Next morning she has her recurring nightmare (shared by Vronsky) about the "old man with a tangled beard" who was "leaning over some iron while muttering senseless words in French . . . paying no attention to her but . . . doing something dreadful to her with the iron." Later that morning when Vronsky has gone out after a quarrel, the two images join: she asks "Is it finished?", and in answer to that question, "the impressions left by the darkness when her candle went out and by the terrible dream, merging into one, filled her heart with icy terror." When she goes out her disordered mind sees its appropriate environment: Kitty's jealousy, boys buying dirty ice-cream, a tradesman crossing himself "as if he were afraid of dropping something," cabmen swearing, lies and greed and hate everywhere.

There is constant movement: she goes to Dolly's, then back home to get Vronsky's telegram which has crossed with her note. She goes to the station, catching glimpses of "the struggle for existence and hatred" which she sees as "the only things that unite people." She turns "the bright light in which she saw everything" upon her relations with Vronsky, and sees what is true and what is not true. The image punctuates this vision of despair: "the piercing light which now revealed to her the meaning of life and of human relations." The things she sees in the immediate scene or in her memory are very sharply engraved: the complacent "rosy-faced shop-assistant who was riding a hired horse," Vronsky's face as it was in their early days together, "suggestive of a faithful setter's," Karenin with his "mild dull, lifeless eyes, the blue veins of his white hands, his into-nations, his cracking fingers." The last train journey begins, and on the platform the vision continues to pierce, the ugly bold-faced young men, the misshapen woman in a bustle, the affected girl, and—at last—"a grimy, misshaped peasant in a cap from under which his touzled hair stuck out . . . stooping over the carriage wheels." "There is something familiar about that misshaped peasant," she thought, remembers her dream, and almost leaves the train.

Her last companions are affected, insincere, weary of each other, "and it was impossible not to hate such wretches." She "directs her search-light upon them," seizes on the woman's words about reason being a means of escape, and asks, "Why not put out the candle, if there is nothing more to look at? If everything is repulsive to look at?"

The candle and the nightmare come together again in the last words of her last chapter:

> A little peasant muttering something was working at the rails. The candle, by the light of which she had been reading that book, filled with anxieties, deceptions, grief, and evil, flared up with a brighter light than before, lit up for her all that had before been dark, flickered, began to grow dim, and went out for ever.

But the novel is not over. Anna made her first appearance, at the station where she first met Vronsky, in Chapter xviii, and after her death there are nineteen chapters to follow—fair symmetry for a large loose baggy monster. Tolstoy's artistry becomes very conspicuous towards the end of the novel, in this subtle interplay of image and symbol which we have just seen. The development of the imagery is part of the portrayal of character: its distorting flickering light becomes clear and piercing, Tolstoy peoples Anna's world with ordinary figures who can enact her nightmare, and the disordered sickness of her last hours is presented with poetic intensity which is the appropriate form. The contrast between the sick vision and Levin's affirmative faith concludes the novel.

It began with the drift of ordinary life and after Anna's tragedy comes a return to the normal flow. There is symmetry here, even in the detail, for we return to yet another railway journey and end, where we began, with the domestic scene. Part VIII opens with Koznyshev, a character we have not seen for some time, and there is an apparent diversion which tells us of the frustrating reception of his great book, into which has gone so much devotion and labour. With the typical natural movement of Tolstoy's narrative we encounter Vronsky's mother and then Vronsky himself, on his last desperate journey, which once more involves the individual destiny in the larger movements of history. From a Jamesian point of view, this transition involves a very substantial piece of intrusive action and feeling, but Tolstoy is evidently choosing to make an undramatic shift from Anna's death to Levin's life by using a character who is neither central nor deeply involved in the main action, but whose personal life has its hopes and losses too. There is the sense of continuity, a lowering of tension, loose ends tied up but not too neatly, Koznyshev is on his way to visit Levin.

Life turns into new channels. We move back to Levin and follow his climactic progress and the conversion to a sense of meaning and purpose. Like Anna he is tempted by suicide, unlike Anna, he turns away from the solicitations of reason and of despair. But this is no triumphant flourish in conclusion. The novel is at its most formal in this concluding antithesis.

As far as one can judge from a translation, symbolism, rhetoric and structural relations are as pronounced and conspicuous here as they are in a novel by Henry James. And yet—in the very presence of such insistent repetition and balance—the novel is also at its most free and fluid. It is as if the frankly artistic contrivances are there to draw our attention to their own inadequacy. This seems to me one of the most important and interesting features of artifice and formal assertion in the expansive novel, and it is to be found in George Eliot and Meredith as well as Tolstoy. In Henry James and Virginia Woolf and E. M. Forster it seems roughly true to say that where the formal elements become most conspicuous, the human substance is at its most thin and sketchy. The reverse is true in Tolstoy and George Eliot, where a symbolic assertion of fable or category has the function of freeing the human material. The function of Mary Garland or Maria Gostrey is assertive at the expense of plausibility, whereas the functional relationship of Lydgate and Dorothea, or Anna and Levin, only makes the individual variations more apparent. The novelist's artifice may be held in tension with his "love of each seized identity" or it may compete with it. The novelist's skeletal moral framework may show clearly in order to reveal the density and complexity of the flesh, or it may show itself by unfleshing identity. This is one reason for avoiding generalizations about novels and novelists and regarding always the individual form.

In Tolstoy the artifice and the moral fable show through more clearly at some points than at others: the loose bagginess may be apparent in places, tight organization at other places. The ends of novels are frequently places where a summary of value or an aesthetic completion will appear, and in the end of *Anna Karenina* there is a remarkable combination of the artifice which makes the moral categories absolutely plain, and the expansive life which resists facile conclusion. Candlelight distorts, and Anna's disgusted nihilistic vision finds perfect expression in the image of the candle, in its phenomenal aspect and in its actual nightmarish origin in her life. For Levin, light has a different source, larger and clearer in fact and associated not with despairing insomnia and drugged sleep but with great clarity. Its source is chiefly in the vision of the vault of the sky picked out by stars, but it comes too from other diffused images. In Chapter xi, which describes the sensation of converting faith we have the last moving description of peasants at work, and light and darkness are important terms in the scene which makes such an impression on Levin:

> He looked now through the open doorway into which the bitter chaff-dust rushed and whirled, at the grass round the threshing-floor lit up by the hot sunshine and at the fresh straw that had just been brought out of the barn, now at the bright-headed and white-breasted swallows that flew

in chirping beneath the roof and, flapping their wings, paused in the light of the doorway, and now at the people who bustled about in the dark and dusty barn; and he thought strange thoughts:

"Why is all this being done?" he wondered. "Why am I standing here, obliging them to work? Why do they all make such efforts and try to show me their zeal? Why is my old friend Matrena toiling so (I doctored her after the fire, when she was struck by a girder)?" he thought, looking at a thin peasant woman who pushed the grain along with a rake, her dark sunburnt bare feet stepping with effort on the hard uneven barn floor. "She recovered then, but today or tomorrow, or in ten years' time, they will bury her and nothing will be left of her, nor of that smart girl with the red skirt, who with such dexterous and delicate movements is beating the chaff from the ears. . . . What is it all for?"

There follows the brief description of actual routine—as in the hunting scenes, life goes on and man attends to work or play even in moments of grief or acute questioning. Then comes the brief mention of Daddy Plato, "the upright old man" who "lives for his soul and remembers God" and lovingly lets people off.

At the peasant's words about Plato living for his soul, rightly, in a godly way, dim but important thoughts crowded into his mind, as if breaking loose from some place where they had been locked up, and all rushing toward one goal, whirled in his head, dazzling them with their light.

The actual imagery of light continues, as it did for Anna, but more naturally, present in fairly obvious metaphors like the last one in the passage above, or associated with Levin's vision of space and "high cloudless sky" which is both the limited rounded vault which his eyes can see, and the unseen "limitless space." It is the image of the sky rather than of mere light which corresponds to Anna's candle, and here the larger contrasts are more important than imagery. There is the pastoral contrast in his peasants and her townsfolk, his sky and her ceiling, in the sources of his stability—"the old beehives, every one familiar to him," for instance—and her rootless existence. There is his outward vision and her sick obsession. Both are presented in terms of clear sight, though Anna's disturbed mind clings to "reason" while Levin tries to see his faith in the context of ordinary life where he will not be greatly changed, where his relationships will still be difficult, where no miraculous transformation scene will make everything different. But what Anna sees is not merely her own distorted vision, like Kay's in The Snow Queen, but the actual sickness and dirt and pretentions and competitiveness of the city. What Levin sees, more realistically, is again not his own blinding vision, but men at work, the stability and demands of the land and labour. What they see is what exists—at least in Tolstoy's belief—and, more important, it is what has made them what they are. This is perhaps why both are given light, and from appropriately different sources, manmade and Godmade, tiny and large, temporary and enduring.

There is no clear answer, and the very last appearance of the image of light blurs the antithesis between the two people, the two ways of life, the negative and positive vision. But this is only a blurring, not a disheartened questioning. The end is like the end of *Women in Love,* but more affirmative. It is like the last strong contrast between the mirror-gazing Rosamond and the far-seeing Dorothea, but less optimistic. It enacts Levin's realization that faith in life's meaning will not transform human relationships or break isolation. At the end he, like Anna, is alone, but his is a sane acceptance of the conditions of living.

In the last chapter of the novel, storm continues, and Levin looks at the lightning which does not illuminate:

> Levin listened to the rhythmical dripping of raindrops from the lime trees in the garden, and looked at a familiar triangular constellation and at the Milky Way which with its branches intersected it. At every flash of lightning not only the Milky Way but even the bright stars vanished; but immediately afterwards they reappeared in the same places, as if thrown there by some unerring hand.

Levin goes on questioning, feeling that solution is not yet discovered but is near, and he accepts both reason and its limitations, in a way which draws us back to Anna's last moments in contrast:

> "Do I not know that it is not the stars that are moving?" he asked himself, looking at a bright planet that had already shifted its position by the top branch of a birch tree. "But I, watching the movements of the stars, cannot picture to myself the rotation of the earth and I am right in saying that the stars move."

Anna's sickness seems appropriately figured in the candle's distortions which she takes literally, Levin's sanity in his ability to entertain reason and faith, using the image of light and space with conscious detachment. He is joined by Kitty, who peers at his face in the starlight, and is able to see his calm and happy expression in a flash of lightning which also shows him her answering smile. "She understands" he thinks, and feels that he can share his thoughts. Just as he is about to speak she begins:

> "Oh, Kostya! Be good and go to the corner room and see how they have arranged things for Sergius Ivanich! I can't very well do it myself. Have they put in the new washstand?"

Levin is left to realize that there is no total illumination, no change, no communication, even though his life is now, for him, invested with a sense of purpose. His course and Anna's are opposites, divided in despair and faith, insecurity and stability, death and life. This final suggestion reminds us that human destinies are not quite so distinct. The pattern of the three marriages cannot be described as normal, tragic, and happy. The pattern of different energies cannot be described as normal, frustrated, and successful. Faith is not isolated and given a glorious climax, but brought into steady relationship with the difficulties of life. This is not only Tolstoy's admission of the free flow of life, made because he, like Lawrence, does not take the novel beyond the stage he had reached in actual experience. It is also an assertion of dogma in an undogmatic form, the last pulse of a slow and irregular rhythm which is a faithful record of the abrupt, the difficult, the inconclusive.

JOHN BAYLEY

"What Is Art?"

The primitive vitality in this sense of possession reminds us of childhood, and almost everything in *War and Peace* springs out of the childhood world and returns to it for judgement. It is the source of life and sensation, the setting of the idyll. The idyll has all the capacity of childish appetite—"more, more yet"—Anatol Kuragin shouting for *more* troikas, *more* champagne, *more* gipsy music reminds us of the piercing, senseless cry of ecstasy which the small Natasha used to utter. Kuragin's is the spoilt version of that eagerness which keeps every stage of Natasha's life in correspondence with her life as a child—her marital communication with Pierre echoes the communication between children in the family. This depends upon *understanding*, a particularly Tolstoyan quality, which he explains in *Youth*.

> Apart from the general faculties, which are more or less developed according to the individual, of intellect, sensibility, and artistic feeling, there exists a special capacity that is more or less developed in different circles of society and especially in families, which I call mutual *understanding*. The essence of this capacity lies in an agreed sense of proportion and an accepted and identical outlook on things. Two members of the same set or the same family possessing this faculty can always allow an expression of feeling up to a certain point beyond which they both see only empty phrases. Simultaneously both perceive where commendation ends and irony begins, where enthusiasm ceases and pretence takes its place—all of which may appear quite otherwise to people possessed of a different order of apprehension. People of the same understanding see everything they come across in an identically ludicrous, beautiful, or repellent light. To facilitate this common understanding the members of

a circle or a family often invent a language of their own with expressions peculiar to them, or even words which indicate shades of meaning non-existent for others. . . . Dubkov fitted into our circle fairly well and *understood*, but Dimitri Nekhlyudov, though far more intelligent, was obtuse in this respect.

In *Childhood, Boyhood,* and *Youth* this understanding between the members of the family is also an understanding—intimate, sometimes almost incoherent—between Tolstoy and the reader. He depends on us to see the point of the private jokes that produce screams of happy, senseless, sometimes malicious laughter. "Katya, the *Russians?*"—cries Volodya, on a particular note of interrogation, meaningful only to himself and his brother the narrator; and the narrator goes crawling through the raspberry canes, repeating endlessly to himself "And by twenties and by sevens." This bid for *understanding* has often been imitated since by other writers. Its dangers are inconsequence, drift from one kind of intimate accuracy to another, and eventually to boredom. Moreover, there is a discrepancy between the intimate bid for understanding and the generalising, retrospective tone of the narrator: it is this that Tolstoy probably had in mind when he later spoke of the book as "insincerely written in a literary sense," and why he broke off without completing the whole work, to be called *Four Epochs of Growth*, which he had planned. In *War and Peace* the narration is unified, the incoherencies of family life organized and concentrated into the traditional patterns of idyll and epic. Instead of the appeal to understanding followed by the slightly pompous explanation of it, we have a plain descriptive transparency. We learn for instance that when the young Rostovs are talking, Sonya (like Lyuba and Katya) "did not quite keep pace with them though she shared the same reminiscences." But "she enjoyed their pleasure and tried to fit in with it."

There is an immense gain in clarity and purpose in the family life of *War and Peace*, but at the expense of that wonderful, maddening, inconclusive accuracy which reigns in *Childhood*. Since everything in the great book must be followed up, much must be left out. Its completeness is a magnificent illusion, and its steady pulse bears us onwards before the idylls can settle into poses that would reveal the artifice of their structure and what they omit. One of the most striking omissions is the kind of sexual awareness which permeates *Childhood*. We must remember, of course, that the version of *War and Peace* which we have was prepared for the press by the Countess Tolstoy, and that the early drafts are much more outspoken than the finished product was allowed to be. "Needs a husband, even two?" Tolstoy wrote in his notes about Natasha, and Hélène is described as "a beautiful piece of meat in a skirt." These frank comments have no place in the book, where the sexuality even of Hélène is generalized and idealized on the epic scale. But with men Tolstoy is less successful in the idealization process; male sexual desire is curiously furtive. The decorum of life so essential to the great work would be bothered by it; there seems no place for it in the great harmony of family and nation. The significance of this is considerable. Tolstoy only created a world that seems to embrace all reality by sealing off things that worried and disturbed him.

One might say that Tolstoy enjoyed contemplating female sexuality (with all that "enjoyment" implies in such a creative intelligence) but he detested contemplating his own or that of other men. His marvellous marriage sequences are seen entirely in terms of the sexuality of the woman, to whom the man is merely a passive instrument. Both Pierre and Levin in *Anna Karenina* are surprised by the total subordination to family needs which their wives require of them, but their vanity is gratified by it and they submit. It is part of the nature of things. And not only in the marriage sequences.

> He half rose, meaning to go round, but the aunt handed him the snuff-box, passing it across Hélène's back. Hélène stooped forward to make room, and looked round with a smile. She was, as always at evening parties, wearing a dress such as was then fashionable, cut very low at front and back. Her bust, which had always seemed like marble to Pierre, was so close to him that his short-sighted eyes could not but perceive the living charm of her neck and shoulders, so near to his lips that he need only have bent his head a little to have touched them. He was conscious of the warmth of her body, the scent of perfume, and the creaking of her corset as she moved. He did not see her marble beauty forming a complete whole with her dress, but all the charm of her body only covered by her garments. And having once seen this he could not help being aware of it, just as we cannot renew an illusion we have once seen through.
>
> "So you have never before noticed how beautiful I am?" Hélène seemed to say. "You had not noticed that I am a woman? Yes, I am a woman who may belong to any one—to you too," said her glance. And at that moment Pierre felt that Hélène not only could, but must, be his wife, and that it could not be otherwise.

Like a composer Tolstoy converts even the angularity of real life—like the touch of Hélène stooping forward while the snuff-box is passed behind her—into the flowing rhythm of the passage. It was bound to happen; it was as right as a tune, and the gathering is caught up, as by a tune, into "the attraction of a healthy and handsome young man and woman for one another." "The human feeling dominated everything else and soared above all their affected chatter."As in the troika drive in which "a voice told Sonya that now or never her fate would be decided," the dominant note in the harmony is female, and Prince Vasily presides as an epic host on one level and as an epicene procurer on the other. His face, generally full of benevolence and good will, is apt on occasion "to assume the coarse unpleasant expression peculiar to him." Although his daughter resembles him, his attitude is hardly parental. He addresses her "with the careless tone of habitual tenderness natural to parents who have petted their children from babyhood, but which Prince Vasily had only acquired from imitating other parents." So, after all, have most parents! But the whole scene, which in *Ivan Ilyich* would be a nightmare of hypocrisy and ugliness, is here harmonious and full of delight. The Trollopian expedient by which Prince Vasily compels Pierre to accept his fate acquires in Tolstoy's hands a Mozartian brio, as if the prince were a conductor executing the final flourish. And Hélène manages the absurdity of sexual urgency as gracefully as when she stooped forward to allow the snuff-box to be passed behind her back.

> "Oh, take off . . . those. . ." she said, pointing to his spectacles.
> Pierre took them off, and his eyes besides the strange look eyes have from which spectacles have just been removed, had also a frightened and inquiring look. He was about to stoop over her hand and kiss it, but with a rapid, almost brutal movement of her head she intercepted his lips and met them with her own. Her face struck Pierre by its altered, unpleasantly excited expression.
> "It is too late now, it's done; besides I love her," thought Pierre.
> *"Je vous aime!"* he said, remembering what has to be said at such moments.

Well, perhaps not quite so gracefully! She is her father's daughter. And Tolstoy ends the scene on a note that suggests he is about to revert to his ironic technique, the technique that the Russian critic Shklovsky called "making it strange."

This suggestive phrase refers to Tolstoy's use of an eighteenth-century satiric device much favoured by his admired Voltaire, who describes soldiers playing on a drum as "murderers six foot high, clothed in scarlet and beating a distended ass's skin." The intention is to reveal what reason or "unclouded common sense" show to be true about a subject wrapped in romantic nonsense or ancient prejudice. It is highly important in *War and Peace* and we shall often have cause to notice it again. Obvious instances of its extended use are Natasha's visit to the opera, and Pierre's induction into the masonic rites. It is common in battle scenes, where it merges with what Tolstoy learnt from Stendhal's factual style and lack of emphasis, as in the scene when Nikolai's horse is killed under him at Schön Grabern, or when at Ostrovna he hits the French dragoon with his sabre and captures him. Tolstoy not only uses it in many variations but interspersed with other methods of narrative to provide shades of contrast. At Schön Grabern, for example, Nikolai is enchanted to find just before the fall of his horse begins to "make it strange" that war is just like what he had hoped and imagined; that he is charging forward waving his sword—just as in the battle pictures— shouting "Hurrah" and full of the intoxicating hope of killing somebody.

Voltaire and Swift use the method of "making it strange" as satire: Tolstoy uses it dramatically. For the satirist it shows the object as it really is, but for Tolstoy it shows one way of seeing it. His other methods of narration put it on record that other ways of seeing the thing exist. At the end of the engagement scene Pierre says to Hélène " 'Je vous aime,' remembering what has to be said at such moments." The implication is that such scenes are utterly insincere and fatuous, and that Tolstoy is recalling us to a sense of this. We certainly need to be recalled, for our impression of the scene, with all its comedy and harmony, was very different. The ludicrous and the beautiful appeared, as in *The Rape of the Lock,* as the substance of art and life. At such moments Tolstoy shows himself as very much a complete man of the eighteenth century: Mozart and Voltaire counterpoint one another and the music of the narrative depends on their alliance even more than it does on epic association.

The next scene, though shows old Prince Bolkonsky on his estate, awaiting the arrival of Prince Vasily, and now the poised glitter of the ballet gives way to a sober epic domination. No doubt this patriarchal country life was for Tolstoy the real thing, and the frivolous social life of the capital a mere excrescence, but the change does not mark a deliberate moral contrast. The old Prince is monarch of all he surveys; he refuses to play the social game, and when his steward incautiously reveals that he has had the avenue swept because a "minister" is coming, he flies into a rage and gives orders for the snow to be shovelled back again. It is a gesture worthy of the epic man, as Prince Vasily's device to make Pierre declare himself was worthy of the Mozartian social one; and as Pierre's shame for himself, when he says "Je vous aime" because it has to be said at such moments is worthy of the rational and Voltairean man. The three methods, the three modes of living, are given the stature of originals, and contribute together to the greater harmony of the novel. . . .

Anna Karenina does not only contain its own qualification and contradiction of Tolstoy's attitude to art—it also gives unexpected support to the examples of good and bad art that Tolstoy choses. When we read *What Is Art?* we may assent to many of his general propositions, but we are staggered by the apparent perversity of his taste. *Hamlet* and *Lear* are notorious instances, but even more disheartening is the offer of Hugo, *Uncle Tom's Cabin,* his own stories *God Sees the Truth but Waits* and *The Prisoner of the Caucasus* (his only works of good art according to Tolstoy) and the crudest kind of *genre* painting. He singles out for special praise a sketch by Kramskoy (the Mikhaylov of *Anna*)

> showing a drawing-room with a balcony past which troops are marching in triumph on their return from the war. On the balcony stands a nurse holding a baby, and a boy. They are admiring the procession of the troops, but the mother, covering her face with a handkerchief, has fallen back on the sofa sobbing.

In spite of the different moral, this sounds horribly like the modern Russian *genre* painting *The Letter from the Front,* said to be Khrushchev's favourite. But when with Anna and Vronsky we suddenly catch sight in a corner of Mikhaylov's studio of his picture of two boys angling, we are, like them, completely won over by it. Tolstoy makes a picture seem good which cited as an example in *What Is Art?* would seem awful, and the reason is that he can make the picture alive for us in the novel by the element of *participation.* We are vividly aware of the attitudes of the three spectators, of their ennui with Mikhaylov's big religious work and their need to say something intelligent about it; of their attempt to express appreciation by means of the word "talent," "which they understood to mean an innate . . . capacity, independent of mind and heart, and which was their term for everything an artist lives through"; and of how their bogus appreciative vocabulary is extinguished by spontaneous delight at the sight of the angling picture, which Mikhaylov has forgotten all about, as he has forgotten "the sufferings and raptures" he went through while painting it. The point is not that the painting is "good art"—the novel does not pronounce on this—but that it gives these people whom we know real pleasure instead of merely engaging with their aesthetic expectations; that it leads us, therefore, into a true and penetrating study of the relation of artist, art and spectator. Tolstoy has made it come alive "with the inexpressible complexity of everything that lives."

It is precisely the absence of this life which condemns the examples thrust down our throats in *What Is Art?*. Tolstoy had little experience of pictorial art and less education in it. He saw it in terms of the bad painting of his own time, but given this large limitation (of which he admittedly seems unaware) his taste is singularly just. He preferred the bad picture with feeling to the bad picture with none. Though he might not have cared for Piero della Francesca, and still less for Cézanne, he none the less urges upon us the considerations in art which makes those artists great; the dependence of skill upon "mind and heart"; the true invitation to the whole of human experience. He detests art that stops short at beauty, or indeed that stops short anywhere.

All treatises on art are unsatisfactory—the issue is at once too simple and too complex for any theorist to do justice to—and Tolstoy's is no exception. What he says is profoundly true, but it is not the sort of truth which can be set out in the way he chooses to do so. As polemic, the effectiveness of *What is Art?* lies not so much in its positive assertions as in its rejection of much that was taken for granted in the aesthetic theories of the time, particularly as these relate to the story and the novel. Tolstoy explicitly rejects Kantian isolation of art as the realm of decoration and play, and all the nineteenth-century doctrines of art for art's sake which stem from it. He points out that the word for beauty in Russian, *krasota*, applies only to what is seen, so that it makes no sense to speak of beauty in an action or a novel, or even in poetry or music. The interchangeability of words meaning *good* and *beautiful* in Western languages has, he implies, resulted in the notion of some sort of beauty, verbal or aesthetic, as the goal of art.

The admired literature of the nineties could hardly defend itself against a charge like Tolstoy's. Even Wagner and Ibsen—to say nothing of Maupassant, Huysmans, Mallarmé, Rilke, Bryusov and the symbolists— they *are* inferior to great writers and for the reason Tolstoy gives, a lack of that wide and involuntary humanity which unites the writer's consciousness with the human experience that "knew the thing before but had been unable to express it." We are reminded of the eighteenth-century pre-Kantian view of art here—"what oft was thought but ne'er so well expressed"—"and we remember the reaction of Vronsky to Anna's portrait by Mikhaylov (where the general point is characteristically sharpened by Vronsky's unconscious assumption of his superior background and culture).

> "One needed to know and love her as I do to find that . . . expression
> of hers," thought Vronsky, though he himself had only learnt to know it
> through the portrait. But the expression was so true that it seemed both
> to him and to others that they had always known it.

Tolstoy perceives with great clarity the connection between "art for art's sake" and the new morality associated with Nietzsche and his followers. "It is said that art has become refined. On the contrary, thanks to the pursuit of effects, it has become very coarse." Art for art's sake aims for the pure "effect," but because art cannot but mirror the religious feeling of the age, the new aestheticism has become the prophet and religion of a new barbarity; and this applies not only to trivial works like the *Contes cruels, Salome,* Andreyev's *The Red Laugh,* and so forth, but to such otherwise dissimilar writers as Flaubert, Kipling and Gerhart Hauptmann. Tolstoy detests the notion of the *Zeitgeist,* and with some justification sees the new aestheticism as pandering to it and dependent upon it.

Even when the moral is supposedly good, the craze for what Tolstoy calls "physiological effect" vitiates it—the writer is concerned not to infect the audience but to play upon their nerves, as at the climax of Hauptmann's play, *Hanneles Himmelfahrt.* It is instructive to compare Tolstoy's caustic comments on this piece, in which the part of the ill-used girl might have been expected to arouse his sympathy, with the enthusiastic preface he wrote for a German novel—Von Polenz's *Der Büttnerbauer*—with its similar part of a meek and injured wife. In the play there is "no infection between man and man" but only a deliberate attempt to excite the audience. The novelist on the other hand "loves his protagonists," and in an equally pathetic and terrible scene compels the reader not only to pity but also to love them.

Irrespective of the merits of the actual play and novel, Tolstoy's criteria are cogent. He considers the play form more subject than the novel to the crudity of the author's intention and desire for effect and it is notorious that he considers Shakespeare as guilty in this respect as Hauptmann. As in the case of pictorial art, it is his lack of knowledge that is at fault here rather than his critical sense. He supposes that Shakespeare, like other playwrights is chiefly concerned to secure an effect, and he denounces such an intention untiringly. "You see his intention," he observes of a new composer, "but no feeling whatever, except weariness, is transmitted to you." And again—when attacking Kipling and Zola—"from the first lines one sees the intention with which the book is written, the details all become superfluous, and one feels dull." When praising Chekhov's story *The Darling* he asserts that Chekhov intended to make fun of "the darling," "but by directing the close attention of a poet upon her he has exalted her." The best books, the most full of infectious feeling, are those in which the author's intention is lost sight of, or even contradicted by, the close attention of "love" which he devotes to his characters. Tolstoy is here implying a criticism of himself and revealing why we feel as we do about Stiva or about Anna.

Only once does he come near to perceiving that Shakespeare might have the same gift of "close attention," and that is when he observes that

Falstaff is his only non-theatrical character, the only one who does not behave like an actor. "He alone speaks in a way proper to himself." It is an illuminating comment. Again we feel that the novel, and in particular the naturalism of the Russian novel, is being called in to condemn the theatre. Falstaff is the only occasion when Shakespeare, like a novelist, set out to do one thing, and by becoming involved with his hero, did another. Such is Tolstoy's view, and he implies that Falstaff moves us for this reason, and that Lear and Cordelia do not move us because they are not seen in this way and not, as people, involuntarily loved. For this to happen they must be seen (like Falstaff) as if in real life and surrounded by the complex detail of real life. Tolstoy is of course committing here the common critical fault of attacking a work because it has not the form that he prefers and refusing to understand the form in which it is actually written. And even on his own ground he is wrong, for the most obvious thing about almost all Shakespeare's characters is how continuously—and often, in terms of dramatic requirement, how unnecessarily—like "real people" they are! Had Tolstoy known it, Shakespeare was really on his side.

Moreover, his criticism of Lear indicates not, as Tolstoy holds, what is wrong with the play, but what is remarkable and unique about it. It is true that Lear and Cordelia are actors whose parts are almost impossible to present and sustain, and that when Tolstoy speaks of "Lear's terrible ravings which make one feel as ashamed as one does when listening to unsuccessful jokes" he describes with uncomfortable accuracy the kind of embarrassment we feel at pretentious acting and an insensitive production. But we never know where we are with the play, as Tolstoy wished always to know where he was. Edging bathos and weird farce, it confounds our instinctive desire (which in Tolstoy had become an obsession) to see life steadily and whole. There is no clarity or security in which close attention might be paid to the individual—indeed the most unnerving thing about the play is the irrelevance of the character indications that do none the less appear, to be burnt up in the human reduction. Edmund's flashy comprehensibility gets us nowhere, nor does the puffing humanity of old Gloucester so brilliantly hit off in the opening scene—a scene that might well prelude a different kind of work altogether. Strangely enough, the openings of Lear and Anna are by no means so different: we feel we know Gloucester as we know Stiva, but it would be unthinkable for Stiva to surrender his personality in some extraordinary metaphorical climax, to be blinded and driven to despair for his misdemeanours with governesses and ballet girls. For Tolstoy this would indeed be a flagrant case of a character being made to "do what was not in his nature," or to suffer what was not. But it is at once Tolstoy's strength and limitation that he will not relinquish his grasp on the individual nature—he cannot tolerate the thought of a total human reduction. On the retreat from Moscow Pierre still remains Pierre, and hence there is "nothing terrible": Father Sergius cannot renounce his pride and desire to excel; and in spite of his moment of impersonal greatness Karenin cannot shake off his old persisting self.

This is certainly true of human beings in society as we usually know it. But in *Lear* Shakespeare presents us with another truth, no more profound but equally convincing. He could have understood and rendered Auschwitz in art: Tolstoy could not have done. When men are indistinguishable in animal evil and animal suffering, love and goodness seem no longer qualities connected with the whole complex of a personality but as graces entering as if from outside. Tolstoy's final charge against Shakespeare—curiously echoing Dr. Johnson's less censorious comment—is that his reader "loses the capacity to distinguish between good and evil." His plays, and plays generally (Tolstoy specifically includes his own), have "no religious basis," and because they depend on effect and sensation "even lack any human sense." One sees what he means, but "human sense" is not everything, and religion—in Tolstoy's use of the term—most certainly is not. In his passion for common sense and common virtue he turns his back on the extreme situation which deprives us of personal differentiation, of the habit of being ourselves. For Tolstoy "the capacity to distinguish between good and evil" must come out of close attention to the individual self. In Shakespeare it can also come from prolonged exposure to his poetic art, and from the range of apprehension—in the widest sense of religion—with which he can infect us as Tolstoy cannot.

There is much to be learnt from Tolstoy's dislike of Wagner and Shakespeare, though in both cases what really counts is his refusal to educate himself into their created medium. When Tolstoy says that from the first reading "I was at once convinced that it is obvious Shakespeare lacks the main, if not the only, means of portraying character, which is individuality of language—one can only suggest that he should have read more Shakespeare and learnt more English. If all art were simple, transparent, and international it would not even be necessary to attack Shakespeare and Wagner—they would hardly have been heard of. Tolstoy's method of attacking them is the same: he describes the action of *Lear* and of *The Ring* in his Masonic "making it strange" language, a kind of seemingly guileless esperanto, so that the whole complex appeal and participation through music and language is lost. When he tells us that though *Lear* may sound absurd in his version it is even more absurd in the original, he speaks truer than he knows: but the real absurdity of *Lear* is that of life, not that of basic English. None the less, Tolstoy did show up the chorus of nineteenth-century European pedants who proclaimed Shakespeare's beauties and pro-fundities without any regard for the living complex of linguistic and national sensibility in which they have their being: just as he showed up *The Ring* worshippers who went into mass hypnosis at Bayreuth without understanding of what Wagner was trying to accomplish in the tradition of Germanic self-awareness and Germanic dream. By being deliberately insensitive himself, Tolstoy revealed the insensitivity of those who profess to adore the great, but this is not the same as revealing that the great are not great at all.

"Great works of art are only great because they are accessible and comprehensible to everyone." By insisting on this principle Tolstoy asserts that a Vogul hunting-mime is far superior as art to *Hamlet*. The mime may indeed be true art, but its level of operation is sufficiently summed up by Henry James's comment on the pupper show: "What an economy of means—and what an economy of ends!" Moreover, "everyone" is not—though Tolstoy would no doubt like to have him so—in a fixed state of being but in a state of becoming. His level of participation rises with education, becomes more complex and more demanding. "Groaning, weeping, and holding their breaths with suspense," the primitive audience of the mime were clearly participating much more than the average audience of *Hamlet*; but one can be sure that they would respond to *Hamlet*, in so far as they understood it, with just as much interest and enthusiasm, and more so as they got to know more about it. The trouble with drama is not the art but the audience, and the uneasy and pretentious relation between drama and audience—the desire to shock and be shocked—which Tolstoy saw as characteristic of nineteenth-century drama, and which he would recognize in drama today. That is why he returns, perversely to the most primitive audience/drama relation. He ignores the fact that the vogul audience would have delighted in the climax of *Hanneles Himmelfahrt*, and by their delight would have purged it of those elements of invited embarrassment and planned sensationalism which he rightly detected in the relation between Hauptmann and his audience. The gruesome thing about modern Shakespeare productions is precisely the mutual wish to shock and be shocked, to give and take gimmicks, but that is not Shaespeare's fault, though Tolstoy said it was. His real target, to a greater extent perhaps than he realized, is not counterfeit art that has been mistaken for great art, but the bad taste that has become accepted and standardized between producer and consumer. This is why much of what he has to say about art is so relevant today.

Unexpectedly, *What Is Art?* is an assertion of the solitude of good art in the modern age. It leads us back, deviously but unmistakably, to Tolstoyan solipsism. Tolstoy's shame before the speeches of Lear, or before a performance of Beethoven's Ninth Symphony, reveals an overwhelming fastidiousness, a refusal to find the communal art of his own day anything but false, coarse and embarrassing. His solution—a return to primitive mime and to communal story-telling like that of Karataev in *War and Peace*—is of course a hopeless one, and there is no reason to suppose Tolstoy did not realize it. He disliked public art as much as public government, and the television age would not have given him cause to change his mind about either the one or the other. Tacitly he accepts the novel—the most private form—as the form in which good art still appeared in the modern age, and again and again in his criticism he makes things easy for the novel, allowing it a degree of sophistication which other forms—poetry, music, drama— are not allowed to share. Chekhov's *The Darling* and Von Polenz's novel are cases in point: can Tolstoy really have thought that his hypothetical "everyone" would grasp the issues that he draws attention to in them, the grounds of appreciation which he indicates? The great irony is that he did not perceive how, with the decay of public art, Shakespeare's works—by one of those transformations of form in time of which supreme art is capable—had come to exhibit themselves, and to be treated, as the most comprehensive of novels—or non-novels perhaps, like *War and Peace* itself. The great unadmitted and perhaps unconscious assumption and conclusion of *What Is Art?*—all the more evident from his rejection in it of his own best work—is that art is the novel, Tolstoy's novel.

W. GARETH JONES

A Man Speaking to Men: The Narratives of "War and Peace"

Entranced by a night spent outside a military camp in the Caucasus in 1851, the twenty-three-year-old Tolstoy wrote in his diary, "I thought—I'll go and describe what I see. But how to write it? One needs to go and sit down at an ink-stained desk, take some grey paper and ink; get one's fingers dirty and trace letters on the paper. The letters make up words, the words—sentences; but is it possible to convey the feeling? Is it not possible somehow to pour into another man one's view at the sight of nature?" The young soldier was discomfited by the artificiality of writing, by an awareness of the fallibility of words. But in this jotting he had already signalled that the aim of writing for him went beyond composing something of intrinsic worth, poetry so well wrought that it could pretend to an independent existence. Parable would later be exalted by Tolstoy over poetry; not merely because the former carried a moral message, but because the parable was an art of performance, "pouring one's view into another man," demanding an attentive and responsive listener. Writing for him, as for Wordsworth, meant "a man speaking to men," and Tolstoy would occasionally enhance this sense of public performance by equating writing with singing to his fellow men. In the sketches for his *Childhood*, for example, it was to music that he turned for an analogy to explain his new kind of writing that would avoid stale convention in its direct "anti-poetic" appeal to his reader. Significantly, it was not the musician as creative composer that suggested himself to Tolstoy but the *performing* artist; the image that he held of himself was not that of the song writer, but of the singer, intent on affecting his audience.

What is remarkable about Tolstoy is that he never saw himself as a solitary singer set apart from a world of passive listeners. His world's stage was peopled by men and women with their own voices, speaking and singing parts they had fashioned for themselves, listening as responsively as an audience for parables. So were his novels. For it was this Tolstoyan understanding that inspired his works: human society consisted of men, each pouring his feelings into another. His creatures live on the page because they too, like him, make sense of existence by narrating their experiences to each other. One must see *War and Peace* not as a single narrative issuing from one author, but as a dynamic pattern of many narratives, constantly varied and inter-reacting. To be Tolstoy's reader, so far as this novel is concerned, one's response must be not to the author's tale, but to the work's many narratives.

For Tolstoy was accustomed to imagine his fictional characters, like himself, as performers; often his creatures, in contrast to those of other novelists, do not engage in private conversation, cogitation or reflection but hold forth publicly, narrating, recounting or "telling stories"—*rasskazyvat'* is the Russian verb for which it is difficult to find a single English equivalent. They speak to a company who respond as a distanced audience to a ritualised performance. So at the beginning of *War and Peace*, Prince Vasily talks "like an actor speaking lines from an old play," Anna Scherer enthuses "in order not to disappoint people's expectations," the vicomte de Mortemart is introduced as "un parfait conteur." Much time and mental energy was spent by Tolstoy in the search for a beginning that would set his *War and Peace* in motion; over a dozen false starts are recorded. What is significant about the final choice—the description of a soirée at which the main protagonists are guests was hardly a fresh solution—is the way in which modes of narration, or communication between people, are presented and examined. It is as if Tolstoy, on the threshold of his own story-telling, wished to put his reader on his guard against its conventions and artifice by demonstrating to him different kinds of narration. First there is the polish and assurance of the vicomte de Mortemart's refined reciting of a scabrous anecdote about Napoleon and the duc d'Enghien, a piece of society gossip greeted with delight by his audience. Set against that, the earnest conversation of Pierre and the abbé Morio on the balance of power is shown, for all its sincerity, to be out of place and awkward. In Anna

Scherer's salon, the *well told* anecdote, however superficial, always wins more attention than any attempt to bumble out the truth. Even a nonsensical buffoon's tale from Prince Hippolyte gains more respect than Pierre's honest theorising.

What is happening in these early scenes, as the reader commits himself to the long journey through Tolstoy's novel, is that the author is signalling to him some of the curious relationships between the man who tells the story and his listener. An attempt to tell the honest truth unconventionally, as by Pierre, is met with resistance; there may be more real communing, not only in the retailing of superficial gossip related with polished art, but even in twaddle such as Hippolyte's nonsense tale which makes everyone stop to listen and applaud.

Without making any separate declaration on the nature of his art, Tolstoy had embedded within his own narrative the awareness that had come to him under the Caucasian night sky: experience cannot be conveyed directly to another; the paraphernalia of art is necessary for any human communication. The same realisation had been fused into the narrative of *The Raid* (1853), where Captain Khlopov, so rich in life's experiences, can only seek to convey those experiences to a young volunteer by suggesting that he read the historian Mikhaylovsky-Danilevsky and chat to a young poet in the regiment. Aware that experienced truth was invariably modified by the artifices needed for its transmission, Tolstoy felt impelled to alert his reader to the extent to which he was being manipulated by fiction's conventions. So, as *War and Peace* was set in motion, its reader was warned to distrust its apparent solidity and fascination.

This insinuation into his fiction of passages that encouraged the reader to determine consciously his own attitude to narrative (whether to listen avidly along with most of Anna Scherer's guests, or turn away in disgust as Prince Andrey did from the anecdote about Napoleon) was not new for Tolstoy. If the examination of the relationship between narrator and audience is there at the beginning of *War and Peace* as it was in *The Raid*, it lay too at the foundation of Tolstoy's first published work, *Childhood*. In the sketches for that work, it is apparent how much more important enthralling and moving his reader was for Tolstoy than weaving verbal patterns. By the final version, a perusal of the bond between author and audience had been incorporated into the fiction in the central chapter "Verses" where the boy, Nikolenka, faced with the task of producing a present for his grandmother's name-day, recites a poem for her. It is not as an entertainer that Nikolenka is presented but as an embryonic Tolstoyan narrator, beset with disgust and self-doubt, and fearful of his reception.

In the boy's composing, Tolstoy revealed to his reader the inspiration, doggedness, plagiarism, and posing involved in producing an inherently false communication to the listener of an initially sincere impulse.

There are times in *War and Peace* when Tolstoy becomes almost Brechtian in the relentless warning to his readers against being swept along by his narrative, particularly of the historical and military events. Again, however, no separate artistic manifesto is apparent; rather we are allowed, as in *Childhood*, to see the relationship between narrator and audience developing between the fictive characters. Inevitably, in such a work as *War and Peace*, with characters and episodes embedded in a historical chronicle, the registering of event, time, place, conversation bears the novel along. Is Nikolay Rostov's arrival in Tilsit significant because he arrived there on 27 June 1807? Tolstoy's noting of that day is reminiscent of the conventional chronicler: "That day, 27 June, the first conditions of peace were signed. The Emperors exchanged orders: Alexander received the Légion d'Honneur, and Napoleon the St Andrew 1st Class, and that day a dinner was arranged for the Preobrazhensky regiment given to it by a battalion of the French Guards." Yet this sort of brisk narrative of Tolstoy's, making immediate the public, historical framework for private happenings, had just been put in question in the previous chapter where Boris Drubetskoy's habit of noting down particulars, even at the Tilsit meeting between the Emperors, had been mocked. It is Boris here who stands for the typical writer who stores up material with which he will later seek to affect an audience. Not only does he make a note of the persons present and their uniforms, but is meticulous about logging time: "At the very moment when the emperors entered the pavilion, he looked at his watch and did not forget to look again at the moment when Alexander left the pavilion. The meeting had lasted 1 hour 53 minutes: that is what he noted that evening among other facts which he supposed had historical significance." This ironic comment on memoir writing that concentrates on surface detail while telling nothing about the true condition of human relationship is again made through a narrating character, one of the "performers" in the fiction, and not by Tolstoy himself. Ironically, it gives the reader an eloquent warning against narrative chronology used with effect by the author of *War and Peace*.

If Tolstoy wished to warn his reader against the conventional chronicling of diplomatic history, he was even more intent on setting him on guard against the narration of military exploits. And on guard against the reader's own craving for the conventional. It is through Nikolay Rostov—

as much, surely, an emanation of Tolstoy's self as Prince Andrey and Pierre—and his recital of Schöngraben, that Tolstoy persuades his own reader to understand that however truthful a narrator would wish to be, he is swayed from the truth by his audience that is bound to rely on conventional signals. Transparent truth cannot be seen. Art's untruth springs not necessarily from the maliciousness of an embellishing narrator, but is demanded by an audience that relies on the conventional. So does Nikolay's audience: "They expected an account of how he was all on fire, beside himself, how he rushed like a storm at the square; how he was hacked at, while striking to left and right; how a sabre cut into his flesh and he fell into oblivion, and so on. And he recounted all that for them." It is interesting that Tolstoy had once shared Rostov's feelings. In his note to the fourth volume of the Tolstoy Centenary Edition *Tales of Army Life*, Aylmer Maude recalled that "One day, when talking about Sevastopol, he [Tolstoy] told me that when writing these sketches he was aware that, contending with his desire to tell the truth as he saw it, there was another feeling prompting him to say what was expected of him." The point is made clearly to the reader of *War and Peace* that there are conventional ways of recounting battles that are inherently false; paradoxically it is only these false strokes that can shape an experience for an audience. Tolstoy does not propose to spurn these conventions, but would like his reader to be aware of them, and see *through* them to the real experience.

The lesson is well placed: the probing of Nikolay's "imperceptible, involuntary and inevitable" slide into untruth must modify the reader's acceptance of the description of Andrey's wounding which follows shortly. At Austerlitz, from the moment that Prince Andrey shouts "Hurrah!" and raises the standard to rally his men, the charge is recounted in a conventional manner. It is with the panache of jingoistic literature that the scene is told initially: the banner is held aloft, bullets whistle, men fall to left and right of our hero—it is as if we are listening again to Nikolay entertaining his audience. Already prepared by the insight into the gap between the conventional style of Nikolay's story of Schöngraben and the true experience which it obscured, the reader, following Andrey's charge, is swept along by the vigorous conventional description, but simultaneously suspects the truthfulness of the account. He may remember that it was this same Prince Andrey who had stemmed Nikolay's increasingly impassioned narrative, borne beyond convention into cliché, silencing him with is unexpected appearance. The reader is, therefore, prepared for the sudden dissolution of the conventional here as the same Andrey asks "What are they doing?" on seeing the wordless but mortal tug-of-war between a French and Russian soldier. From that point on, we are subject to a new narrative technique—but not at the expense of old conventions.

If the experience of warfare, as indeed all human experience, was beyond man's ability to comprehend and narrate, why should Tolstoy have persisted so long with his writing? Tolstoy mediates his answer through a Nikolay Rostov made fully conscious of the perils of communication between men. After his experience of Austerlitz and the 1807 campaigns, Nikolay had realised that "in recounting military events, men always lie, as he himself had lied while recounting." So it is with shame that he listens to an overblown account of a patriotic exploit by General Rayevsky while providing his own debunking gloss to the narration in his mind. Yet he does not object to the narration. And the reason that Nikolay gives to himself might well be Tolstoy's apologia for continuing to write fiction, despite his rage for the truth. Such narration, he came to realise, even if it failed to communicate experience fully, had a particular justification: despite its falsity it exerted an independent moral force and enabled men to commune with each other in society. For Tolstoy this was no new revelation. The earlier Nikolenka of *Childhood* had also realised, as a consumer of literature, the way in which the lie of art enhanced the art of living. The vividness of the children's games was sharpened by their imitation of *Swiss Family Robinson*. Although Nikolenka knew as well as his supercilious elder brother Volodya that a stick was not a gun, his play was all the more intense if he pretended. The rhetorical question posed by the child to close the chapter "Games" in *Childhood*, might still be the one for Nikolay Rostov to ponder over: "If one is to judge by reality, then there would be no play. And without play, what would remain?"

II

If the Nikolenka of *Childhood* was unsettled—and the reader in consequence—by his growing awareness of the fictive fluidity of verses, and story-based games, he was no more secure in the language, or it would be more correct to say languages, that shaped the expression of his experiences. *War and Peace*, which has been called a bilingual novel for its large use of French, was by no means the first work in which Tolstoy had troubled the reader with a foreign language. If *War and Peace* begins in French, then the first spoken dialogue in *Childhood* is in German between Karl Ivanich, the family tutor, and Nikolenka. While the use of German may be explained as historical colouring, as the work progresses we become aware that Tolstoy intended to present his child as one conscious of the lack of security afforded by human speech. Although the mother speaks Russian with the children, her own mother tongue, and the one she employs for her intimate thoughts, is German. The shift of language is noticed by the child as he perceives that French is used at the dinner table formally to exclude Grigory, the holy fool, from the community around the table. Foreign idiom was a means for Tolstoy to intimate to his reader his sense of the fragility of language as a means of communication.

The use of French, and to a lesser extent German, in *War and Peace* as well, is a means by which the reader is made aware of the linguistic texture of the fictional work. Too aware, perhaps, for many early reviewers—not only the young radical nationalist critics, but also Tolstoy's aristocratic friends—protested against an apparent over-indulgence in French. Indeed the novel begins with a sentence whose single Russian word is used as a calculated disparagement, "Eh bien, mon prince, Gênes et Lucques ne sont plus que des apanages, des *pomest'ya*, de la famille Buonaparte." Since it is Anna Scherer who speaks these words, it would seem natural for her to speak French and so it seemed to the editors of the Jubilee Edition who maintained that *War and Peace* would make no sense without French since French was an "integral accessory to the way of life of the upper class at the beginning of the nineteenth century." Had they chosen to follow the 1873 edition in which the French had been translated, they argued, many of the characters, such as Anna Scherer, Hippolyte Kuragin, Bilibin, Napoleon, Kutuzov, Alexander I, would lose some of their individual quality. It was roughly these reasons—historical and dramatic—that Tolstoy himself gave as a rational justification for his apparently excessive use of French. Prompted by subsequent criticism from friends, however, Tolstoy allowed the 1873 edition to appear not only with the removal of his philosophical and historical discussions, but with all the French translated. This he did, however, with some regret. The use of French, despite what Tolstoy's editors and Tolstoy as editor of his own work suggested, goes far beyond the need for local colouring. Could he not have merely indicated the use of French, as contemporary critics suggested? There are times when Tolstoy does indeed state that his characters whose dialogue is given in Russian, are conversing in French; this is true even in the case of Andrey and Natasha. Furthermore the abundant gallicisms of the novel might have been sufficient to preserve the local historical colouring. However, French is not merely used for historical *vraisemblance*. Sometimes it would appear that French is used to stress artificiality of sentiment and attitude, as opposed to the genuineness of Russian: it is the language in which Pierre proposes to Hélène, the language in which Hélène addresses Natasha at the opera. For Andrey, it is not only Natasha's gaiety and shyness that are a mark of her naturalness, but her mistakes in French. However, some characters manage to be intensely Russian despite their French, such as Kutuzov with is fondness for Madame de Genlis' novels and French proverbs, or Bilibin who showed an "exceptionally Russian fearlessness before self-judgement and self-mockery" in a long letter to Prince Andrey despite his writing it "in French with French jokes and turns of phrase." Bilibin is one of the most conscious of Tolstoy's narrating characters, producing memorable phrases in his "inner laboratory" that insignificant people could carry from drawing-room to drawing-room. And one of the features ensures that the reader grasps the mechanical precision of Bilibin's narrations is his skill at mixing French and Russian, "saying in Russian only those words which he wished to emphasize disparagingly."

It is this mingling of French with Russian which is met in the novel's first sentence, rather than the use of French itself that makes the reader linguistically unsettled, as were the early critics who would have felt more comfortable in the presence of *War and Peace* had Tolstoy spiked his Russian with less French. It was an experience that the English reader of Jane Austen, or even Dickens with his idiosyncratic idiom, never endured: English, the common mother tongue of writer and reader, ensured some stability in their relationship. Even this bedrock of communication was deliberately undermined by Tolstoy. The insidious French in his narrative is subversive, alerting the reader to the transience of language and the words used by the writer to communicate with him. In excusing his use of French in *A Few Words about "War and Peace,"* Tolstoy drew ananalogy with the formal texture of a painting. The French, he explained, was akin to the dark patches used by a painter: they may be perceived as shadows, but the naive eye sees them as black blobs. "I would only wish that those who find it amusing that Napoleon speaks Russian and French in turn, would realise that they find it so only because they, like a man looking at a portrait, see not a face with light and shade, but a black patch under a nose." However, what is striking about the analogy is how Tolstoy reveals his awareness that his use of French actually encouraged his reader to see through the conventional deceptive shadows of the artist to the dark, crude blobs of paint at the base of his craft. Language, too, may be as inexpressive as a paint pot.

Differing languages disturb the reader; he shares the experience of Prince Andrey, conscious of confusion on the battlefield when he hears the Babel of a multi-lingual exchange. "Pfuel . . . shouted angrily even at Wolzogen 'Nun ja, was soll denn da noch expliziert werden?'—Paulucci and Michaud in a duet attacked Wolzogen in French. Armfelt addressed Pfuel in German. Tol explained it in Russian to Prince Bolkonsky. Prince Andrey listened in silence, and observed."

III

It is that cooly observant listener, like Andrey, that Tolstoy would have liked his reader to be. Our discussion to this point has attempted to bring out the way in which, through is "narrating" characters, Tolstoy has warned his reader against the deceit of story-telling. In wishing to make the reader aware in this way of the ritual of narration, Tolstoy seeks to elicit a special response from him, engaging him in the particular conspiracy in which the true novelist would wish to embroil his reader.

Readers of *War and Peace*, will, of course, object that they are surely not always treated by Tolstoy as cool, aristocratic observers of the world's stage. Sometimes there is a direct appeal to us as one of a mutinous mob. The coarse demagogic address is particularly apparent in Tolstoy's excursions into historiography. By showing the absurdity of other versions of historical events, he suggests that it must follow that "ours"—that is, the author and reader in collusion—our version must be true. Dealing with the battle of Borodino, Tolstoy gave his own precis of the view of "all historians" and then declared with the most conventional of debating ploys: "That is what the histories say, and all that is completely unjust, which can easily be vouched for by anybody who wishes to look into the essentials of the matter." In then giving a revised account of Borodino, Tolstoy flatters the reader; we feel that we are privileged to know more about the battle than any learned historian. Again at the beginning of part iii we have the same tub-thumper's appeal to his audience: historians are wrong is the message, the implication being—and it is never more than an implication—that Tolstoy is right. And the debater's claim is supported by crude, simplistic mechanistic images: any fool can realise that it is not the hands of a clock that cause church bells to ring, nor is it its whistle that sets a locomotive running.

Yet even when his demagoguery is at its most effective, we find Tolstoy recoiling from it and subjecting it to the same criticism as other forms of conventional communication. One of the most effective of the scenes debunking historiography is that in which Lavrushka, Nikolay

Rostov's servant, falls into the hands of the French. This interlude was based on a passage from Thiers' history which recounted the capture of a Russian whom the French took to be a Cossack, "un enfant du Don," who showed a child-like wonder at being in the presence of the great Napoleon; the Emperor responded by freeing the Cossack and sending him back to the Russian lines, an action which is described by Thiers in an overblown, romantic and, consequently for Tolstoy, false phrase to which the reader's attention is drawn: "Napoléon . . . lui fit donner la liberté, comme à un oiseau qu'on rend aux champs qui l'ont vu naître." In reality Tolstoy would have us believe, it was not a noble savage of a Cossack that the French had captured, but Nikolay's wily lackey who, far from being impressed by Napoleon, realised that his role was to pretend astonishment and veneration. If the scene had ended there, then it would have been unconvincing, another example of Tolstoy's crude haranguing. Even if we are led to distrust Thiers' narrative, common sense suggests to us as we read the passage that there was little likelihood of Thiers' historical "Cossack" being the fictional Lavrushka.

But the scene did not end with the freeing of Lavrushka. And as Lavrushka returns to the Russian lines, Tolstoy submits his own previous narrative to a critical appraisal through the mind of his character. Even more striking than Lavrushka's hoodwinking of Napoleon are his thoughts as he rides back: "he galloped towards the forward posts, thinking up beforehand everything that had not been and that he would recount to his own side. Everything which had really happened to him, he did not wish to recount just because that seemed to him unworthy of a narrative."

As Lavrushka returns to his lines, the point is forcibly made—strikingly soon after Tolstoy's attempt to "tell the truth" by debunking Thiers and his "enfant du Don"—that the substance of man's life is incommunicable. Lavrushka knows, as his master Nikolay did, that conventions which channel the flow of communication from narrator to listener will inevitably frustrate any stories he cares to tell based on perceived events. What he "thinks up," or what comes to his mind, as he gallops back is a story to tell, not wholly unrelated to his experience, but "worthy of being recounted." Lavrushka and Nikolay like Nikolenka of *Childhood* and Captain Khlopov of *The Raid* before them are aware that what is recognised as "worthy of recounting" is the only possible way for one person to communicate through speech with is fellows. Lavrushka is here, like his master previously, involuntarily and inevitably moved into untruth, despite his desire to tell things as they had happened.

For Tolstoy perhaps, Lavrushka could have only given voice to the truth through instinctive song—if he had been indeed Thiers' "bird restored to its native fields." Tolstoy had anticipated many writers who would feel how words are so much more haphazard and fugitive as a medium of expression compared with song. In the drafts for *Childhood* where he had sought an analogy for writing in music two types of singers were described—the "head singer," bound by technique, and the "chest singer," who sang more directly to his audience. The latter, the instinctive performer rather than the trained musician, reappears a number of times in *War and Peace*. So Natasha at the end of the second volume's first part is the typical, intuitively physical, "chest singer":

> Natasha took her first note, her throat widened, her chest straightened, her eyes took on a serious expression. She did not think of anyone or anything at that moment, and from the lips, set in a smile, poured sounds, those sounds which anyone can produce at the same periods of time, the same intervals but which leave you a thousand times unmoved, and at the thousand and first make you shudder and weep.

Again it is not the beauty of Natasha's art that Tolstoy wished his reader to appreciate, since Natasha with her "untrained voice, with her incorrect breathing and strained phrasing" is as "anti-poetic" as Tolstoy wished to be. But techniques can never be a substitute for sincere human expression such as the singing voice. "Her voice had that virginal inviolability, that unawareness of its strength and that unpolished velvet quality which so merged with the mistakes in the art of singing that it seemed impossible to change anything in that voice without spoiling it." There is an assurance in Natasha's singing, stressed by the set of her stride—a firm heel to toe movement—as she takes up her position. This same stride is repeated when she finds so much delight in the sound of her own voice as she goes through her singing exercises while waiting for Andrey: the rhythm of the voice exercises here gives way to the more elemental rhythm, in which she finds equal pleasure, of her heel and toe striking the parquet, "just as joyfully as to the sounds of her voice, she listened intently to the measured tap of her heel and the squeak of the toe." Tolstoy was clearly fascinated by the primitive naive instinctive art of singing which somehow was not aimed at communication, was not therefore circumscribed by technique, yet somehow communicated directly with listeners—the type of folk singing practised by the Rostovs' uncle: "Uncle sang as the peasant folk sing, in the full and naive conviction that in song all the meaning is in the words alone, that the tune comes of itself and that there is never a separate tune and that the tune is only there to hold it together." So the tune was unconscious, "Like the tune of a bird." The idea of song bursting forth from man's lips as from a bird's throat, as an unconscious affirmation of self, is again suggested in the description of Platon Karatayev's singing: "He sang songs not like singers knowing that they are heard but sang, as birds sing, evidently because it was as necessary to emit these sounds, as it is necessary to join in song or break off." For Karatayev, and the uncle, for the people, singing is a means of self-affirmation and there need be no thought of the audience. It is not a prerogative of the common folk, however. It is the same unconscious delight that Natasha experiences in her voice exercises in the resonant drawing-room. For her, a failure to sing becomes a signal of her collapse after the break with Andrey; her restoration to health is marked by the renewal of the ability to sing. What Tolstoy shows in these singing passages is the necessity for human voicing of a reality which may be expressible but not wholly communicable. The listeners—one might even say the eavesdroppers on these naive, bird-like effusions—can only be stirred by the contagion with a deeper reality so distant from the surface manifestations of existence, such as those noted and registered by Boris Drubetskoy. Song is heard at climactic moments in *War and Peace*, and it would appear that Tolstoy was as taken by the idea of pure expression being possible through music as was Paul Valéry in his conviction that music was the ideal art.

Tolstoy's medium, however, was words, even if words did not spring so freshly from men's lips as song. Sometimes they may: they fell naturally from Platon Karatayev's lips so that he could not understand words taken in isolation, nor could he repeat what had been said. Language could, as in his case, flow along as an integral component of the life of the moment. Just as Natasha, unable to explain her experiences *in words* to Andrey when their love was at its most intense, made Andrey understand her despite the lack of articulation. As in love, so in war: Kutuzov at the height of battle does not rely on words alone but on the expression of the narrator and his tone. So the reader, following the words on the page, paradoxically is alerted to the dimness of words at climactic moments in man's life.

Thus, while using the full power of his rhetoric to sustain his fiction, Tolstoy intimates to his reader through Karatayev, Kutuzov, and Bilibin, through the mingling of French with Russian, the insignificance and deception of words. In writing history with irony and persuasion, he alerts his reader, through Boris Drubetskoy, to distrust all historical narration. In reading Tolstoy's magnificent set pieces of adventure, heroism and love, the reader is reminded of Nikolay Rostov's and Lavrushka's realisation that it is only possible to mediate a modicum of true experience through narration. In the end, the reader puts his trust in Tolstoy, since he is being fashioned by an author who endeavours to let him take a critical stance. If Tolstoy as an omniscient narrator plays God with his creation, then he

sets out not to predetermine his reader's responses but to endow him with
critical free will.

IV

The passages where Tolstoy seems to reach out to his reader to alert and
instruct him are remarkable for not being set apart from the main narrative.
The problem of commmunication for Tolstoy was never reduced to a question of mere technique but was fully integrated into a particular Tolstoyan
vision. So, although Tolstoy may use the chapter "Verses" in *Childhood* to
mediate his views on literary composition and its reception, that chapter
is simultaneously a central scene in the work, placed at the point where a
farewell has been sung to childhood as the boy became conscious of self in
relation to others. Time after time, the reader finds that the characters'
narrative performances within Tolstoy's main narrative are fused with emotional points of crisis in the novel. It is indeed a feature of Tolstoy's fictional
universe to find characters at a high emotional pitch reading or writing,
being in an audience or telling a story. At life's turning points, the art of
narration intrudes. Two examples from the second volume of the second
part will suffice: Pierre, on his way to Petersburg after his duel and break
with his wife, is beset with nihilistic thoughts which are reinforced by
his reading of an epistolary novel by Madame Suza (a writer despised by
Tolstoy) which prompts him to compare his own situation and that of
Hélène with the story of "some Amélie de Mansfeld." By the time Pierre
arrives in Petersburg, after his conversion to freemasonry, he spends whole
days reading Thomas à Kempis. From Madame Suza to Thomas à Kempis!
Their narratives are shown to have influenced Pierre's life, revealed his
instability and moved him from nihilistic despair to certitude. When
shortly, in chapter 10, we cut to Prince Andrey at Bald Hills, *War and
Peace* appears briefly to become an epistolary novel as Andrey opens two
letters, one from his father and the other from Bilibin. Off stage, Andrey's
son is hovering between life and death in the nursery. Yet Bilibin's letter,
written in French, bristling with sardonic irony, consciously a literary creation aiming for effect, manages to capture Andrey's whole attention so
that it is only with an effort of will that he can shake off his bondage to
Bilibin's artificial narrating, and return to the solid reality of the nursery.
Throughout the ensuing scene, the reader is conscious that this father,
despite his deep feelings for his son, has been infected and somehow modified by his recent reading, so that he preserves—even in the private solitude

of the nursery—some of Bilibin's diplomatic restraint: "Prince Andrey wanted to seize, squeeze, press to his breast this small helpless being; he did not dare do it."

What we should recognise is that the narrative mode itself is often employed to precipitate feelings. In both the above cases we have stock figures from fiction: the despairing cuckold of a cold wife, the distressed father of a dying son. The reader would expect the conventional novelist to limit himself to a description or dramatisation of that despair, of that distress. Tolstoy, however, does not attempt to describe these states directly; the ultimate reality of distress, pain or joy is indescribable. They are too complex. Mingled with Pierre's despair unto death is an irritating enjoyment of his emotional state; with Andrey's brimming paternal love, there is an admixture of cold aloofness and male exasperation at being shackled to domesticity. These complexes of emotion may be vented in such acts as intuitive song, or mutely in a brisk walk, such as Natasha's heeling and toeing in her drawing-room. But if they are to be cast into words, then such states are best given shape through the medium of some formal address or narration which may well be tangential to the real experience. So the nature of Pierre's *pleasurable* despair is made evident in his reading of Madame Suza. It is Bilibin's letter, exquisite in its artificiality, that brings out the full complexity of Andrey's genuine emotional state.

The second volume from which the above examples are taken is a section of *War and Peace* where the love affairs of the novel are developed, if not resolved: Pierre is reunited with Hélène, Prince Andrey asks for Natasha's hand in marriage, Nikolay declares his love for Sonya, Boris Drubetskoy and Julie Karagina make their match, and Natasha is seduced by Anatole. It appears that Tolstoy had set out to examine the thousand faces of love in tracing these matches and mismatches. Again a framework of novelistic convention can be seen around each affair: faithful love being put to the test of absence, love triumphing over impediments of social station, a marriage of convenience, a conventional seduction. However, once more Tolstoy shows how rapport is made not in discussion or even conversation, but emerges through men's use of those many forms of narrative that have been elaborated in human culture. Before following these manifestations of love it is worth noting at the outset that the reader is reminded of the futility of trying to transfer one's vision directly to another. During Pierre's address to his brother freemasons on a way of regenerating the world, the reader is told that Pierre was driven by the need "to convey his thought to another exactly as he understood it." That, for Tolstoy, is the impossibility. The lodge reacts as negatively to Pierre's honesty as Anna

Scherer's salon had: not only those opposed to his views reject him, but even those in general agreement misunderstand him. The result of this confusion is that Pierre is awkwardly reunited with is wife. The awkwardness of that dutiful cohabitation is, of course, an unstable foundation for the love affairs that follow. If the cohabitation had been made possible by a rational address, then it is other forms of narrative—song, mumming, sentimental literature, music, opera and dramatic readings—that determine the relationships that ensue. Their common feature is that they are all addressed to an audience. They are all performances.

Without being informed by the narrator, the reader realises that Prince Andrey comes to full realisation of his love for Natasha when she sings at the clavichord. His falling in love is fixed in time and place as if it were a religious conversion. One is reminded of Paul Claudel's memory of his own conversion, so rooted in the Christmas of 1886 in Notre Dame "on the right, opposite the vestry by the second pillar before the choir" as he responded to the singing.

> Prince Andrey stood at the window, conversing with the ladies and listening to her. In the middle of a phrase Prince Andrey fell silent and had a sudden feeling that his throat was filling with tears whose possibility he had not known in himself. He looked at the singing Natasha, and something new and joyful happened in his soul. He was happy, and also he was sad. He had nothing to cry about, but he was ready to cry. For what? His earlier love? The little princess? His disappointments? His hopes for the future? . . . Yes and no. The main thing that he wished to cry for was his sudden vivid awareness of the terrible contrast between something infinitely great and indefinable within him and something narrow and corporeal which he was himself and even she was. This contrast brought him distress and joy during her singing.

Again the response to the song has allowed Tolstoy to transform a conventional love scene into a searching examination of a complex of emotions.

Some time later the apparent superior naturalness of a Russian national life, uncontaminated by Western ways, is conveyed to Natasha during her visit to her uncle after the hunt, mainly through the music of balalaika and guitar, and the Russian dance, the instinctive movements for which had not been stifled by the *pas de châle*. It is this music that first causes doubts and worries about her relationship with Andrey to come to Natasha. Would *he* appreciate this music-making that she so enjoys? The refrain of that music, now linked with worrying thoughts about Andrey, re-echoes in the Rostovs' drawing-room. It is the picking out on her uncle's folk guitar of a phrase she had heard in a St Petersburg opera with Prince Andrey that users back first memories of her distant betrothed, and then, when she plays for Sonya, the despair at her enforced parting from him.

The examination of the love relationshp between Andrey and Natasha continues with music. Even the mother's complicated response to her daughter's match is brought out by music. The mood of that scene is set by Dimmler playing Countess Rostova's favourite Field nocturne on the harp by moonlight (there is no indication that "European" music is any less potent than Russian folk music in its ability to promote the transference of thought and emotion). Then Natasha sings at the clavichord her mother's favourite song to the assembled gathering. Again it is the complexity of the listener's emotion, in this case, that of the old countess, that resonates to the formal song. Feelings are apprehended which could not be expressed in any conversation with her daughter or in cogitation.

> The old Countess sat with a happily melancholic smile and tears in her eyes, shaking her head from time to time. She thought of Natasha, and of her youth, and that there was something unnatural and frightful in Natasha's forthcoming marriage with Prince Andrey . . . Her mother's intuition told her that Natasha had too much of something and consequently would not be happy.

The ominous feelings called forth by the resonance of the singing voice are interrupted by the sudden arrival of the domestics as mummers who launch into their traditional songs, dances, choruses, and games. Drawing-room music yields to the rude gaiety of folk traditions: yet the mumming provides the same type of artificial background fostering human intercourse as Field's nocturnes. The only difference is in a register of culture. Yet it is through these artificial conventions alone, however varied they may be, that Tolstoy informs his reader that men may communicate. Despite their living closely together, Nikolay had found it impossible to declare his love for Sonya. It is only when released by the grotesque artificiality of the mumming from their conventional selves that Nikolay, in an elderly lady's farthingale, and Sonya, as a moustachioed Circassian, seal their love with a kiss redolent of burnt cork from Sonya's mock moustache.

That their love was not expressed sufficiently in truth, but in the rigmarole of mumming, does of course suggest its instability. Yet the mumming is not treated by Tolstoy in as harsh a fashion as the rigmarole of sentimentalism through which Boris and Julie have to arrange their match. The sentimental verses with their melancholic descriptions of gloamings and graveyards, penned in Julie's album, the doleful nocturnes on the harp, the emotional reading of Karamzin's *Poor Liza* together, all necessary signals in Boris's plan to make a rich match—but the literature of sentimentalism

had fooled neither Boris nor Julie. Whereas in the previous chapters arti-
ficialities had managed to crystallise human relationships which were dimly
felt but had not found their expression, here there was an emotional emptiness between Boris and Julie that not even the heightened emotionality
of a forced sentimentalism could fill. Despite the album verses and the
harp's nocturnes, the marriage would remain one of cool convenience:
The betrothed, without further mention of the trees plunging them in
gloom and melancholy, made plans for the future setting up of a splendid
home in Petersburg, went visiting and made full preparation for a splendid
wedding."

With the excesses of sentimental literature apparently mocked, it
would not seem strange for Tolstoy to find operatic conventions more
laughable. Towards the end of this volume, there is the passage describing
Natasha's visit to the opera which has become a classical reference in
Tolstoy criticism. Yet our response to that opera visit may be distorted if
we peruse that performance in isolation from the preceding ones. The fresh
young girl from the country is apparently made to see through artificial
staginess.

> They all sang something. When they finished their song, the girl in white
> went up to the prompter's box and was approached by a man in tight silk
> trousers over his plump legs, with a plume and dagger who began to sing
> and wave his arms.
> The man in the tight trousers sang alone, then she sang. Then
> both fell silent, the music struck up and the man began to finger the arm
> of the girl in the white dress, evidently waiting for the beat again in order
> to begin a new duet with her. They sang together and everyone in the
> theatre clapped and shouted and the man and woman on the stage who
> represented lovers, took their bows, smiling and extending their arms.

The visit to the opera has often been quoted in support of the view that
central to Tolstoy's method was *ostraneniye* "estrangement" or "making
strange," a term coined by Shklovsky to define Tolstoy's specific ironic
detachment, a view as piercingly fresh as that of the boy who refused to
see the Emperor's clothes. Yet here, it is not Tolstoy but Natasha who
refuses to form the opera in her mind, from her perception of its conventions. There is no reason to suppose that Natasha was incapable of grasping
the peculiarities of the opera: although fresh from the country, she had
received voice training, had been credited by Dimmler with "a real European
talent," and had lovingly recalled a visit to the opera in St Petersburg with
Prince Andrey. What causes her to reject the opera is not so much its
absurdity—if ironic detachment had been rigorously applied, the folksy

balalaika strumming at the uncle's could be made equally absurd. Tolstoy does not grade the ritual ways of communication into ones which are more or less artificial, or more or less genuine. It is the reaction of the audience to a performance that for him is crucial: a melancholy nocturne played at the Rostovs' can elicit real feelings, whereas the same nocturne played by Julie Karagina for Boris would echo in the emptiness of their relationship. The opera is another "performance" in the series of performances which have illuminated the variety of sexual bonding in this part of the novel. The description of the opera in that context is not intended mainly to show the absurdity of artifice, or the superiority of Natasha's naive vision. Her failure to take in the opera results from the cruel rebuff she has just experienced from the Bolkonskys and the impossibility of having any reassurance from the absent Andrey: her rejection by them is turned into her rejection of the opera. The highly-strung Natasha, put more on edge by the tension of the operatic event, becomes hysterical: "She looked and thought, and the strangest thoughts suddenly, without cause, flashed through her head. Now the thought presented itself of jumping behind the footlights to sing the aria which the *artiste* was singing, now she wanted to flick the old man sitting near her with her fan, lean over towards Hélène and tickle her." It is at this moment that Anatole Kuragin, her seducer, makes his appearance in the theatre: one might almost see it as a dramatic operatic entry. Motivating the seduction of Natasha by Anatole and making it plausible was undoubtedly difficult. Again though, as with all the other sexual bondings in this part of the novel, it is the ritual performance that acts as a catalyst: slowly Natasha begins to accommodate the conventions of the opera, and eventually as she begins to be fascinated by the male peacockery of Kuragin, she joins in the mass hysteria for the male dancer Dupport. That the final storm is an artificial creation of chromatic scales and diminished seventh chords is no longer a barrier: "Natasha no longer found it strange. She looked around her with pleasure and a joyful smile." By accepting the star performer, she had shown herself ready to accept Kuragin. And Natasha's new response to the final act is what informs us of the strength of the bond forged between her and Anatole Kuragin during the interval:

> Again the curtain rose. Anatole left the box composed and happy. Natasha returned to her father's box completely subject to the world in which she found herself. Everything which took place before her already seemed completely natural; but on the other hand all her previous thoughts about her betrothed, Princess Marya, life in the country not once entered her head, as if all that was in the distant, distant past.

On the next occasion when Natasha meets Anatole at a soirée at Hélène's, it is again a performance, this time a declamation by Mademoiselle Georges of some French verse "about her criminal love for her son," presumably from *Phèdre*, that causes Natasha to return to the "strange, senseless world, so far removed from her previous one," where she is open to Anatole's advances. Finally the seduction is completed by Natasha's trusting acceptance of a letter from Anatole. From all the artful performances the reader has witnessed, the truthfulness of the written word, carefully weighed for the benefit of the audience—we may remember Natasha's own letters to Andrey written almost as school compositions with the spelling mistakes corrected by her mother—cannot be trusted. Ironically, Marya's sincere letter of apology to Natasha does not find any response in its addressee, rather as Pierre's honesty is invariably misunderstood. What Natasha accepts as the truth is a letter, apparently from a passionate lover, but in fact composed for Anatole by Dolokhov: yet it is in that sham that she finds "echoes of all that she thought she had felt herself." It is the literary fake that turns Natasha: " 'Yes, yes, I love him!'—thought Natasha rereading the letter for the twentieth time and searching for some special deep meaning in its every word."

From the above, we see that "performances" by their inherent fraudulence pervert human relationships and particularly sexual bondings. Honest, straightforward communication on the other hand—such as Pierre's address to his masonic lodge or Marya's letter to Natasha—do not find a receptive audience. For Tolstoy, communicability is possible only when narrator and listener both understand the futility of transferring thought and emotion through words alone. And of course, this is the accord that he would wish to make with his reader. Again such understandings, brought about by the recognition that full communication is not possible, occur at high points in the novel such as Andrey's recollection of a communion with Natasha on the eve of the Battle of Borodino. For Andrey to admit to such understanding is particularly remarkable since throughout the novel he is one who spurns vain attempts at relating experience from the moment when he shies away from the anecdotes in Anna Scherer's salon. He is the one who brings Nikolay's tale of Schöngraben to an end, and the most poignant example of his failure to relate to others through "performance" is his breaking off the tale of Bluebeard to his son. Yet on the eve of Borodino, unable to sleep, he remembers Natasha recounting the story of being lost in the forest while mushrooming. Exasperated by her apparent failure to tell her story, Natasha keeps explaining this to Andrey: "Natasha was not content with her words—she felt that the passionately poetic experience which she had felt that day and which she wished to bring to the surface was not coming out." Yet in her failure to tell it as it was, Natasha communicated with Andrey. He consequently understood and loved her. But the man of war only came to understand this as his final battle approached.

V

All these narratives and performances are, of course, enfolded within Tolstoy's own great narrative which holds forth to an audience in the same way. It is remarkable to find as the novel is brought to a resolution that the story of *War and Peace* is, as it were, retold within the novel. And it is retold through the mouth of Pierre who eventualy is able, through the reprise, to achieve real communicability while preserving his honesty. Central to the resolution of the novel is the fact that the Pierre who, throughout the course of the novel found his rage for honesty an impediment to communication, is at last able to transfer his thoughts to another in his love for Natasha.

In the treatment of Pierre's realisation of his love for Natasha Tolstoy demonstrated in a powerfully ironic way the force of an insincere tangential narrative in crystallising real emotions. Pierre's full understanding of his love comes when he acts as an audience to Captain Ramballe's risqué recital of his amorous adventures: nothing could be more absurd than that the tipsy captain's recital should bring Pierre to a realisation of love. Pierre reciprocates with a telling of his own story—which in a way is a retelling of the story that the readers of *War and Peace* know—and again Pierre fails to communicate. What Ramballe grasps as the main import is not the essence of Pierre's love for Natasha, but that he was rich with two palaces in Moscow. Ramballe is made to appear as a comically misunderstanding audience with which the reader of the novel can compare himself to his own advantage.

If his story told to Ramballe ends in a fiasco of non-comprehension, Pierre finally is able to achieve communication when in chapter 17 of the last volume he tells his story—again a reprise of what we have learnt from the novel itself—to Marya and Natasha. Pierre begins by giving expression to all those problems of evaluating experience and communicating it, which we have discussed: "I am told about such miracles which I have not dreamt of. Marya Abramovna invited me to her house and kept on telling me what happened to me or what should have happened. Stepan Stepanych also taught me how I should tell my stories." Repetition, as R. F. Christian has demonstrated, is one of Tolstoy's most powerful techniques, and this chapter reverberates with the repetition of the verb *rasskazyvat'* (to narrate) and its cognate noun *rasskaz*. Pierre is being importuned to tell a conventional story (what should have happened) in conventional terms (Stepan Stepanych taught me how I should tell my stories). But at last Pierre is able to turn away from self-mockery and tell of *real experiences* naturally; what had made his narrations so awkward previously, from the first one in Anna Scherer's salon, was that he had been only able to speak honestly of abstractions or, at best, of half-digested experiences. Now he began to speak "with the restrained enthusiasm of a man experiencing strong impressions in his recollections." Pierre at last understands that true communication, "man speaking to man," is akin to Wordsworth's celebrated understanding of poetry, originating in "emotion recollected in tranquillity . . . till by a species of reaction, all tranquillity gradually disappears, and an emotion, kindred to that which was before the subject of contemplation, is gradually produced and does itself actually exist in the mind." Again, of course, the act of narration, the "performance," marks a climactic moment in the novel. Whereas previously the performances were flawed and the accompanying sexual bondings insecure, finally, in the closure of *War and Peace*, we find that the union of Pierre and Natasha is made manifest by a perfected narration fused with a most sympathetic reception. What effects the union is not eloquence (even at this moment Tolstoy launched into a scathing aside at *intelligent* women who listen to words to retell them or to use them as starting points for their little "laboratorial" thoughts), but the whole narrating experience whose significance Pierre had grasped with Platon Karatayev whose stories were told with the naturalness of a singing bird.

And in this new-found way of telling, he finds his ideal listener in Natasha, who responds in the way that Tolstoy would probably have wished any reader of his to react. By look and gesture she indicates to him that "she understood exactly what he wished to transmit"; and more than that, "It was evident that she understood not only what he was telling but also what he would wish to tell but could not express in words." It is in the telling itself that Pierre became fully aware of the significance of experience—as Tolstoy himself had become aware of the significance of his own experiences during the long writing of *War and Peace*—and Natasha in her reaction personified the ideal reader that Tolstoy would have wished to reach out for: "Natasha, without knowing it, was all attention: she did not let slip a word, a tremor of the voice, a look, a shudder of a facial muscle, nor a gesture of Pierre's. She caught in flight the as yet unexpressed word and carried it straight into her open heart, guessing the secret significance of Pierre's whole spiritual world."

At the novel's end, having pleaded with his reader and hectored him, having shown him the futility of seeking to transmit experience, and the fluidity of human language, and having also demonstrated to him that only in his narrations and performances to his fellows could man hope to give form to his existence, Tolstoy too, through Pierre, rests content in the knowledge that in making *War and Peace*, he had also made his reader.

GARY SAUL MORSON

The Reader as Voyeur: Tolstoy and the Poetics of Didactic Fiction

Of course, I myself have made up just now all the things you say . . .
can you really be so credulous as to think that I will print all this and
give it to you to read, too? . . . I shall never have readers.

—From *Notes from Underground*

R eaders of Russian fiction accede
with special haste to Stendhal's dictum that "politics in a work of literature
is like a pistol shot 'n the middle of a concert, something loud and vulgar,
and yet a thing to which it is not possible to refuse one's attention." There
are countless histories of Russian literature that divide its authors and critics
into two irreconcilable camps, those who judge art "in its own terms" and
those who insist on a moralistic or political framework external to art. The
nihilist's assertion that boots are more important than Shakespeare, Maia-
kovskii's self-destructive pledge to step on the throat of his song, Turgenev's
plea to Tolstoy to remain a belles-lettrist and leave religion to the church—
these are the usual landmarks in the history of Russian literature. Attempts
to save radical critics like Belinskii from opprobrium usually take the form
of arguing that he was not so Stalinist as the Stalinists say; when we praise

From *Canadian-American Slavic Studies* 4, vol. 12 (Winter 1978). Copyright © 1978 by
Charles Schlacks, Jr. and Arizona State University.

the late Tolstoy we marvel at the great art he was able to produce *in spite of* his moralistic strictures.

It is an account on which the new critics and the Soviets can agree, although their values are reversed. And yet it is possible that both sides misstate the question. It is simply inappropriate to ask whether great art *can be* didactic; the fact is, that it often is. I do not know many scholars, whether formalists or new critics, who would deny *The Possessed?* and *The Death of Ivan Il'ich* the status of "great literature"; and to argue that they are such despite their dicacticism is simply to force reality into a theoretical mold. I simply cannot imagine what would be left of *The Death of Ivan Il'ich* or *The Kreutzer Sonata* without their moralism: perhaps something like the *War and Peace* Percy Lubbock wished Tolstoy had written—without the lectures on history and the polemical story of Napoleon. The right question, however, should not be *whether* great art can be didactic, but *how* it can be didactic; what we need (and what formalism and new criticism have prevented us from finding) is a poetics of instruction. Only then can we begin to appreciate Russian literature on its own terms.

There is perhaps no better place to start than with the new critics themselves. "We reject as poetry and label as mere rhetoric," write Wellek and Warren, "everything which persuades us to a definite outward action. Genuine poetry affects us more subtly. Art imposes some kind of framework which takes the statement of the work out of the world of reality. Into our semantic analysis we thus can reintroduce some of the common conceptions of aesthetics: 'disinterested contemplation,' 'aesthetic distance,' 'framing.' " An absolute gulf separates art from reality, for art is framed—as surely as a physical frame surrounds a picture—by an implicit set of conventions which remove it from the world of "is" to that of "as if." Literature is implicity preceded by what Gregory Bateson has called metacommunicative statements, statements of the type "take this as a joke," "read this as a metaphor," or "this is only a story." We are not asked to believe, but to suspend our disbelief. The reader takes the text which follows *as fiction*, and does not judge its "truth" in literal (or referential) terms. We must be able to understand this language about language, or we will resemble Dostoevskii's Smerdiakov, who objects to Gogol because his stories are "not true," or like the judge at the Daniel trial who equated fiction with slander on simple literalist grounds. Conversely, the formalist insistence on the absolute, ontological division of fiction from reality also separates persona from biographical author, and text from reader. That is why, indeed, it rejects as "mere" rhetoric (rhetoric is here opposed to art, to "genuine" poetry) works which insist on being evaluated by non-aesthetic criteria. A poetics of didacticism (as distinguished from a study of how ideas can become material for fictive discourse) would seem to be a contradiction in terms.

The present article suggests a model for a poetics of didactic literature, a model derived from a study of the Russian tradition (though not limited to it). I choose Tolstoy as emblematic of that tradition, and "Sevastopol in December" as a fiction in which his devices are most conspicuously "bared." My thesis in brief is that Tolstoy's violation of the principles of "framing" and "aesthetic distance" is strategic; he assumes that his readers expect to read fiction with a set of conventions that separate it from reality and he therefore deliberately encourages those expectations *so that* he may violate them later. For it is precisely aesthetic detachment that these stories seek to challenge. Their recurrent theme is that the aesthetic experience is itself immoral, that to observe is to act—and act badly. There are not only "speech acts," but also listening acts. These fictions therefore work by morally implicating the reader in the experience which is in process as he reads that very fiction. The reader of the story is culpable *because* he is a reader of the story. He responds by trying to reassert the conventions of fiction, and so to separate the aesthetic experience of the story from the aesthetic experiences he is led to condemn in the story; but he comes to learn that this act of distancing has also been planned and is, indeed, part of the story's strategy of implicating its reader. A series of metafictional devices constantly break frame; and we are allowed to reconstitute the frame only so that it may be broken again. Involuntarily, the reader *of* the fiction becomes an actor *in* the fiction. If the reader still rejects the story's anti-aesthetic, he has nevertheless defined himself in terms of the story's own set of choices.

In other words, these fictions do not ignore literary conventions, they defy them. Structured as patterns of violated expectations, they first ask us to read them as literature and then lead us to reject the conventions on which such a reading is based; and this structure implies that they rely on those conventions every bit as much as Turgenev's works do. Tolstoy's fictions are deliberately paradoxical, and we can only appreciate a paradox if we already hold beliefs that the paradox challenges. Their strategy is both to be and to deny being "mere literature," a strategy that is closely related to Tolstoy's frequent rhetorical device of asserting that his stories are not stories, but reality. In the middle of his fiction "Lucerne," for instance, Tolstoy breaks frame and tells the reader that "this is not a fiction, but a positive fact, which can be verified by anyone who likes from the permanent residents at the Hotel Schweizerhof, after ascertaining from the papers who the foreigners were who were staying at the Schweizerhof on the seventh of July. The reader is trapped between conflicting sets of conventions, as the story alternately insists on being read as fiction and as journalism; and to rest with either side of the contradition is to misread the work.

Consider, for instance, Tolstoy's first Sevastopol story. No better refutation could be provided to Wayne Booth's assertion that "efforts to use the second person [form of narration] have never been very successful, but it is astonishing how little real difference even this choice makes." "Sevastopol in December" is written almost entirely in the second person, and one need only try to rephrase it in the first or third person to see that it depends for its effectiveness on that form. "The radical unnaturalness" of the narration is disturbing, and is meant to be. For it seems to violate an essential convention of fiction which normally distinguishes it from rhetoric, a distinction succinctly stated by John Stuart Mill: "eloquence is *heard,* poetry is *overheard.*" The speech of fiction takes place within the fictive frame; we the real historical audience, as distinguished from the implied or fictive one, are mere eavesdroppers. So far as the fictive speaker of the work is concerned, we do not exist at all. (This is the device that is "bared" in the quotation from *Notes from Underground* with which this essay begins.) But the strikingly "unnatural" second person address momentarily seems to break the frame, to be addressed to *us,* as if the author wanted us for once not to eavesdrop, but simply to listen. If we are experienced readers, we try to regard even this address as a literary device, and so to reconstitute the frame, but our effort is never fully successful and our position as audience remains problematic. The strategy is symmetrical to the ambiguous position of the narrator in "Lucerne," who alternately claims to be persona and biographical author, and the reader's uncertainty about his own ontological position becomes a central element of his experience of reading this didactic fiction.

This work is written in the second person because it really is addressed to the second person, its reader. While it is fiction, it is also Mill's "eloquence," Wellek and Warren's "rhetoric." The second-person address constantly threatens to make the reader a character in the story, a participant in an unmediated dialogue with the author—a threat that is the first of the work's many strategies to overcome the aesthetic distance it assumes we "assume." The work is addressed directly to the reader because it is about the reader, and the act of reading. This story is, in Henry Sams' phrase, a "satire of the second person."

To read a text as literature is to apply aesthetic criteria to it: we judge it as performance, we detach ourselves from personal involvement. As Shklovsky observes, "art is thus without compassion, or outside it, except in those instances when the feeling of commiseration serves as material for an artistic pattern." Now, it is precisely this act of distancing, our ability to turn horror into "tragedy," that is the theme of Tolstoy's story. The aesthetic experience stands in opposition to the ethical; and this opposition applies to our apprehension of this work as well. The very fact that its reader is able to appreciate the artistic transformation of an ongoing battle into art makes him morally suspect. " 'Well, you know, I wanted to see . . . ' " Pierre explains his presence as gentleman tourist at Borodino. "Mounting the steps to the knoll Pierre looked at the scene before him, spellbound by its beauty. . . . the sound of the firing produced the chief beauty of the spectacle. . . . and for a long time [Pierre] did not notice the killed and wounded, though many fell near him. He looked about him with a smile which did not leave his face." The strategy of the second person address in "Sevastopol" is to turn its reader into just such a tourist of death, to make him see the act of reading is an *act* of reading. We learn too late that this is a reflexive fiction and that we are its protagonist. The reader becomes voyeur. This text does not so much have an "implied" reader as an implicated one.

Tourism is the controlling metaphor of "Sevastopol in December." The story is, indeed, a fictive tour guide and that is why it is written in the second person (and second person imperative). As in real tour guides, whose language the story imitates, this form of address works as a set of directions (quite literally) for seing a museumized world. I quote from George W. Oakes' guide *Turn Right at the Fountain*: "Carrying a raincoat or umbrella . . . start at *Piccadilly Circus*." "Just past Lloyds . . . you will have an amusing time. . . . As you turn back toward *Traitor's Gate* and contemplate the great personalities . . . you may be in the mood for something out of the ordinary." Here the underscoring of names of places, like the titles of books and paintings, renders them and the people in them (whose "typical" conversations "you will enjoy") into a kind of sculpture: they are "picturesque." The tour guide is a subset of "how-to" books (which are also written in the second person) that tells us how to *see*. It teaches us not simply to look, but what to look *at*. The world becomes theatre (its setting is "authentic") and you have the script; its people are actors in your "play." "From the stream of action," writes Dean MacCannell in his recent study *The Tourist*, "select bits are framed" so that they can be "savored." If MacCannell is right that the quintessential moment of tourism is the "instant replay," then a tour guide is an "instant pre-play."

But a walk through Sevastopol is no promenade through Lucerne. The central iron of Tolstoy's fictive tour guide derives from the description of war as one might describe such a promenade, a battleground where men are still dying as a historical landmark. "You" expect to see the site of "beautiful historical legends," and you try to appreciate the "majesty" of heroism in process. Buy "you are mistaken": there are things to which art is not adequate, events which we must not even try to view with equanimity. The form of a tour guide becomes singularly inappropriate to the "sights" of this tour, and we must read its descriptions *against* the conventional expectations we have of such forms: "You enter the large Assembly Hall. As soon as you open the door you are struck by the sight and smell of forty or fifty amputations and most seriously wounded cases, some in cots but most of them on the floor." As he described the smell of the sea, your guide now evokes that of putrefying flesh. "Now if your nerves are strong, go in at the door to the left; it is there they bandage and operate. . . . The doctors are engaged in the horrible but beneficient work of amputation. You will see the sharp curved knife enter the healthy white flesh; you will see the wounded man come back to life with terrible, heart-rending screams and curses. You will see the doctor's assistant toss the amputated arm into a corner and in the same room you will see another wounded man on a stretcher watching the operation, and writhing and groaning not so much from physical pain as from the mental torture of anticipation." Characteristically, in this drama of observation, "you" are made to watch someone watching, and inevitably to remind yourself that there are observers and observers; and "you," thankfully, are one who does not have to undergo what he witnesses. "You" are pleased that for you these deaths are only objects to be seen; and here the moral problems of watching already begin to be apparent. *You take comfort* in the fact that for you these amputations are only sights, are objects, and that you are as detached from their pain as that arm is from its former owner.

The kind of time in which a tour guide is written also multiplies the horror of the scene. The tourist simply does not exist in the same kind of time as the people he observes, and he sees them across this time difference (it is the consciousness of the separation which frames them). The present tense of a guidebook does not mean "now," but "whenever." Its present tense is an absolute present. For the point of a guidebook, indeed the very possibility of writing one, depends on the sights being constants. People are not present, they are re-present-ative. Indeed, it is *because* all the sentences of a guidebook contain an implicit "whenever" that the word may be omitted. A Russian guide (and Tolstoy's fictive one) is made up of iterative verbs because its action may be reiterated as often as one likes; its imperfects point to the possibility of repeating its actions (as do some future perfects, e.g., *uvidite*). But the very idea of repeating this promenade is grotesque, as is the implicit repeat "performance" of amputation. The effect of the tour-guide narration in this case is to juxtapose the specificity of the pain that each soldier suffers with "your" knowledge that it might be seen at any time. The author of the guide describes what you would like to believe are exceptions as utterly unexceptional, so unexceptional that "you" have come knowing the pain you will witness at each point. The topology of pain is mapped out with geographical precision.

If this text has a subtext, it is *The Inferno*. There, too, an omniscient guide shows the way through the house of torments; and this text also chronicles its "tourist's" reaction: "Now the notes of pain begin to reach my ears; now I am come where great wailing breaks on me." When he wonders if he may speak to the sufferers, Tolstoy's tourist is echoing Dante. "Poet," Dante addresses his guide, "I would fain speak with these two. . . . 'O wearied souls, come and speak with us if One forbids it not.' " It is only necessary to rewrite these passages in the second person and the absolute present to turn Dante's singular account into Tolstoy's repeatable tour. This difference redefines the reader.

Here we begin to approach a still more significant inversion of the form of a guide: the relation of its implied reader to its text. For in a real guide the second person form of address is no more than form: the text emphasizes not the one who sees, but what he will see. Though it "plots," it is plotless; though it may be told as a narrative, we understand that to be a transparent device for rendering the immediate apprehension of space in the sequence of language. No "story" is in fact being told. That, indeed, is why a guide may be opened at any point. One may progress to that page not only by reading the preceding pages, but also by simply reaching the physical place it is then describing; and guides are usually written assuming that they will be used that way (thus the wealth of cross-referencing, the repetition of necessary information, the division into brief, easily digested sections). But Tolstoy's "guide" is in fact not a guide at all, but the story of its reader. We learn not so much about the sights of Sevastopol as about what will happen to "you" when you see them. The observer changes because of what he observes. One cannot read the same guide twice.

What the tourist of Sevastopol learns to see is himself. This is a story of his growing self-consciousness, his rite of "passage." As the journey progresses the tourist begins to realize that he himself is one of the sights of Sevastopol, an expected part of the scene for which provisions have been made and which he must consider in his survey of the battleground. He begins to watch himself watching, just as he has watched other watchers.

And in the process of growing self-observation, "you" come to realize that seeing is an action and keeping one's distance a relation.

"You" begin secure in your role as tourist, and your point of view is unself-consciously asethetic. As you approach the harbor, you hear "the majestic sound of firing" and are prepared for picturesque scenes of heroism and valor. At first, this is what the tour guide seems to promise, beginning with its initial paragraph's deceptively placid description of the dawn that will soon make "the dark blue surface of the sea" begin to sparkle "merrily." But your disillusionment begins early, though at first on purely aesthetic grounds. "Your first impression [of the camp] will certainly be most disagreeable: the strange mixture of camp-life and town-life—of a fine town and a dirty bivouac—is not only ugly but looks like horrible disorder." You are wrong again, however, and as you heed your guide's command to "look more closely" at the faces of the soldiers, your impression of Sevastopol once again changes. Twice mistaken, you now reflect on your errors and on yourself. "Yes, disenchantment certainly awaits you on entering Sevastopol for the first time," the omniscient narrator predicts your inner monologue. "Perhaps you may reproach yourself for having felt undue enthusiasm and may doubt the justice of the ideas you had formed of the heroism of the defenders of Sevastopol, based on the tales and descriptions and sights and sounds seen and heard from the North Side." But of course this re-evaluation will itself soon be re-evaluated in your constant process of learning through a series of planned errors—the "pitfalls" of your guide's uneven tour.

Expectation, disillusionment, self-reflection, and new expectation—this is the pattern "you" constantly repeat. Your tentative expectations repeatedly prove false (and so they become more and more tentative). The narrator then corrects you: "But look more closely," "But you are mistaken," "Do not trust the feeling that checks you." You then reflect upon, and reproach yourself, "you . . . begin to feel ashamed of yourself in the presence of this man," and so learn not only about Sevastopol, but also about "you" who observe Sevastopol. And as the process of vision and re-vision, analysis and self-analysis, unfolds, you become more and more implicated in the horror you watch.

Your painful self-discovery gradually becomes the center of your attention. You see less and less of Sevastopol as you (an unattractive you) enter your field of vision. " 'What matters the death and suffering of so insignificant a worm as I, compared to so many deaths, so much suffering?' But the sight of the clear sky, the brilliant sun, the beautiful town, the open church, and the soldiers moving in all directions, will soon bring your spirit back to its normal state of frivolity, its petty cares and absorption in the present." But do not trust this normal state. As you approach the bastion, and death ceases to be a "remote" possibility, a less self-indulgent "self-consciousness" begins to supersede the activity of your observation: you are less attentive to all that is around you and a disagreeable feeling of indecision suddenly seizes you. But silencing this despicable little voice that has suddenly made itself heard within you . . . you involuntarily expand your chest, raise your head higher, and clamber up the slipper clay hill. What you are most closely observing now is you; and when you look at the enemy ("him"), that is now the distraction. And it is a welcome distraction, because its very intensity is (perhaps) capable of drawing your attention from the "despicable little voice" to the already "regular and pleasant whistle . . . of a bomb." You try simply to look (just look) to prevent yourself from looking at your self looking. So you go to the bastion, lean out of the embrasure, and stare.

It is here that the climax of the story takes place. For your benefit, the naval officer "will wish to show you a little firing." And the exchange of shells will please you, the narrator predicts; "you will experience interesting sensations and see interesting sights." Distracted from yourself, "you revive and are seized, though only for a moment, by an inexpressibly joyful emotion, so that you feel a peculiar delight in the danger—in this game of life and death—and wish the bombs and balls to fall nearer and nearer to you."

But just as you are enjoying this game, it kills a man; and the "scarcely human appearance" of the mutilated, dying soldier is the next sight on your tour. His death is the last event in the story. The text breaks, and the narrator now summarizes "the principal thought you have brought away with you": the heroism of the soldiers in contrast to "that petty ambition of forgetfulness which you yourself experienced." When the guide ends his tour on a pacific description of the evening, we recognize the apparent parallelism with the story's opening as ironic. Since the death of the soldier, "you" are not the same "you," and cannot take the same aesthetic joy as before.

It is of the utmost importance to understand what has happened in the story's climactic scene: the tourist has literally become implicated in a death, a death which has taken place for his aesthetic pleasure. Looks kill. "Your" story is your growing awareness that (literally and metaphorically) you are responsible for what you look at. It is this growing awareness that may "seem to inspire a dread of offending" the wounded in the hospital by looking at them, a dread that makes you want to look away. But that reaction, the narrator immediately corrects you, is precisely the wrong one, for it repeats the moral error by further denying your relation to the sufferer. "Do not trust the feeling that checks you at the threshold, it is a wrong feeling. Go on, do not be ashamed of seeming to have come *to look* at the sufferers, do not hesitate to go up and speak to them. Sufferers like to see a sympathetic human face." The only way to redeem looking is to acknowledge it as an action, to make it a form of relation and not of separation. And that will mean going through the painful process of listening (again like Dante) to the wounded man's litany of pain, a process which "you" wish to cut short as soon as possible. One *bears* witness.

Now, reading is also a form of tourism, and a particularly cowardly form of it, since it distances us all the more. Unlike the reader, the tourist at Sevastopol momentarily enters the time of the soldiers, because he can die in it. But as readers, we take no risks by leaning out of an embrasure. We protect ourselves from ever having to see men in agony and, more important, from ever having to see them watching our tourism and compelling us either to talk with them or show we are only "looking." The key point I wish to make is that we gradually come to learn that what applies to "you" also applies to *us*, that we are simply tourists through the written word. As "you" come to observe yourself while trying to see Sevastopol, we learn equally involuntarily about ourselves while trying to *read* "Sevastopol." The pattern of reluctant advances and cowardly resistances that are enacted between this omniscient tour guide and his tourist is repeated in a similar tension between the author of the story (Tolstoy) and his historical, real readers. There is "leakage" of the narrative out of its frame. The story is double; the text creates its own context. The narrative projects out of itself a second story in which we are actors, in which we gradually come to realize that as readers we are implicated in the crime of "disinterested" observation. We resist that leakage; but that very resistance is simply a form of "looking away" and implicates us (as it implicates the tourist at the hospital) still more. There is no way simply to "read about" Sevastopol. As "you" come to look at the act of looking, we come to look at the act of reading.

The real story, therefore, may be described as the story of our encounter with what we at first *think* we are reading, the story of the "plotted" failure of our attempt not to apply the "you" to us. Like the confidence game it is, "Sevastopol in December" exists by making its audience its unwilling participants. It is primarily for this reason, I think, that the effects of its passages are lost when rewritten in the first or third person. (I invite the reader of *this* article so to rewrite the passages I have cited.) Confined in its frame, the double-level story would turn into a single-level account.

Consider again the striking form of the second-person narrative. The address implies the immediacy of direct discourse rather than the mediated language of fiction; it threatens to make us listen when we want to eavesdrop. Precisely because this is not the conventional way to construct a story, we must remind ourselves that the conventions of storytelling do still apply, that the fictional frame encloses the first part of the Sevastopol trilogy as surely as the third. This imitation tour guide constantly seems to alternate with a real tour guide and appears on the verge of claiming not real*ism*, but reality. This ambiguity of genre, it seems to me, is the reason for the journalistic title, the documentary quality of the first two sketches (which footnote linguistic data), and the original intent to publish the narrative in a new military, rather than a literary, journal. The fiction constantly threatens to deny its own fictiveness; and to the extent that it succeeds in doing so, we become not readers of a fiction in the form of a tour guide, but real tourists through the medium of non-fictive journalism. And as tourists, the condemnation we have made of the immediate observer in the fictive guide becomes applicable to us, since we are now in the same position.

We therefore try to resist the identification with the implied reader, to remind ourselves of the story's fictiveness, and so to distance ourselves from it. We attempt to appreciate it aesthetically, and so to assert a comforting aesthetic distance. But in so doing, we justify the very accusation whose applicability we hope to deny. Our attempt to look across a fictive frame means we insist on being disinterested, not responsible for artistically rendered pain. " 'Blood' in art," to quote Shklovsky, "is not bloody." In the hospital, the tourist encounters an amputee who describes how he managed to avoid pain. " 'The chief thing, your Honor, is *not to think*,' " he declares. " 'If you don't think, it's nothing much. It's most because of a man's thinking.' " It is advice that the tourist accepts all too quickly to distance himself from his pain of looking, until the wife of the wounded man interrupts to say that her husband was indeed in dreadful agony and to imply that the advice is extended for "your" comfort. And so "for some reason [you] begin to feel ashamed of yourself in the presence of this man." Now, "your" mistake is precisely our mistake. We, too, try "not to think" of the concrete pain of real sufferers, but only of characters in narrative; and the narrative corrects its reader as surely as its character corrects its tourist. Not to think, not to look—this is the natural reaction to other's horror, precisely because it classes it as *other's* horror; and the aesthetic distancing made possible by the classing of a work as "only a story" is simply another way of "not looking."

It is, in fact, a response that the tourist in the story also makes. When pain becomes unbearable, he tries to apply an aesthetic standard, to judge events as if they were performance. When you leave the "house of pain," you will be in this state of mind. "You may meet the funeral procession of an officer. . . . The funeral will seem a very beautiful military pageant, the sounds very beautiful warlike sounds; and neither to these sights nor these sounds will you attach the clear and personal sense of suffering and death that came to you in the hospital." The removal of the personal sense of suffering, is of course, precisely what the aesthetic frame is designed to do; and this is why the narrator interjects his reproach for "your" relief at your spirit's return to its "normal state of frivolity. It is a reproach he repeats several times, whenever "you" attempt to see this tour as tours are usually seen. "Your" appreciation of the "beauty and majesty" of the "sights" betrays you.

But the same process betrays us; we also come to look with discomfort at our initial appreciation of the majesty of the sunrise in the first paragraph. Indeed, our very attempt to read this story as a story, to admire *its* artistry repeats the tourist's error. "Sevastopol in December" contrasts aesthetic and personal approaches to suffering, and is therefore structured to force its readers to experience both in turn. The story plays us false. It tells us to read it as fiction, then reproaches us for doing so. The reader is caught between contradictory characterizations of the text he is reading, between "this is a story" and "you are culpable for reading this as a story"; between "as if" and "as if as if." The structure of the reader's experience therefore fits the pattern of what Gregory Bateson has called a "double bind." And the double bind is essential to its strategy to reach beyond the text to "infect" its reader with a personal sense of the pain it describes, to make him present.

The story includes the story of reading it. It works much like Velasquez' meta-painting, *Las Meninas* (here I follow Foucault's interpretation). The canvas portrays an artist painting a canvas, whose subject lies outside the canvas. But we can guess who that is, because a mirror in the back of the painting points to the place where the subject is standing, and reflects a royal couple. Since the place where the subject stands is also the place where the viewer must stand to see the painting, this projection beyond the frame constitutes an elaborate compliment to the viewer, to us. What is happening here is that the position where we must stand to observe the painting has become part of the painting—just as the process we must go through to read "Sevastopol in December" becomes part of it. Crucial differences also obtain. The portrait of us in Tolstoy's narrative is humiliating. More important, since a narrative must be read in sequence and over time, the process of reading can itself be "plotted" in advance. Tolstoy constructs a pattern of repeated humiliations for us, makes us construct the story of our encounter with ourselves as readers. We are "taken in."

The story we think we are reading, therefore, turns out to be an enclosed narrative, and we are the protagonist of the frame tale. Our reading of this outer tale is its central event, and our discovery of it becomes a double discovery of the self. Like "you," we learn (against our wishes) about ourselves. Indeed, this unwilling self-knowledge, this change we have not expected and perhaps resisted, is the goal towards which all instructive literature strives. Didactic fiction is reader-implicating fiction.

Some generalizations about the poetics of didactic fiction are in order. Instruction seeks to change its audience, perhaps to move it to specific action. Fiction, on the other hand, only states in the subjunctive; its "truths" obtain only in possible worlds, but not in the actual one. "The poet is least of all men liar, for the poet nothing affirmeth," writes Sidney; and his statement may be neatly contrasted with the closing line of the second Sevastopol sketch: "The hero of my story," writes Tolstoy, "is the truth."

Didactic fiction, then, is something of an oxymoron, and its best practitioners work not by avoiding but by taking advantage of its necessary contradiction. The didactic story-teller doubly encodes his text as fiction and as truth, and manipulates the reader's experience through code-switching and an ambiguous frame. He realizes that fiction is an effective means of seduction precisely because it is defined as counterfactual, as "only a story"; and so we willingly make ourselves into its implied audience as we might not when listening to a sermon. For the duration of our reading, we suspend our beliefs (not just our disbelief). We allow our expectations to be shaped not by what we think about the real world, but by what the author tells us of his. We give up metaphysics for genre, exchange principles for conventions. The strategy of the didactic fiction-writer is to make this assumption of his view carry over into the reader's real world, and so to abuse convention to induce conversion. He must make orthodox (if disingenuous) use of the opening frame ("this is only a story") but elude, as much as he can, the power of the closing frame. He must, in a sense, not allow the curtain to fall. In this particular sense, the story strives to remain open, as its ontological status seeks to be (in the full etymological sense of the word) indeterminate.

The didactic poet exploits the doubleness of the moment of reading. The plot of his story may unfold in a fictive, infinitely repeatable time, but the reading of the story takes place in a unique time, continuous with the rest of experience. It is this peculiar kind of simultaneity that the poet uses to create "leakage" of text into context: and so, doubleness becomes duplicity. The poet is most of all men liar, for he affirms he is only a poet.

The poetics of didactic fiction, therefore, does not essentially challenge formalist assertions about the autonomy of the literary function. On the contrary, it assumes we necessarily hold these beliefs, however intuitively, in order to read fiction at all. Its violation of our expectations is strategic: if we ceased to understand the fictiveness of fiction didactic art might be impossible.

Though it seems paradoxical, then, there may be no better formalist text than *What Is Art?* (unless it is *The Republic's* justification for banishing the poets). The perception of art as seduction—and that is the metaphor which controls Tolstoy's *The Kreutzer Sonata*—implicitly affirms that we assume an absolute separateness of art from life. That, indeed, is why those who fear art point out the dangers to which that assumption can lead. Shklovsky and his Soviet censor may have had more in common than either one knew.

We may take the argument one step further. Not only is formalism a fruitful way of studying didactic fiction, but the analysis of didactic fiction can tell us much about the limitations of early formalism—precisely because early formalism is so well suited to it. Briefly put, formalism fails to explain how texts can live when the conventions by which they are originally encoded do not survive; and didactic texts do fail at that point. In its initial concern with the conventionality of literature, formalism insists that texts be read according to the conventions of their times. Implicitly it denies the leakage of signs and ignores the renewal of readability in unexpected ways. A text must die with the wearing out of its "devices," and with the passing of the readership that sustains them—and didactic fiction does in fact die at that point. If the second person form of narration should ever become too commonplace to shock, or fictionality ever cease to be a central category of narrative, "Sevastopol in December" would fail in its plotted instruction. It might, however, survive on other terms. For we do re-author our texts and make them mean in unforseen ways: didactic literature is reread, in that emasculating phrase, "as literature." The final irony will belong to the high culture Tolstoy despised when it can comfortably and unself-consciously incorporate even *What Is Art?* into its canon.

If the limitations of formalism suggest a model for didactic fiction, we must, nevertheless, take those limitations into account. For in an important sense, there may be no such thing as didactic fiction, just as there is no fiction which is securely framed from context. Shklovsky's *mots*—that literature is always free from life, that there is absolutely nothing that can be learned from a work of literature—are at best useful overstatements. The very opposite may be the case. There is no literature from which we do not learn, and in that sense, all fiction is didactic. I think we must ultimately speak not of a class of texts that are didactic, but of the didactic strategies of all texts. Then we can read stories like "Sevastopol in December" as narratives in which the didactic element is the "dominant," and our explication of them will also serve to make us aware of less obvious, but essentially similar, strategies in even the least "instructive" of narratives.

The false framing of the narrative and the consequent "framing" of the reader—this is the strategy of didactic fiction. "Sevastopols" duplicitous use of the second person, as both fictive and real reader, may therefore stand as archetype of reader-implicating narrative. For Tolstoy, the reader of fiction implicates himself simply by being a reader of fiction: he is therefore a member of the leisure class and lives the sort of life that allows him to indulge in the artifice of art. As Dostoevsky's underground man tells his readers that they do not exist, Tolstoy tells his that they should not exist (at least, not as readers). Tolstoy wants us to reject Tolstoy as Tolstoy rejected Tolstoy.

It follows that we can understand fictions like *The Kreutzer Sonata* best if we treat them as anti-fictions. *The Kreutzer Sonata* is a brilliantly contrived aesthetic masterpiece that teaches us to despise such contrivance and mastery—and that is its duplicitous strategy. Tolstoy's didactic fiction is in a perfect position to manipulate the experience of reading because the object of his attack is the aesthetic experience itself. Even if we are sophisticated enough to understand and still ultimately reject his lesson, the process of reading his anti-fictions at least makes us experience the choices involved in the act of reading fiction—beginning with the choice to read fiction at all.

Tolstoy's characteristic device for implicating the audience of his fiction is to depict an audience in his fiction: the audience in the narrative becomes the reflection of the audience of the narrative. In condemning it, we unwittingly condemn ourselves; too late, we recognize ourselves in its unexpected mirror. So we are invited to *The Death of Ivan Il'ich* as our fictional equivalents are invited to his funeral. As they invoke social conventions to deny the applicability of the death to themselves, we invoke those of fiction. We make ourselves the "proper" audience that art requires.

If we are sophisticated—*comme il faut?*—we will frame the narrative "as a story" about Man and his death. That is, in our socially defined role as readers, we will think away the "inappropriate question" of our own death. But Tolstoy's story is not literature, it is anti-literature; and the conclusion of its syllogism is not that "Caius is mortal" but that *you* will die. To the extent that we recognize this breach of literary decorum, we like Pëtr Ivanovich at the funeral, take this "reproach to the living" as somehow "out of place, or at least not applicable to him." Our reading condemns us. Even if we imagine that we do agree with the story's lesson, the very fact that we are at that moment reading fiction belies us. The only person in the story to whom its lesson does not apply is the one who could not read it, the peasant Gerasim.

EDWARD WASIOLEK

"Resurrection"

By the time Tolstoy had finished *Resurrection* he was more than an author: he was a prophet in search of his crown of thorns. The picture of the noble old man with a white beard, dressed in a linen blouse and Turkish trousers, humbly wielding his scythe, working the fields with his peasants, and persecuted by the autocratic tsar and the orthodox church, was irresistible to the world and to Tolstoy too, who played his part to the full. His fame was disseminated throughout the world in cheap editions of his work in all major languages, and endless streams of pilgrims came to assure him that he had seen the truth and that the truth was needed. Until the 1880s the world honored his art but was indifferent to his preachings; Tolstoy remained the artist first and the teacher second. But by the end of the eighties and certainly by the nineties the world wanted both his art and his truths, and Tolstoy made them the same.

Since the world wanted his opinions on the political and social situation of Russia, he obliged them by scalding rhetoric on the legal system, the prisons, private property, the bureaucracy, and every conceivable institution of contemporary tsarist Russia. There had always been a rhetorical bent in his writings; even the early works are interlarded with pronouncements on marriage, education, agriculture, and various other subjects. But never had Tolstoy's pedagogical bent assumed such gargantuan proportions as in *Resurrection,* nor had it ever posed so grave a threat to his art. George Steiner, among others, has seen the novel as seriously flawed because of the massive intrusions of political and social commentary: "When Tolstoy

From *Tolstoy's Major Fiction.* Copyright © 1978 by The University of Chicago. The University of Chicago Press.

came to write *Resurrection*, the teacher and prophet in him did violence to the artist. The sense of equilibrium and design which had previously controlled his invention was sacrificed to the urgencies of rhetoric. In this novel the juxtaposition of two ways of life and the theme of the pilgrimage from falsehood to salvation are set forth with the nakedness of a tract." It is easy to see why one would find these denunciatory essays harmful to the aesthetic quality of the novel. They are too many and too long; the person of Tolstoy is found in them too bluntly and directly; they touch too directly on the issues of the time; and they seem to have only the most external and mechanical relationship to the romantic tale of Nekhludov and Maslova's love. Yet the teacher and the prophet had not spoiled such magnificent works as *The Death of Ivan Ilych* and *Master and Man*, and they did not mar *Resurrection*—at least not as seriously as Steiner and others would have us believe.

But if the novel is not spoiled, then the tale and the tracts will have to be joined. The artistic integrity of the novel turns on this question of how one can justify the essays of social commentary—their number, length, the rhetorical anger that pervades them, and the mechanical way in which they are connected with the dramatized tale of love between Maslova and Nekhludov. The novel is structured most visibly on the alternation of visits by Nekhludov from government office to prison and from visits to officials to visits to Maslova. The point of both journeys is the pursuit of justice, and most specifically the pursuit or effort of Nekhludov to right a wrong that he has committed on the person of Maslova. We have Nekhludov's efforts to combat injustice as well as Tolstoy's efforts to combat injustice in the vituperative essays: the tale of personal injustice and the generalized exposition of injustice. One of the functions of the "tracts" surely is to multiply the significance of Nekhludov's perception and recording of the injustices he finds in society. Nekhludov's perception and sense of injustice—not only that which he has committed but also what he sees—would be too small a thing if they were not environed by the magnitude of Tolstoy's perception and wrath. Tolstoy takes what Nekhludov perceives into abstraction; yet at the same time Nekhludov concretizes what Tolstoy surveys. One apparent connection between the essays and the personal tale, then, is "illustrative," and "generalizing": the concretization of what is abstract and intellectual and the multiplication of what is personal and seemingly exceptional. One of the parallels—perhaps the most important—that Tolstoy establishes between tale and tracts by way of the structure of generalizing and illustration is the class nature of the evils that beset contemporary Russian life, a concern that Tolstoy belabors about the same time in *What Is Art?*

Tolstoy's concern with the class nature of contemporary society can be seen in the way he structures both tale and tracts about the problem of the haves and the have-nots. One part of society has arrogated to itself all the privileges, degraded the other half, and then, as portection of its privileges, has punished the other half for degradations that it itself has engendered. Tolstoy does not deal in subtleties in the essays. The representatives of the ruling class are presented as uniformly corrupt, physically and morally repulsive, lacking in human feeling, and uniformly the servants of a monstrous bureaucracy. They are gluttons, philanderers, murderers, liars, and drunkards. Those in prison are also drunkards, murderers, liars and swindlers, but they have been punished for what they have done. The haves are rewarded for it.

The debasement for Tolstoy works both ways: the haves corrupt, but they are in turn corrupted. When we first meet Maslova, she is smoking, drinking, and engaged in prostitution. But Nekhludov, too, drinks, eats, smokes, and engages in prostitution. He has been carrying on an affair with the wife of the Maréchal de Noblesse, and is contemplating the prostitution of himself by marrying Missy Korchagin. The differences of corruption between haves and have-nots are those of manner, privilege, and sensitivity. The sensitivity lies with the have-nots. Those in prison are shown to have passively adopted much of the predatory character of the society, but the suffering endured has endowed many of them with dignity and the capacity to feel the suffering of their fellow human beings. As the novel progresses, it become clear that by and large the real criminals are outside prison and the martyrs are inside prison.

It is, too, in the light of class privilege and its consequent cruelties that Tolstoy presents the personal injustice that Nekhludov inflicts on Maslova. Nekhludov acts as he does because he has been so taught and formed by the class he belongs to. He is pictured first as pure and innocent— a lover of truth, unsullied by predatory instincts, and a lover of the world and its people. After several years in the army he becomes a drunkard, a gambler, a sensuous, predatory beast. It is the military life that teaches him to drink, to talk coarsely about women and exploit them, to kill what had been true and pure in his being, and to exalt what is corrupt and unfeeling. For Tolstoy the process of corruption of individual life by social codes is always signaled by the substitution of generalized, mechanical, and impersonal feeling for personal, specific, immediate, and constantly new feeling.

One's personal life is obliterated by the general life of society. This is why, during the night of the seduction, Nekhludov moves as if in a dream, mechanically. It is not his own thoughts and feelings that move him to prurience but the voices of his fellow officers. When his love for Maslova was pure, his feelings for her were natural. They were his and not the generalized feelings of his class. Maslova and he had played as equals on that spring day when their lips first touched, but when Nekhludov returns for the Easter visit, Tolstoy is careful to remind us of the class difference of the two: she serves the family, makes beds, brings towels, food, and water. When Nekhludov first puts his arm about her, she is putting a pillow case on a pillow. On the day of his departure, he stands outside the maid's room to give her the hundred rubles. The fall of Maslova is presented as the consequence of the sexual misuse of a servant-ward by a nobleman officer, and that misuse is multiplied many times over, as Maslova is preyed upon by others again and again. The confrontation in the courtroom is between officer and maid, the misuser and the misused, the debaser and the debased; and something of the quintessential mechanism of the society is caught in the irony of the corrupter there to judge the person he has corrupted.

Nekhludov is in the courtroom to complete the fall he began many years before. If there seems little connection between the original seduction and the judicial error, it is there nevertheless. The judicial error which takes place with Nekhludov's inattentive cooperation is an example of that indifference that runs the mechanisms of society. Without the explicit intention of individuals, that indifference results in prison and degradation for many. Nekhludov need only shrug his shoulders, wash his hands, and go to dinner to the Korchagins, which indeed is what he attempts to do, after indulging in the luxury of arranging for a legal appeal. But something had moved in his soul that day, altering his perception. The dinner at the Korchagins and the people present appear to him to be grotesque, a reaction that signals repulsion with himself. Marx said that man is in his essence a social being, but what for Marx was a desirable truth was for Tolstoy only a partial and repulsive truth. Man, for him, begins to reach for his true essence only when he gives up his social being and becomes conscious of his personal being. This is what begins to happen to Nekhludov in the courtroom. It is also the fact that man's true nature lies in the realization of his individual essence that takes the locus of the novel necessarily from the problem of class conflict. Marx saw true consciousness as the awakening of the individual to class consciousness; Tolstoy saw true consciousness as an awakening to individual consciousness. The opposition in the novel between the haves and the have-nots is in the most essential respects an evasion of the real source of corruption, just as Tolstoy's thundering denunciation of the institutions by which Russia is organized is an evasion of the real source of corruption.

The class problem, as all the social and political commentary, are moral hieroglyphics betokening something beyond the institutional framework of the corruption Tolstoy rails against. Tolstoy's rhetoric at the vileness of the institutions and the men who run those institutions would seem to be a call to action. Yet a reading of these vituperations as a call to institutional reform would be grossly in error. To be sure, Tolstoy was in favor of eliminating the degradations of Russian life, was against the lumbering bureaucracy and the spiritually dead rites of the Orthodox church. But to the extent that rhetoric should move one to work for the replacement of vile institutions with better institutions, then it is a call that leads nowhere, just as the presentation of class corruption in such detail does not lead to institutional change. It takes no special emphasis to remind ourselves that it is not "bad" institutions for Tolstoy that corrupt people, but institutions themselves, whether "good" or "bad." The rhetorical wrath is a call to avoid what is the real source of both public and private corruption. In a sense, Tolstoy's "tracts" are a gargantuan misleading of the reader, an evasion he tempts us with, and as such the form of the novel proceeds largely by offering the reader more and more subtle evasions of the truth. If many of the officials in their various roles take their corruptions to be justice, so too does Tolstoy offer us a variety of injustices to be taken as justice and falsities to be taken as truths. Nekhludov is our guide, and he runs the gamut of evasions of truth.

Nekhludov's first evasion is the longest: his attempt to seek justice in the courts that condemn Maslova. He looks for what is not there. The government, offices, lawyers, and civil servants are wrong, but Nekhludov's quest is also wrong. Nekhludov is persuaded that if he makes the proper appeals, sees the right people, takes the right steps, the error in justice will be corrected. The irrelevance of his quest for justice becomes increasingly apparent in the course of the story. Nekhludov seeks what Maslova becomes increasingly indifferent to. When he tells her that he has exhausted every avenue and that everything has fallen through, she hardly hears him and answers perfunctorily and truthfully that none of it matters. She is concerned rather with his reaction to the slander that has been spread about her cavortings with the hospital attendant. What is important to her is what she is in Nekhludov's soul, not what she is in the eyes of the law. It becomes apparent that Nekhludov has sought so earnestly for justice for

Maslova because such justice was perhaps another obstacle in his making a complete commitment to the other truth: the truth that he carries within himself.

If he had succeeded in correcting the judicial error and in setting Maslova free, he would have "freed" her to continue the debased, corrupt life she had led and to which he had led her. Nekhludov would have given to the impersonal processes of justice what was his to redeem. He will not buy his redemption at the small price of taking steps to reverse the verdict, nor even at the larger price of giving up his property, alienating his friends and class, leaving his settled, luxurious life, and following Maslova to Siberia. Nor will he buy it at the still larger price, which is to link his life to her irrevocably through marriage. There are even larger prices than that, and near the end of the novel Nekhludov and Maslova are ambiguously aware of them. It is not justice that will free Maslova and Nekhludov, but truth, and truth has nothing to do with judicial error and rectification. It has everything to do with what goes on in the souls of Maslova and Nekhludov. But what goes on there is almost as tangled, complex, and misleading as that which goes on in the labyrinths of officialdom. Some of this tangle is caught in the responses of Maslova to Nekhludov's efforts at redeeming the hurt he has caused her. At first when he seeks her out in prison she has no trouble understanding him: he is one of the predators and she one of those preyed upon, and she meets him with her customary defenses of sexual manipulation. She is interested in the alcohol and tobacco his money will buy and in the judicial steps he is taking to reverse the verdict. But as she begins to grow spiritually, she gives up alcohol, tobacco, faith and interest in the judicial system. She knows that the prison outside is no different from the prison inside. Maslova and Nekhludov meet in evasion of the truth.

The offer of marriage would seem to be a decisive spiritual step beyond the efforts on his part in officialdom to reverse the verdict. It is a personal act of great proportions and consequence for his life. It is too the most appropriate "redemptive" act, because it is what Nekhludov failed to do in the first place, and it is his failure to do so that condemned Maslova to the depraved life she has subsequently led. Yet it is an act that makes Maslova recoil in anger the first time Nekhludov brings it up. She explains this to herself and to him as a reaction against being used by him a second time,—not physically as before but spiritually. There is both truth and blindness in this remark. It is true that then and now Nekhludov is concerned with is feelings: then with the predatory feelings of sex and physical enjoyment and now with the feelings of moral self-cleansing. The offer of marriage is, whatever other significance it may have, threatening to Maslova. The threat comes from the pain that is recalled from the first experience and the fear of remembering that pain.

As Nekhludov's first corruption of Maslova was his possession of her, so the offer of marriage is another move to possess her. Maslova will be redeemed when she "repossesses" herself, which happens when she begins to believe in herself and realizes that she is not the captive of the society she lives in, nor of past Maslovas and not the captive of Nekhludov's magnanimity. Nekhludov's sacrifice of his name, position, and public esteem is the right journey for him, but not necessarily for Maslova. The efforts at self-cleansing provide Maslova to remember herself as she was, but Nekhludov's efforts to sacrifice himself for her become a net into which Maslova is gently but persistently drawn. She becomes progressively the object of that magnanimity, sacrifice, self-cleansing, and as such a part of it. What Nekhludov must finally do is divest himself, too, of the self-imposed duty to sacrifice himself for Maslova. *Maslova is not his to ruin or to save.* She belongs to no one but herself, and to the God that is within her. This is why, I am convinced, Tolstoy has Maslova reject his offer of marriage when he repeats it after the reduction of her sentence and the fixing of her official fate. We have very little insight into her motives, and perhaps it doesn't matter, but her rejection of Nekhludov is a sign of her consciousness that she belongs to no one but herself.

It may very well be that Maslova is in love with Nekhludov and even possible that some form of love—other than the redemptive pity that he has pursued and that has pursued him—has grown in Nekhludov for her. There is certainly obligation on both sides: on Nekhludov's part to redeem both himself and her by remaining with her whatever her lot, and on Maslova's part to be grateful for what he has given up for her. But it is a sign of spiritual perfection that Maslova should want to leave that gratitude behind and to leave her benefactor too and tie her life with Simonson. More is involved here surely than Maslova's desire to release him from his promise to link his life with hers, thus sparing him the ruin that would follow. This speculation of Nekhludov's may be looked on as a remnant of the pre-redemptive thinking. For in Tolstoy's moral vision no ruin would come to Nekhludov in continuing to be by her side and abandoning his privileged and corrupt life.

What Nekhludov discovers and what Maslova discovers, although perceived and understood only dimly by both, is that the process of true redemption is a return to what one has been. What Nekhludov and Maslova were at the beginning is preserved in that faded picture that Nekhludov brings Maslova, which she looks at with dismay, hunger, and then affection. He brings her pain in reminding her of what she was, but he also brings her hope. The true love that they enjoyed for a short time as equals and young people with little consciousness of class is caught in the game they play on that thoughtless summer day. There is no doubt that Tolstoy wants us to contrast the image of Nekhludov and Maslova on that day and on the night when he seduces her: to contrast the spontaneity, self-possession, and naturalness of the first love and the premeditated, artificial, abstract, impersonal nature of the second love. The meeting with Maslova behind the lilac bush is "accidental" and not deliberate, and the force that bends her toward his kiss and his toward hers is unpremeditated too. But on the night that Nekhludov seduces Maslova, he forces his way past doors, implorings, and physical resistance. The innocent love is prompted by play and the personal impulses of joy and immediate sensation. The guilty love is prompted by the voices of others and the remembered gestures of others. The innocent love is crowned by sunlight and natural scents and sounds. The guilty love is shrouded by a deep mist and fog, through which Nekhludov moves as if demented and lost.

But as good and true as was the first love, something else is communicated by the flowering of first love in the summer scene, and this something tells us that if the better love is the first, it is not the best. If the lips barely touch, then it would be better if they had not touched at all. If the scene takes place within nature, the nature is not entirely benign: Nekhludov stumbles on nettles, and the blossoms that crown the love are beginning to fall. The true garden of Eden comes before he kisses or even becomes conscious of Maslova. It is when he awakens at dawn and roams the fields alone, and when as "a young man for the first time, without guidance from any one outside, realizes all the beauty and significance of life." The journey toward the purified and redemptive self is a journey toward the self, untouched by and untouching of people.

It is no accident that Simonson's interest in Maslova is not sexual; and if there is no mention of sexuality in Nekhludov's interest in a redeemed Maslova, it cannot be absent, if only in memory and recall. Tolstoy's views on sexuality had come, during the period in which *Resurrection* was written, to the point of seeing chastity as the highest form of spirituality. If such a view is foolish, it is nevertheless in keeping with the dynamism of Tolstoy's moral vision of the world, something that was already implied in *Anna Karenina* and in some of the tales after the conversion. This is not because of some personal distaste of sex—although there were doubtless personal reasons here too—but because such a view is consistent with the way Tolstoy looked upon corruption and redemption. Tolstoy has given us in *Resurrection* a fallen and a redeemed world or a demonic and paradisiacal world, which turns on an axis of self and unself. There is something of Dante's inferno in the journey that Nekhludov takes through officialdom, where every virtue has become a vice, where the natural world has become distorted, and where beasts and madmen rule. In a society where the insane are outside the prisons and the humane are inside, it comes as no great shock that the prophet of redemption is to be found in prison.

The prophet is the old man that Nekhludov first meets by the river and later in prison. He may stand as epigraphic of the novel. In his "mad" words of serving oneself and the God in oneself, he is making a summary statement not only on Tolstoy's moral vision in *Resurrection* but also in Tolstoy's vision before and beyond *Resurrection*. The old man believes in no one but himself and the God in himself, refusing to acknowledge any authority. He has no country, God, or tsar. He says: "Everyone be himself and all will be as one." Nekhludov's interest in the old man is a sign that he is touched by some sympathy, but his silence too is a sign that he does not fully understand his significance. What the old man tells us is what Maslova is beginning to understand and to embody; it is what Nekhludov possessed as a young man but sought in vain in his journey through officialdom and in his impulses of magnanimity, self-sacrifice, and self-denigration. Maslova does not need his sacrifice, for his sacrifice is part of her prison. Maslova does not need Nekhludov, Nekhludov does not need Maslova, and none of us need each other. This is the paradoxical conclusion to which *Resurrection* leads; but if we don't need each other, brotherhood is the consequence of our redemption. For men relate best when they don't relate, just as they love best when they don't love. When they strive for brotherhood by way of conscious ideals and premeditated actions, they take brotherhood into abstraction, coercion, and separation. When they become themselves, they touch others with an immediacy that is not possible otherwise.

This is why Tolstoy's fulminating tracts are a misdirection, for the path to social improvement is no more by way of institutional reform than the path to personal reform is by way of intentional brotherhood. The tracts are the illumination of the demonology that reigns in the contemporary world, shocking us into the consciousness of impersonal, abstract participation in evil, as Nekhludov is shocked into what he has done to another person without meaning to do so. It is doubtful that the demonology could have been adequately expressed without the tracts. Nekhludov, it is true, could have made his journey from no consciousness, to false consciousness, to true consciousness, just as he could have conveyed to us the callous indifference of the officials who administer the machinery of this hell. Yet it would still be a single journey, still fiction. The tracts take the fiction into time and fact; and if this is usually the death of fiction, it is not so this time. Something of the urgency of Nekhludov's agonizing quest, as well as that of Maslova, would be lost if it did not take place in the desperations of contemporary time. We have today left behind, to be sure, that particular demonology, but past facts have a way of fictionalizing themselves and thus preserving themselves. If *Resurrection* has not gone the way of Disraeli's *Sybil*, it is because Tolstoy's facts were already reaching out to fiction and his fiction to facts.

One cannot leave the novel without pointing out once again how optimistic Tolstoy's vision of life is and how it permeates this last major work of his. The title is not to be taken ironically. Although there is hardly to be found on the pages of Russian literature a more scathing attack on the corruptions of contemporary life, there is no despair. For Tolstoy, men have created the hell and misunderstood their true nature, and it is men who, by understanding themselves, can create their redemption. No matter how much men may degrade the earth—and themselves—as the first pages of the novel show, they touch only the surface of the earth and of themselves. Nature pushes forth its healing shoots in the vile air of the corrupted city, as well as in the noxious inner citadel of man. In this sense *Resurrection* is of one piece with the later works. There may be in the lives of men lechery, debauchery, self-deception, and dishonesty, as we have in *Hadji Murad*, but there are also beautiful flowers and men who lead their lives with grace and beauty as does Hadji Murad. Kautsky in *Father Sergius* may go from the vanities of fashionable life to the vanities of monastic life; he may pursue what seem to be numberless wrong paths, but he finds the right path. The journey of life for men may be across the great wasteland of the universe, fated to end by way of ever smaller circles in death, as in *Master and Man*, but it is also across the space from one heart to another. Men can give comfort to each other. The distance between despair and hope may lengthen in the late works, but it will always be traversable for Leo Tolstoy. There are no irredeemable sins in his world—no Dostoevskian tragic and uncorrecting chemistry of the soul. There is *Resurrection*.

W. W. ROWE

Some Fateful Patterns in Tolstoy

Although Leo Tolstoy is famous for his treatment of historical causation and predetermination in *War and Peace*, a variety of fateful patterns can be discerned in many of his works. These patterns include recurrent images, numbers, words and phrases, and a series of what may be termed unlikely prophets.

In *Childhood, Boyhood, and Youth* the question is raised: Will the "predictions" of the holy fool Grisha prove true? Nicholas Irtenev's mother, at least, declares that she has "good reason" to believe such predictions: "Kiryusha foretold the exact day and hour of death for deceased papa." The apparently meaningless mutterings of a holy food afford a rich opportunity for unexpected predictions: the mental deformity of such a person renders the accuracy of his predictions quite ironic.

In *War and Peace*, the one-eyed Kutuzov (who is often called "blind") sees considerably farther than many others. In *The Cossacks*, Lukashka's dumb sister tells him by hand signals that he must kill another Chechen. Later, a Chechen whom Lukashka is trying to capture alive critically wounds him.

One would scarcely expect Dolly Oblonsky, deceived by her husband in *Anna Karenina*, to be an expert forecaster of marriages. Yet as Oblonsky himself tells Levin, Dolly has "the gift of prophecy," especially concerning marriages. Then, having cited an example of Dolly's accuracy, he reveals

From *Nabokov and Others: Patterns in Russian Literature.* Copyright © 1979 by Ardis Publishers.

her prediction that Kitty will be Levin's wife "for sure." At this point, of course, the marriage is by no means "sure"—and soon appears still less so.

Mary Bolkonsky, in *War and Peace*, also seems an unlikely marriage forecaster, yet she correctly predicts that Andrew will not marry again, especially Natasha. Somewhat similarly, Natasha's "prediction" about Dolokhov's hope to marry Sonya "proves true." Moreover, Natasha correctly prophesies that Nicholas will not marry Sonya. "God knows why I know," she remarks. The accuracy of Natasha's humble, unselfish predictions seems especially appropriate in *War and Peace*, where smug, selfish predictions often prove false. Early in the novel, there is also the oddly prophetic question (*"vous trouvez que l'assassinat est grandeur d'ame?"*) put by Lise to Pierre when he is discussing Napoleon. Of course, this strange interconnection with Pierre's eventual decision to assassinate Napoleon seems quite natural in context. Yet the very naturalness of Lise's motivation tends to render her words more unexpectedly prophetic.

Tolstoy's most remarkable unlikely prophets not only lack logical insight but even reveal motivation tending to belie accuracy. As *Childhood, Boyhood, and Youth* opens, for example, Nicholas Irtenev invents a reason for crying: he pretends that he has just dreamed of his mother's death. The "dream" of course soon proves true. In *War and Peace*, Petya Rostov says that Natasha "was in love with that fat one with the glasses"—presumably for no other reason than that Natasha has just called Petya a fool. Clearly, Natasha realizes this "love" (for Pierre) only very much later. And when Sonya makes her famous predictions before the candles and mirrors, she merely feigns to see the future. "Why shouldn't I say that I saw something?" she wonders. "Others really do see!" As is well known, she unwittingly predicts not only Andrew's death (including the expression on his face?) but also Pierre's marriage to Natasha. After describing Andrew lying down, Sonya feigns to see "something blue and red," and Natasha had already told her mother that Pierre was "dark blue with red."

Early in *Anna Karenina*, Kitty enthusiastically persuades Anna to come to the ball. Anna repeatedly likens Kitty's own expectations of the ball to a blissful "fog" (*tuman*). Then, at the very moment when Kitty, in anguish, perceives the intense feeling between Anna and Vronsky, we are told that the entire ball was covered by a "fog [*tumanom*] in Kitty's soul."

Later in the novel, Dolly manages to comfort Kitty, who is suffering because of her previous passion for Vronsky. Kitty then says that she will visit Dolly to help cure her children of scarlet fever: "I have had scarlet fever," she declares. Soon after this, an ambassador's wife likens passion to scarlet fever in conversation with Vronsky. "One must pass through it," she says. Sidney Schultze has connected the passion simile with little Tanya's scarlet fever.

A fateful image pattern common to both of Tolstoy's major novels involves suggestions of childhood and fairy-tale-like pleasure. Early in *War and Peace*, Pierre is compared to "a child in a toy shop." He later plays at being Napoleon, piercing an invisible enemy with his sword. Natasha, age thirteen, runs in with her doll, and she hides in the conservatory "as if under a cap of invisibility," a Russian fairy-tale image. Such descriptions tend to unite Natasha and Pierre long before it is clear that they will marry each other.

Somewhat similarly, Levin is struck at the skating rink by Kitty's expression "of childish clarity and goodness" and by the "childishness of her face." Her smile, we are told, always carried him off to "an enchanted world where he experienced tender, soft feelings like those he recalled from rare days of his early childhood." He is also reminded of how he used to associate Kitty with an English fairy tale. Levin himself is compared, early in the novel, to a "boy," a "twelve-year-old girl," and a "child." These similar introductory descriptions tend to unite Kitty and Levin even though she soon refuses his first proposal of marriage. In a vague, suggestive dimension, the two remain subtly associated until they are in fact united.

The Cossacks affords an early example of Tolstoyan fateful patterning. In this story, after drinking wine with Olenin, Uncle Eroshka watches moths flying into the candle flame. "Fool, fool!" he says. "You're destroying your own self, and I pity you." At the end of the story they again drink, and Olenin leaves, saying: "Farewell, Uncle!" Eroshka replies: "Is that any way to say goodbye? Fool! fool! . . . You see, I love you, I pity you so!" The parallel wording may be seen to suggest that Olenin has been "destroying his own self" like a "piteous" moth, flying blindly into the passion of his love for Maryanka.

The famous description of Anna Karenina's suicide as a dying candle flame may be traced from the warm shining expression that she cannot "extinguish" upon meeting Vronsky, which grows stronger as she dances with him, to the metaphorical light at the train station as he follows her to Petersburg: "a red fire blinded her eyes," and finally, to the question she asks just two pages before the description of her death as an extinguished flame: "Why not put out the candle?"

This association of fire with Anna could cause us to wonder about the other three main characters and elements. Levin, who constantly works in the fields, can easily be associated with earth. Kitty, who is advised "to drink the waters," regains her health at "the little German waters." But is it possible to associate Vronsky, the fourth main character, with the fourth element, air? When Anna is on board the train to return to Petersburg, we may recall, she finds it "very hot" and goes out onto the platform "to get some air." There she finds that: "The wind seemed to have been just waiting for her; it joyfully whistled and wanted to seize her and carry her off. . . ." Anna breathes deeply of the cold air and looks around. She then takes "another deep breath in order to get her fill of the air"—and meets Vronsky. Why is he following her? He must be with her and "cannot do otherwise," he declares.

> At that moment the wind, as if overcoming an obstacle, scattered snow from the carriage roofs and rattled some kind of torn-off sheet of iron, and the hollow whistle of the steam engine roared mournfully and gloomily in front. All the terror of the storm seemed still more beautiful to her now. He had said what her soul desired but her reason feared.

Twice here the air seems associated with Vronsky, especially since the wind is twice appropriately personified. First, Anna feels that she needs air; the wind, waiting for her, wants to carry her off. Then, just as Vronsky says that he must be with her, the wind is said to have overcome an obstacle; he has clearly declared his intentions. And of course Anna's view of the storm as "beautiful terror" aptly suggests her attitude towards an affair with Vronsky.

These proposed elemental associations seem supported by several other factors in the novel. First, we may note that the primary elements are Anna and Levin: fire and earth are fed by air and water, respectively. And surely, Anna and Levin are the main characters; Schultze has demonstrated that the entire novel may be seen as thirty-four segments, seventeen alternately devoted to Anna and to Levin. Even on the most general level, our attention shifts back and forth, focusing on their twin arrivals in Part One, following their twin loves throughout, and merging, intensified, when they finally meet in Part Seven.

More specifically, we may note that just as fire needs air, Anna needed air when she met Vronsky on the station platform. And as earth needs water, Levin seems to need water when he works in the fields, vainly attempting to forget Kitty. Mowing with his peasants, Levin enjoys a drink of water from the river more than any drink he has ever had. And the rain unexpectedly gives him "a pleasant sensation" as he "joyously" feels it upon his shoulders. Elsewhere, as Schultze has observed, Levin is described as "a fish on land." Moreover, he finds new love for Kitty and their son in the rain, when he discovers that they have not been hit by lightning. The two main love relationships in the novel thus seem intensified by the elemental force of storms; Anna–Vronsky, by a winter snowstorm, Levin–Kitty by a spring thunderstorm.

Even the elemental incompatibility between fire and water seems consistent with the initial rivalry between Kitty and Anna for Vronsky's love. And although Anna prevails (air being more compatible with the fire than with water), she feels guilty; subsequently, water is associated with disaster for her. She unwisely reveals her feeling for Vronsky when he causes the death of Frou-Frou (who has frequently been seen to suggest Anna) at "a ditch with water." Later, when Anna thinks of what she has done to Karenin, she is likened to someone in danger of drowning. Finally, she kills herself like a bather "going into the water"—a vestige of Tolstoy's earlier plan to have Anna drown herself in the Neva River. Elementally, the water image is highly appropriate, suggesting an end both to Anna's fiery passion and to the flame of her life. Earlier, moreover, after Anna's display of emotion at the horse race, Karenin is likened to "a person who had vainly tried to extinguish a fire."

In what may be termed yet another elemental dimension of *Anna Karenina*, fire-related images may be associated with each of the four main characters. Besides Anna's image, the flame of a candle, we may note the following. When Levin arrives at the skating rink to find Kitty, she is repeatedly likened to the sun. Levin himself is strongly associated with the stars. In Part Two, various stars (and especially Venus) seem to inspire Levin to ask Oblonsky about Kitty. Later, "having gazed at the stars." Levin sees Kitty in a passing carriage and realizes that he loves *"her."* Finally as the novel ends, Levin gazes at the stars and they seem to help him find direction and meaning in his life. And Vronsky? As Schultze has demonstrated, electricity is associated with Vronsky throughout the novel.

As with the four elements, these fire-related images have several appropriate associations. Electricity is a dangerous force, especially in water—which, we recall, was Kitty's element. And as noted above, Levin fears that lightning has killed Kitty. Lightning, of course, travels through air, Vronsky's element. The sun (Kitty) warms and gives life, which aptly relates to Levin's element, earth. Finally, the flame obviously coincides with Anna's element, fire.

Yet another appropriate aspect of these images may be seen by grouping them as Kitty–Levin and Anna–Vronsky. The former images (sun–stars) suggest permanence compared to the latter (flame–electricity). This aptness even seems to include the four characters' relationships to suicide.

Anna commits suicide; Vronsky attempts it, and he can be seen to be trying to kill himself at the end of the novel. Kitty despairs, and Levin apparently comes close to suicide; but their permanence endures, and they survive.

If such patterns exist in *War and Peace*, they are not as consistent. Pierre seems associated with fire: he himself relates the brilliant comet of 1812 to the condition of his soul. He also makes his famous declaration about the futility of holding his "immortal soul" captive against a quite fiery background: the "fire-like" haze of the rising moon and "the red fires of camp-fires." Moreover, Pierre remains in the burning city of Moscow and saves a child in a flaming building. However, water is suggested by the "globe of droplets" that Pierre sees when Platon Karataev dies. This "liquid" globe seems to inspire Pierre's vision of himself sinking "somewhere into the water, so that the water closed over his head." In addition, Natasha sees Pierre as having emerged from a Russian bath *(banya)* near the end of the novel. Perhaps both Pierre and Anna Karenina may be seen as moving from association with fire to submersion in water, with the difference that Pierre emerges, and then is further cleansed by the *banya*.

Volume Three, part one of *War and Peace* opens to focus on the question: What caused the War of 1812? After arguing that there were an incalculable number of causes, Tolstoy concludes that the war had no single, exceptional cause: ". . . the event had to occur only because it had to occur." His point, as he finally puts it, is that no matter how much control we seem (from our perspective) to have over our actions, they are nevertheless, in terms of historical causation, "determined from eternity" *(opredeleno predvechno)*. This phrase is later combined with the above notion "had to occur" *(dolzhno bylo sovershit'sya)* at a key point in Pierre's life. Having decided that his own name, like Napoleon's, has the fateful numerological value 666, Pierre concludes that his role (as Napoleon's killer) is "determined from eternity" and therefore, that he must not undertake anything (such as joining the army) but rather wait for what "has to occur."

Pierre's calculations are based upon a prophecy taken from the Revelation of St. John. According to the Apocalypse, "the beast" is a man whose number is 666. With very flexible figuring, Pierre manages to match both his own name and Napoleon's to the number 666. He thus deems it his lot to kill "the beast," and he lists what he feels are the fateful forces in his life: his love for Natasha, Antichrist, Napoleon's invasion, the comet, 666, and the two names with this numerological value.

This emphasis upon fateful sixes may cause us to wonder if there are others. The following examples seem to suggest that in *War and Peace*, and perhaps even elsewhere, Tolstoy sometimes associates the number six with a nearness to—and an escape from—death. Pierre of course does not succeed in carrying out his 666-inspired plan to kill Napoleon.

As many have noted, we are quite pointedly told that Pierre's father has his "sixth stroke" while the "sixth anglaise" is being played. These "sixth's" seem quite ominously juxtaposed, yet Pierre's father dies only after one more stroke, so the pattern of six-related escape from death seems to hold.

Pierre himself is close to death twice. Late in the novel, as the French execute prisoners, we are told that Pierre was "the sixth" in line to be shot. The prisoners are then executed *in pairs* until the fifth, a young factory worker, is shot alone: Pierre unexpectedly survives. Earlier at the duel with Dolokhov, Pierre, "having walked about six steps," had somehow managed to wound his adversary, how then fired with great effort and missed. Not only does this "six" typically attend an unlikely escape from death (Pierre has never before held a pistol in his hand), Tolstoy clearly suggests that the outcome of the duel was fated.

Early in *Resurrection*, we learn that Katyusha was the daughter of an unmarried serf woman whose first five children had been allowed to die of starvation.

> The sixth child, fathered by a gypsy tramp, was a girl, and her fate would have been the very same, but it happened that one of the two older ladies . . . gave milk and money to the mother, and the little girl remained alive. And so the older ladies called her "the saved one."

In the overall context of Tolstoy's world, it seems quite appropriate that this "sixth" child comes so close to death and yet survives. Note also the reference to Katyusha's "fate."

As a kind of corollary to the notion that Tolstoyan sixes may be associated with escape from death, the number seven (perhaps one step further?) sometimes seems related to death itself. For example, the old Count Bezukhov does in fact die soon after his seventh stroke. Moreover, on the page following the ominous juxtaposition of sixth's ("stroke" and "anglaise"), we find a juxtaposition of sevens. The old Count is said to be in his "seventh decade," and this is immediately followed by a reference to someone who received the sacrament "seven times" before dying. The crowd that kills Vereshchagin is likened to the "seventh and last wave that shatters a ship." The Freemasons whom Pierre joins have a list of "seven virtues," and number seven is "The love of death."

In *Sebastopol in May*, the fatally wounded Parskukhin decides to count soldiers. He reaches a total of seven before he dies. In *War and Peace*, it is repeatedly noted that General Schmidt was killed "at seven o'clock." Curiously enough, Anna Pirogova, the model for Anna Karenina, arrived at the railroad station "at seven o'clock" and threw herself under "train number seven." In the novel itself, Vronsky is given "number seven" for the race in which he causes Frou-Frou's death.

Seeking out Levin at his hotel, Oblonsky says: "Levin—number seven, eh?" Finding "number seven," Oblonsky enters and exclaims: "Ah! Killed it?" This refers to the bear that Levin has recently killed. The two friends than discuss "death" at some length, and Levin declares that death haunts him.

Returning to *War and Peace*, we may note that if Nicholas's disastrous loss to Dolokhov at cards may be considered a symbolic death, it is the "seven of hearts" that does him in. Tolstoy repeatedly stresses the fateful seven: Nicholas's decision to stake on it, his agonizing wait for a seven to appear, and his refusal to believe that "a stupid chance" would cause "the seven" to ruin him. There is even what could be termed a "life review" of past experiences that flashes before Nicholas immediately prior to his "death" by the seven.

> At that minute his home life—little jokes with Petya, conversations with Sonya, duets with Natasha, piquet with his father and even his peaceful bed in the Povarsky house—appeared to him with such force, clarity and charm that it all seemed a long-past, lost, and unappreciated happiness.

By what seems a coincidence, Tolstoy uses the word "seven" (*semyorka*) seven times in describing this fateful episode.

As R. F. Christian has demonstrated, various kinds of repetition are a major distinguishing feature of Tolstoy's style. Tolstoyan repetitions sometimes form parts of fateful patterns. In *Anna Karenina*, when Levin finally meets Anna, he notices something special about her: "Besides intelligence, grace, and beauty, she also had truthfulness." The Russian word *pravdivost'*, here rendered "truthfulness," also has connotations of sincerity and uprightness. Levin feels "truthfulness" deeply; in fact, it is a dominant characteristic of his beloved Kitty. Kitty's "truthful [*pravdivie*] eyes" are frequently mentioned, for example both times Levin proposes to her. An especially significant reference occurs in Part Three of the novel, when Levin gazes at the sky just before dawn, pondering the changes in his views of life. A carriage passes by, and two "truthful eyes" look out at him. We are told that this was Kitty only five lines later, but by the adjective *pravdivie*, one could have guessed. "There were no other eyes like those in the world. There was only one being in the world capable of focusing for him the entire world and meaning of life." Truthfulness is thus developed as a crucial quality for Levin, and it seems quite significant that he singles out this quality in Anna, especially so late in the novel.

After Kitty passes by in the carriage, Levin decides that a "mysterious [*tainstvennaya*] change" in the clouds confirms a great change in his own life. Then, just prior to Levin's successful proposal, we are told that he and Kitty had "not a conversation, but some sort of mysterious [*tainstvennoe*] communication." Very early in the novel, this same word had been continually applied to Levin's impressions of Kitty, her family, and love.

Schultze has demonstrated that the influence of strange forces upon the characters in *Anna Karenina* is frequently suggested by the repetition of various words and phrases. Perhaps most strikingly, a person is said to act "involuntarily" or "against his will." As the novel opens, we are told twice in one sentence that Oblonsky smiled "entirely involuntarily" when exposed in his affair with the French governess. And when his sister Anna first meets Vronsky, her face displays an immediate, vital attraction that shines out "against her will" and "despite her will." In *War and Peace*, as Pierre begins the duel (discussed above) that he quite miraculously wins against Dolokhov, we are told that the affair was taking place "independent of the will of people."

While such wordings, as Schultze observes, may suggest either positive or negative forces, Tolstoy also employs three other phrases which consistently seem to fit a patterned evaluation. Two are positive; one is negative. In *War and Peace*, Nicholas is told by the Governor's wife that he should marry Princess Mary. Thinking of Sonya, he answers: "Still *ma tante*, this cannot be." Later, as he begins to read Sonya's letter: ". . . his eyes fearfully and joyfully opened wide. 'No, this cannot be!' he said aloud." Near the end of the novel, Pierre has difficulty recognizing Natasha: "But no, this cannot be," he thinks. "This cannot be she." He then realizes that he loves her: ". . . and still more strongly an agitation of joy and fear seized his soul."

With both Nicholas and Pierre, a mixture of "joy and fear" and the feeling that "this cannot be" precede a happy marriage that seems somewhat unlikely. This pattern holds in *Anna Karenina*. When Levin arrives at the skating rink, seeking Kitty: "He knew she was there by the joy and fear that seized his heart." Then, when he proposes, she answers: "This cannot be . . . forgive me. . . ." Later, Levin intensely recalls these words. Finally, when he sees Kitty at the Oblonskys', he feels "such joy and together such fear, that it took his breath away." Soon they both have "a feeling of joyful fear," and Levin proposes again, this time successfully. With only the first letter of each word, he asks Kitty the fateful question: "When you answered me 'this cannot be,' did it mean never, or then?"

Her reply ("Then I could not answer otherwise") echoes yet another patterned Tolstoyan phrase, one that is temporarily negative. When Levin's first proposal is refused, he answers: "This could not be otherwise." These words, in Tolstoyan reality, sometimes appear when a positive, flexible character resigns himself to a temporary setback by a current of fate. In *War and Peace*, Pierre feels "that Helene not only could, but must be his wife, that this could not be otherwise." Then, when the old Prince Kuragan cleverly congratulates the pair, Pierre thinks: "All this must be so and could not be otherwise." Since Pierre is ultimately destined for Natasha, the repeated phrase "this could not be otherwise" attends a fateful setback similar to Levin's unsuccessful first proposal.

To summarize: the Tolstoyan phrases "This cannot be" *étogo ne mozhet byt'*) and "joy and fear" (*radost' i strakh*) tend to signal that two positive characters will ultimately be united. The words "This could not be otherwise" (*éto ne moglo byt' inache*) typically suggest that a positive, flexible character is resigning himself to a temporary setback by a current of fate. The idea of resignation to such a setback is of course central to *War and Peace*. On the largest scale, Russia temporarily and painfully concedes Moscow to the French—only to win in the end. Quite similarly, both Pierre and Natasha give in, temporarily and painfully, to Helene and Anatole—only to find each other at the end. The pattern extends even to the use of the French language at these two key points in the novel. Pierre, resigned to marrying Helene, awkwardly declares *"Je vous aime!"* Anatole, beginning his conquest of Natasha, announces: *"Mais charmante!"* Yet Pierre's and Natasha's Russianness seems fated to triumph eventually.

As we have seen, Tolstoy's works contain a variety of fateful patterns. He favors characters who may be termed unlikely prophets, whose unexpected insights suggest that the future can sometimes be discerned. Other fateful patterns include images of childhood and fairy-tale-like pleasure (which anticipate the union of positive characters), various elemental images, survival- and death-related sixes and sevens, and recurrent words and phrases. As employed by Tolstoy, one of these phrases ("It could not be otherwise") may be seen to suggest that positive, flexible characters are ultimately rewarded for not resisting a temporary setback by a current of Fate.

NATALIA KISSELEFF

Idyll and Ideal:
Aspects of Sentimentalism in
Tolstoy's "Family Happiness"

Of the early works of Lev Tolstoy, none has received less attention than his short novel *Family Happiness*. The neglect may in part stem from Tolstoy's own negative opinion of this work. After finishing the first part, he sent it to V. P. Botkin, his publisher. Upon re-reading the proofs, Tolstoy considered publishing it under a pseudonym; after it appeared in *Russkii vestnik*, he wrote that the novel was "shameful trash, disgusting filth, and a moral and artistic blotch." The novel had been written hurriedly, from January to April 1859. Although there is no definite notation indicating when it was begun, a diary entry in February 1859, after a long hiatus, shows that Tolstoy had resumed writing. The entry reads: "I have all this while been working on a novel and have accomplished a great deal, but not on paper. I have changed everything. A poema. I am quite pleased with what I have in my head. The plot [fabula] unchanged is ready." The indication, poema, seems to intimate that the new work has to be of a lyric nature. Many critics have esteemed the first lyrical part more highly than the second. Botkin, however, found the first part boring and praised the second part highly. The comparison of the lyrical character of *Family Happiness* with the short novels of I. S. Turgenev greatly disturbed Tolstoy, and has since disturbed those who cannot conceive of Tolstoy as writing in the style of the "art for art's sake school."

From *Canadian Slavonic Papers*. Copyright © 1979 by *Canadian Slavonic Papers*.

Apart from a few avuncular comments about "the gentle charm of the work," there have been no attempts to analyse the work or to discuss it in the perspective of its place in Tolstoy's literary development. Most critics have reiterated Boris Eikhenbaum's opinion that *Family Happiness* is a flawed work and that the second part contradicts or negates the lyricism of the first part without leading to a convincing resolution. There is no disagreement either with the view that the novel presents a typical Tolstoyan perspective of marriage and family life as an eventual disillusionment. The biographical nexus of *Family Happiness* to Tolstoy's personal relationship with Valeriia Arsenieva has also commanded more attention than it deserves. Eikhenbaum's magisterial study of Tolstoy's life and literary evolution has greatly influenced critical opinion of *Family Happiness*. Eikhenbaum's consideration of the feminist problem during the 1850s, his regard for the influence of Proudhon and Michelet, and his view that the novel is in part a polemic with the views of George Sand, impose a strong extraliterary perspective on the novel, which has not been corrected. In addition, Eikhenbaum's view that Tolstoy's lyric tone and the adoption of a romantic discriptive style resulted in an inorganic fusion of styles has influenced many subsequent studies, particularly by those who consider that the Tolstoyan objectivity and concreteness of detail does not fit with the form of notes and with the lyrical landscapes created in the spirit of Turgenev or F. I. Tuitchev. The idea that the novel was a projection of Tolstoy's ideal of conjugal bliss marred by the experience he had with Arsenieva also originates with Eikhenbaum; and as R. F. Christian, following Eikhenbaum, sums up: "His letters to Arsenieva (1856) . . . are the best source material for *Family Happiness*." Only a few critical articles have since contributed much to the understanding of the novel. The Soviet view is that the novel was an echo of Tolstoy's volatile relationship with Arsenieva as well as a programmatic novel depicting social problems of nineteenth-century upper-class women in Russia.

The attribution of a specific philosophic influence and the discussion of the Arsenieva–Tolstoy relationship overlooks another more appropriate and more logical source for the novel and for its ideas and characters. The ideal woman for Tolstoy, the standard against which he measured all women, and the model which served him for many of his female characters was his mother, Mariia Nikolaevna Tolstaia. Tolstoy could not have remembered her and not too much is known about her. But, she was venerated and idealized by him. Her life, or what we know of it, centred on her husband and her children. More pertinently, Masha, her namesake of the novel, corresponds in many ways to Mariia Nikolaevna as she was described in one of Tolstoy's diaries: "She was a woman whose life was spent in the care of children, reading novels aloud to my grandmother in the evening, in serious reading such as Rousseau's *Emile* and discussing what had been read, in playing the piano, in teaching Italian to one of my aunts, in walks and in managing the household." The description could as well be applied to the activities of Masha. Her guided development follows all of the activities that circumscribed the life of Tolstoy's mother, as indeed it describes the activities of most of the gentry women of that age. Although Masha moves away from this model of life in Part II, the concluding sentence leads us to imagine her life as being in no way different from that of Tolstoy's mother, and this life was the ideal transgressed by Masha.

> Before this I had read only because I was bored—now books became one of my greatest pleasures, and this only because we read books and talked about them together, and he brought new ones to me. Before this, the time I devoted to Sonia and the lessons I gave her had been a hard task that I forced myself to fulfill only from a sense of duty. Then one day he was present at a lesson and I began to find pleasure in following Sonia's progress. Before this it had seemed impossible for me to learn an entire piece on the piano, but now, knowing that he would hear and it might be, praise me, I played the same passage over forty times . . . and still it did not bore me.

The motivation behind Masha's activities is also in keeping with the Tolstoyan ideal, possibly derived from Rousseau's *La Nouvelle Heloise,* where the moral development of Julie is combined with the sentimental education furnished by St. Preux. With respect to Tolstoy's mother, the legacy of two sentimental poems she left and her dedication to her marriage connect with thoughts that Masha adopts, and which Tolstoy incorporated into other novels, such as *The Cossacks:* ". . . the only happiness was in living for others, and I agreed with him completely. I was sure we should be serenely happy together forever. I did not dream of trips abroad, nor of gaiety and brilliance, but of an entirely different life—a peaceful family life in the country, a life of constant self-sacrifice and love for one another, in which there would always be the consciousness of a gentle and helpful Providence watching over everything."

It is to this Tolstoyan ideal that Masha returns after passing through the crucible of experience. In all of the first part there is very little that is reminiscent of the shallow and flighty Arsenieva, except for the little story that Sergei Mikhailovich tells Masha when he projects their relationship into that of the fictitious A and B: "She imagined, poor thing, because of her inexperience, that she really could love him, and she agreed to be his wife. And he, fool that he was, believed—yes, he really believed—that his life would begin all over again. But soon she saw that she had deceived him and he had deceived her. . . ."

This passage, in essence, describes the Arsenieva–Tolstoy relationship, but it is only a false movement in the novel before the emotional scene in which Sergei declares his love. To see the novel as compensatory for the way Tolstoy treated Arsenieva is to miss the first manifestation of Tolstoy's ideal woman which he projected in many of his fictional works. The ingenuous heroine of the idyllic first part is quite far removed from the vain and frivolous image of Arsenieva that we derive from the letters that passed between them. Masha, reflecting many of the qualities of Tolstoy's ideal, is the future Natasha Rostova in embryonic form, particularly with her impulsive generous nature, her girlish dreams and her musical talent. Her debut into society in Part II is also comparable to that of Natasha with the same subsequent sequence of events: the two are dazzled by the social whirl and have their heads turned. The seduction of Masha differs from the seduction of Natasha by Anatole Kuragin only in the skill with which Tolstoy was able to describe the scene in the later novel. Even the conclusion of Family Happiness is in keeping with the domesticity of later positive heroines, and a return to the idealized life led by his mother: "My old love remained a dear memory of what would never return, but a new feeling of love for my children and for the father of my children provided the beginning of another happy life, but an entirely different one, and this life has not ended to this day." This conclusion is hardly incongruous with the tenor of the work, and it echoes the plan of married life iterated first by Masha and then by Sergei Mikhailovich: "I have found what is necessary for happiness—a quiet secluded life here in the country with an opportunity to do good to others—it's so easy to do good to those who are not used to it; then work that seems to be worthwhile, leisure, nature, books, music, the love of one's dear ones—that is my idea of happiness, and I cannot imagine anything finer."

The pattern of the novel is not the shattering of an ideal of married life. It is, instead, the dream which is recaptured and for which the actual and idealized are brought together. The false ideal is also brought to bear upon the events of the novel. Masha's false ideal is her rather diffuse vision of a slim and spare hero, with a pale and sad face. This image becomes a reality as represented by Marquis D, whose whole purpose is to turn life into a romance. Tolstoy plays with a false romanticism which, in keeping with trends both in his fiction and in his thought, is rejected. In keeping with a false romantic ideal is Tolstoy's sketchy portrait of the Marquis and

the seduction scene utilizing a florid, almost purple prose unusual for Tolstoy, even in his early works. Furthermore, the episode in Part II is a
realization of the remarks of Sergei about love in Part I: "I always picture
to myself what a puzzled expression there ought to be on the face of Lieu-
tenant Strelskii, or of Alfred, when he says, 'I love you Eleanora,' thinking
that something unusual should happen, and nothing does." After all, nothing happens between Masha and the Marquis. Masha, although attracted,
rejects the advances of the Marquis and rediscovers that her real ideal is
her marriage. The contrast between the actual and idealized is not only an
integral part of the novel and of Tolstoy's conception of marriage, it is a
pattern which characterizes the pastoral, sentimental novel and many didactic-moralistic novels of an earlier age, which William Empson delimits
as an "ideal simplicity approached by resolving contradiction." Empson also
posits an embodiment of a fundamental sense of nature for the pastorale,
and Tolstoy, in his use of lyric descriptions and in several other respects,
returns to this tradition of the sentimentalist novel. *Family Happiness* reflects
Tolstoy's search for form and his use of the sentimentalist canon before he
ended his literary apprenticeship in the early 1860s.

In his study of the young Tolstoy, Eikhenbaum discusses Tolstoy's
spiritual and aesthetic affinity not only with Rousseau, Laurence Sterne,
and N. M. Karamzin, but with other writers of the sentimentalist school.
He notes the sentimentalists' practice of merging detailed descriptions with
lyrical digressions, which suffuses everything with a haziness of mood. According to Eikhenbaum, Tolstoy diverged from this practice, but his examples are from the early Tolstoy tales of Cossack raids; he neglects the
obvious use of this type of description in *Family Happiness*. In passing,
Eikhenbaum notes a characteristic of Tolstoy's early work in that the landscape is an element of narrative form which, as in the sentimentalist novel,
was used as a head piece and as a tail piece framing it. It is this device,
which works on an equal footing with portraiture at a time when character
development was less prominent, that fulfills the primary role of structuring
function that I have assigned to it. The schematization for which Tolstoy
has been reproached is the very quality of sentimentalist prose that makes
Family Happiness a novel which looks back to the eighteenth century.

In addition to the points brought out by Eikhenbaum, there are
several other traditions of the sentimentalist novel which have their correspondence in Tolstoy's piece. One is the tradition of the "Rührstuck" or
country piece, which opposed the world and society of the city to the
solitary life of the country. Characteristic of this type of novel were the
emotional conflicts between family members which were resolved in a final

exchange of tender emotion. Another motif was the "implied sense of emotional revenge, where the denial of emotion which opened another source of emotional graitification was finally resolved by the pleasure of forgiveness or reconciliation." During the period of Masha's estrangement from her husband in chapter VII of Part II, both with respect to the emotional confrontation and to Sergei's cold withdrawal, which continues until the last scene, there is a similar emotional tension which Masha describes in her reflections on the past at the opening of chapter VIII. "From that day on our life and our relations changed completely. . . . We both seemed to be aware of the gulf that separated us and were afraid to approach it. . . . I was convinced that he was proud and quick-tempered and that I must be careful not to offend him. He was convinced that I was unable to live without fashionable society, that I disliked country life, and that he must reconcile himself to my low taste."

Moreover, the opening section, where the instruction given to Masha on how to occupy her time initiates the didactic-moralistic line of the novel, has its correspondence in an aesthetic attitude expressed by the eighteenth-century Russian sentimentalist, M. N. Muraviev: Virtue was to know how to master one's own self. Only he who achieved this aim was considered free and would not have cause to quarrel with fate. Every minute would bring him some enjoyment and boredom would not arise. There was a stress on life in and for the family. This attitude lends itself to Sergei Mikhailovich's admonition to Masha that she should not become a pampered young lady, unable to endure solitude and for whom everything is for show and superficial.

The narrative technique of personal reminiscence with frequent interpolated questions ("zachem," "ot-chego," "pochemu"), the use of pastoral elements, the repeated lyrical images (the garden, the lilac, the nightingale), and the quasiallegorical use of the seasons are some other characteristics Tolstoy shares with the sentimentalists. During his literary apprenticeship—when he experimented with different narrative techniques, genres and styles—there are notable analogies with the traditions of the eighteenth century. Not least of these are the characteristics derived from Sterne's works: the general intimacy of narrative tone, the stress on descriptive detail, the absence of complicated plot pattern, the naive or child-like viewpoint, and the frequent mix of gesture with dialogue ("podozhdem ikh,—skazala ia i vyshla na terrasu, nadeias' chto i on poidet za mnoiu."; "kuda ty?—sprosila ia, uderzhyvaia ego.—zdes' tak khorosho"). One of the curious examples of the last device occurs very early in the narrative, when Masha describes the sadness pervading the household:

"Seldom did anyone come to see us, and those who did brought no joy. They all wore sad faces and spoke softly, as though afraid of waking someone; they never laughed, but only sighed and often wept when they looked at me, and even more often when they looked at little Sonia in her black frock." Although it may be regarded as part of the Tolstoyan device of "making strange" (*ostranenie*), the perception of the visitors is closer to the naive view of a very young child than a seventeen-year-old girl, and is furthermore strikingly similar to the perception of the young Irtenev in *Childhood:* "All the outsiders who were at the funeral repelled me. Their phrases of condolence which they expressed to my father—that she had passed on to a better world, that she was not for this earth—aroused some kind of sadness in me."

Tolstoy's observance of a sentimentalist detached point of view and his borrowing from Sterne, Rousseau and possibly Töpfer have been noted too often to require further discussion. However, many of the lexical, rhetorical and stylistic features characteristic of *Childhood* were carried over to *Family Happiness.* The plot and the characters are rather schematically sketched and follow the tradition of the sentimental novel in which the didactic aim, the lyric descriptions and the evocation of emotion are more important than the development of characters. Tolstoy's use of the temp-tation scene and the near fall of the heroine is a standard feature of one type of sentimental novel. The "fall" motif which makes Masha one of Pamela's daughters is presaged in the first part by the episode in the cherry orchard. The relationship between Masha and Sergei Mikhailovich is one of unequals. Their growing emotional attachment reaches its peak in the season of fructification. The locked gate to the garden forces Sergei to climb over the wall. Feeling himself to be alone in the garden, he reveals his feelings for Masha. Masha, who has climbed up, watches him, and her insight into his feelings gives her power. In effect, she invades the forbidden garden of Sergei's private thoughts. Formerly in the position of inferior, Masha asserts her independence and jumps down to pick the cherries herself. In the amatory relationship she becomes an equal, for he fears and loves her now as much as she fears and loves him. The revelation of Sergei's vulnerability is also the beginning of independent life for Masha, but at the same time it is a step toward the expulsion from paradise as she eats of the fruit of knowledge in both a literal and a figurative sense. The second part of *Family Happiness* continues the theme of the expulsion from paradise, and further use is made by Tolstoy of a Rousseauistic motif—that of the innocent or natural man who is corrupted by civilization. The novel about marriage was written when Tolstoy had temporarily abandoned his project of writing about the Cossacks, yet there are connections between these two novels, particularly in relation to the world of nature and to the emotional impact of nature on man.

The use of a natural environment to define character and consciousness is a feature of many of Tolstoy's works. It is a particularly strong feature of his early works, including *The Snowstorm,* part of *Childhood, Boyhood, and Youth, The Cossacks* and *Family Happiness.* In *Family Happiness* the metaphor of the seasons operates on two levels. It serves to create the idyll, but it also serves as a structuring device. The novel encompasses a period of about four years. The cycle of the seasons is tied to the cyclical progress of the relationship between Masha and Sergei. Each stage of emotional rise or fall is specified by the seasonal change. The love affair grows with the coming of spring, and the gathering of the harvest is also the time of Masha's emotional harvest. The first cycle ends with their marriage, when the sheaves have been taken in the rowan berries flame on the bushes, when there is a frost but the sun still pours light. As Masha notes, "There was not a single cloud in the clear cold sky, nor could there have been." Thus, the seasonal movements of one cycle end with the marriage. In the first part, the seasons are tied to Masha's growth and maturation. The second part returns to the winter of her discontent which parallels her restlessness during the first winter. During the second bleak winter, they move to the city where Masha stays until after Easter. The second part of the novel covers three cyclical periods and there is a final return to the season of spring at the end of the novel, which also marks the end of her quest for experience. The reconciliation takes place in the garden which was the locus of the first idyll. The cyclical movement of the novel and the changing seasons describe two arcs: the first is an ascending curve which returns to the season of winter—the low point, while the second describes a descending curve as the relationship deteriorates. The final point brings us back to the same season which began the second cycle. The reconciliation of the couple coincides with the seasonal change to spring.

The first line of the novel, "My nasili trauer po materi," followed by "ostalis' odni s Katei i s Sonei" attaches the gloom of winter to the event that precedes Masha's comment—her mother's death. "It was a sad and gloomy winter we spent in our old house in Pokrovskoye. The weather was cold and windy and the snow drifted up higher than the windows, which were frosted over most of the time. We hardly left the house all winter, and made no calls." The melancholic mood is changed with the arrival of the catalyst of Masha's emotional growth, Sergei Mikhailovich. He comes in March as if to wake the household from its wintry sleep and to stimulate the growth of the young violet, as he calls Masha. The metaphor of the seasons and the use of the lyric landscape descriptions are also tied to the didactic aim indicated by the epigraph from Michelet, "Il faut qu tu crées ta femme," which Eikhenbaum and others have considered as descriptive of Tolstoy's central focus in the novel. In relation to Masha's education, both in the first and second parts, it reaches back to the exemplary novels of Samuel Richardson, which educate the reader while detailing the tribulations of the heroes. The novel of search, illusion, loss and recovery is contained within the narration of past events from a present perspective. The distancing of past events also contributes to the elegiac atmosphere. The replication of the past is not objectively detailed, for there is often a line which further adds to the melancholic reflections of the narrator: "Ia togda eshche ne znala chto eto liubov', Ia dumala chto eto tak vsegda mozhet byt', chto tak darom daetsia eto chuvstvo."

The changing relationship is supported not only by the changing seasons, but is framed as well by the descriptions of the garden at Pokrovskoye and the components of lilacs, nightingales and music. Music, one of the lyric or emotion engendering factors, which was a particularly strong motif in a number of early Tolstoy works, is also connected to Tolstoy's didactic line. The discipline that Masha learns in order to perform a Beethoven sonata is part of her education. Tolstoy makes use of her playing to distinguish between artificial (insincere) art and that which evokes natural feeling. Music and its reception, and the use of music in generating emotion also acts as a barometer of the fluctuating relationship between the two. The nadir of emotion at the beginning of the novel is a time when Masha cannot practice. But with the introduction of Sergei Mikhailovich into the household, Masha renews her interest in music. Her first playing of the *adagio* from the Beethoven sonata (which is appropriately known by its common appellation—the "Moonlight Sonata") is complimented with the remark that she appears to understand music. Masha's mastery of musical technique is matched by her ability to convey emotion through her playing, and until the sounding of the first discordance in her marriage, music is part of the shared emotional experience between Masha and Sergei. Tolstoy stresses that her playing was not perfect, but was infused with an expressive quality. The musical motif is carried over into the second part. As Masha becomes involved with the social life of St. Petersburg and Moscow, she begins to lose all interest in music. Only once is music referred to prior to Masha's return to Pokrovskoye; this happens when she goes out to hear music after her illness. After her return to the familial estate, Masha takes up the practice of playing, and this in turn attracts the attention of

Sergei who comes in to hear her. The return to the locus of their idyll and the resumption of musical study lead to the emotional recovery and reconciliation. The standard cliches of romantic description—flowers in bloom, moonlight, nightingales—are reminders that Tolstoy's writing was not without its banal moments. Even the quiet lyric descriptions, however, attach to the concept of nature of the sentimentalist age where it was at times an idyllic backdrop, but where it was also a pleasant instructor of refined sentiment leading to moral education. The essential difference, which is noted by both René Wellek and Rudolf Neuhäuser, between sentimental and romantic nature-description is that nature functions as an allegory for the sentimentalist (as in the fable), and as a symbol for the romantic. Tolstoy's use of nature is fully in keeping with nature as an allegory, and this is what distinguishes its descriptions from those of Turgenev.

Family Happiness may be considered a lesser novel. It is in many ways, however, a novel that meets the criteria of sentimentalist poetics as defined by one Russian sentimentalist: ". . . the genuine worth of novels has to be understood as this. They should not only be interesting but should not contain anything unnatural, insulting and bad for the tender ear, which might also stimulate vice. To the contrary, [novels] should contain much lively and active moral instruction, which would also be an incentive to do good. Most of all, they should have such scenes, which might move the innermost heart and excite tears of pleasure in the readers, so that the soul would pass through pleasant and delicious excitement."

Family Happiness may have been Tolstoy's leave-taking of the sentimentalist age and of the tradition which influenced much of his early work. It may have been precisely because he was aware of how much *Family Happiness* corresponded to writing which dwelt on the sensibility of man that made him reject it, for in his view it was regressive. That realization may have also caused him to abandon literature, as he did for several years.

ROBERT WEXELBLATT

Symbolism in
"The Death of Ivan Ilych"

Our first attempt to lean over the side of a boat to grab a shimmering fish teaches us that the medium determines the angle of refraction. Though it is clear that Tolstoy's realism and Kafka's symbolism reveal the depths at different angles—the one far more distorting than the other to be sure—even here the differences may be less obvious than they appear.

To avoid the obvious it will be better not to ask whether Tolstoy is less "symbolic" than Kafka than in what respects their symbols differ. Take the pouffe and the apple for instances. The "low pouffe" which shows up in the first chapter of *Ivan Ilych* is a real enough pouffe, located in an overstuffed sitting-room just as one would expect. Certainly it does not seem to us of any immediate importance, let alone a symbol. Ivan's friend and colleague Peter Ivanovich sits down on this pouffe during his rather comically awkward interview with Ivan's widow, Praskovya. We are attending to the behavior of the two people, thinking the pouffe is there for no particular reason other than to serve as a realistic stage property. And yet how the thing acts up, distracting us from the widow and the friend, calling attention to itself. First the springs "yield under" Peter's weight. Then, when he rises to free Praskovya's caught veil, "the springs of the pouffe rise also and give him a push." The same action is repeated, audibly this time, with "creaks." A whole page later we see Peter at the end of the interview bowing while "keeping control of the springs of the pouffe which immediately began quivering under him."

Here is the art which conceals itself fairly well, though not so utterly that we will miss it altogether. The comic routine of the rebellious pouffe turns a realistic object which would otherwise be beneath our notice into a symbol worth remarking. In effect, Tolstoy uses the pouffe to offer us a rather slapstick version of the coming action, much as dramatists once used dumb-shows. Peter, a "little Ivan" himself, is embarrassed and discomfited; the whole scene is robbed of its conventional decorum not only by the spilled ashes, snagged veil, and contradictory concerns of Praskovya, or by Peter's longing to be on the other side of town playing cards, but also and specifically by that commonplace low pouffe. The alien nature of objects of comfort and decoration—who has not kicked an offensive coffee-table?—is thus established right away and we are meant to recollect the episode when we learn of Ivan's fatal fall, as Peter unwittingly does here: "As he sat down on the pouffe Peter recalled how Ivan had arranged this room and had consulted him regarding this pink cretonne with green leaves." We may also think of the pouffe when we read that death is an "It," a force of nature, which undermines all Ivan's complacency and pretension. Peter does not desire the pouffe to push him around—no more did Ivan desire his wife to become pregnant or that he should begin to die. Birth and death, those fearful chances of nature, shatter our plans, so to speak.

So Tolstoy has his symbols too. But it is the apparent innocence of Tolstoy's method which so much contrasts with Kafka's, as well as the number, context, and provenance of his symbols. Tolstoy squeezes the expected, the normal, until it positively creaks for him. His story is controlled both by him and by familiar realities; it is really a collaboration in which the transcendent ideal, the departure from reality, has only the last word in the final chapter. But Kafka has left all that behind in his first sentence. Thus if he wants to present us with a symbol there is no need whatever to conceal its origins or to account for them more than perfunctorily. A fine example of the arbitrary appearance of a symbolic object occurs on the altogether amazing last page of Part Two, when Mr. Samsa is chasing Gregor in circles around the family room:

> . . . suddenly something lightly flung landed close behind him and rolled before him. It was an apple; a second apple followed immediately . . . his father was determined to bombard him.

The apples come as much out of nowhere, the mention of a "dish on the sideboard" notwithstanding, as does the metamorphosis itself, and are almost as full of meanings. The mortal wound Gregor receives from one of these apples puts us in mind of Eden; for the symbol is also an allusion.

"Sometimes I believe that I understand the Fall . . . as no other person," Kafka once wrote. Sin, death, and awareness—the three elements of the Fall—join together in the circle of throbbing pain around Gregor's wound. This circle in turn recalls all the other circles and rotations in the story, from the circular motion of the key in Gregor's lock to the pursuit around the family room, gathering all these images about its dead but excruciating center. This passage is also a fine example of Kafka's characteristic blending of the religious and the psychological, since outside reality all meanings may be present at once. In the context provided by the graphic Oedipal nightmare which follows on its heels—with the half-naked mother "in complete union" with the father, begging for her son's life—the episode of the apple-wound simultaneously represents a psychic laceration. No detail is missed. Even the "small red apples" which roll "about the floor as if magnetized and cannon into each other" hint horribly at castration.

Little wonder that the two stories should feel so utterly different. Nor is it surprising that Kafka's inwardness reminds people of dreams, since in dreams, too, objective reality is turned askew, not always arbitrarily, but often in ways made portentous and significant by inner compulsion. However, in Kafka the dream is never for itself. It was in speaking of this story to his young friend Janouch that Kafka epitomized at once his method and his purpose in all his writing: "The dream," he said, "reveals the reality, which conception lags behind." The case is different with Tolstoy. *Ivan Ilych* is a story in which we feel that conception has won the race long before, as indeed can be proved by examining the passages on death in Tolstoy's *A Confession,* an autobiographical and openly didactic work written three years earlier. Tolstoy's magisterial stolidity derives not just from premeditation but even more from his blessed and mutually respectful relationship with the outward world and its laws. This difference between the two authors is admirably summarized by Philip Rahv in his essay on "The Death of Ivan Ilych and Joseph K."

> Kafka clears at one bound the naturalist barrier to his symbolic art. . . .
> Manifestly in order to get the better of the accepted normality of the
> world, the naturalism of Tolstoy's narrative must come to an end at the
> precise point where the symbolism of Kafka's begins: at a crisis not only
> of conscience but of objective reality.

That the methods of the two men differ is obvious enough. But one must also wonder whether what Tolstoy and Kafka say in their stories is consonant with their respective methods of telling them. I have said that Tolstoy's relation to reality seems to me blessed, but Ivan's departure from reality is itself a blessing. And what, after all, is the message of this exemplum in which three days of screaming can end in a blessing? That one ought to become an idealized peasant like Gerásim or, if that is not feasible, that one should at least be an even better family man and public servant, one who marries for love and has no inordinate love of bridge, one whose life should not be the most ordinary so that it will not be also the most terrible? In the end, even after all the satire and the staring into the face of Nothing in the middle of the night, it is not possible for Tolstoy to condemn "Ivan's world." There is no world that is Ivan's, since there is only one world and it is also inhabited by Gerásim, along with the author and the reader. On such terms Tolstoy's confidence in the final redemption of his Ivan Ilych makes considerable sense. Since reality itself can reveal the dream—that is, the ideal—why should not a conversion take place in a drawing-room? This confidence in reality also helps to account for the immediate and Continent-wide popularity of Tolstoy's story with the very people it attacks. For one thing, Tolstoy has not challenged the middle-class reader's own interpretation of what is real, nor has Tolstoy caused him to see that his reality is merely an interpretation. For another, what real-life Ivan Ilych would hesitate to claim that he was a much better husband or lawyer than the fictional one or would fail to grant (though in a rather abstract way, of course) his own mortality? In short, to read *The Death of Ivan Ilych* could become the occasion for a renewal of self-deception, if not of complacency—exactly as "the reproach and warning to the living" which Peter Ivanovich reads on the visage of Ivan's corpse fails to keep him from even one evening of bridge.

Unlike Tolstoy's, Kafka's relation to reality is not blessed but cursed. The world, void now of any spiritual content whatever, loses even its unity, and is all interpretation or the will to power. Spiritual battle of any sort must be waged through symbols, by armies of parables, with the strategy of the dream. Yet all this would be insignificant fantasy if the dream did not indeed "reveal the reality" and thereby approximate the purity of truth. But what truth is liable to be approached given Kafka's methods? Tolstoy can end his story with a departure from the world because all is as well as can be and the world itself is as full of potential grace as Ivan is finally of joy. Kafka must end his tale with a return to the world just because nothing is well at all and because even Gregor's final peace in it is only vacancy. Since Kafka has so little confidence in reality, his story, unlike Tolstoy's, will only perplex those who do possess that confidence. One can certainly choose to mistake Tolstoy's meaning, but one can hardly fail to comprehend it. Kafka's story, however, is at once more radical, more threatening, and more difficult.

MARTIN PRICE

Tolstoy and the Forms
of Life

I t is difficult to account for the re-
markable sense of depth as well as breadth we feel in reading Tolstoy. Sir
Isaiah Berlin, in describing that sense, has come closer than anyone else
to explaining it. Tolstoy's heroes achieve a kind of serenity through coming
to accept "the permanent relationships of things and the universal texture
of human life." Through them we become aware of an order underlying
and perhaps girding the world of our experience. It is an order which
" 'contains' and determines the structure of experience, the framework
on which it—that is, we and all we experience—must be conceived as
being set":

> we are immersed and submerged in a medium that, precisely to the degree
> to which we inevitably take it for granted as part of ourselves, we do not
> and cannot observe as if from the outside; cannot identify, measure and
> seek to manipulate; cannot even be wholly aware of, inasmuch as it enters
> too intimately into all our experience, is itself too closely interwoven with
> all that we are and do to be lifted out of the flow (it is the flow) and
> observed with scientific detachment, as an object. It—the medium in
> which we are—determines our most permanent categories, our standards
> of truth and falsehood, of reality and appearance, of the good and the
> bad, of the central and peripheral, the subjective and the objective, of
> the beautiful and the ugly, of movement and rest, of past, present and
> future, of one and many; hence neither these, nor any other explicitly
> conceived categories or concepts can be applied to it—for it is itself but

a vague name for the totality that includes these categories, these concepts, the ultimate framework, the basic presuppositions wherewith we function.

Those characters who, like Pierre in *War and Peace* and Levin in *Anna Karenina,* gain a measure of wisdom have learned no new facts about their world. They have come to accept the limits the world sets: "It is 'there'—the framework, the foundation of everything—and the wise man alone has a sense of it; Pierre gropes for it; Kutuzov feels it in his bones; Karataev is at one with it. All Tolstoy's heroes attain to at least intermittent glimpses of it." This is caught concisely in the account of Platon Karataev, who appears at a time when Pierre has lost faith in the meaning of his life. Karataev was always to remain in Pierre's memory "the personification of everything Russian, kindly, and round." When he spoke "he seemed not to know how he would conclude":

> He did not, and could not, understand the meaning of words apart from their context. Every word and action of his was the manifestation of an activity unknown to him, which was his life. But his life, as he regarded it, had no meaning as a separate thing. It had meaning only as part of the whole of which he was always conscious. His words and actions flowed from him as evenly, inevitably, and spontaneously as fragrance exhales from a flower. He could not understand the value or significance of any word or deed taken separately.

Karataev lives without self-consciousness in a world whose unity admits no abstraction. He embodies God for Pierre better than the Freemasons' Architect of the Universe. He helps Pierre recover the simplicity of direct feeling. Pierre feels at last "like a man who after straining his eyes to see into the far distance finds what he sought at his very feet." Beside this spontaneous and unreflecting assurance of Karataev one can set Levin's despair near the close of *Anna Karenina:* "When Levin thought about what he was and what he was living for, he could find no answer and was driven to despair; but when he stopped asking himself about it, he seemed to know both what he was and what he was living for, because he acted and lived in a positive and determined way. . . ." In the midst of many duties that must be performed, Levin has tried to avoid thinking about larger questions, but he is not a man to rest with comfort in evasions: "So he lived, not knowing and not seeing any possibility of knowing what he was and why he lived in the world, and worried so much by this ignorance that he was afraid he might commit suicide and yet at the same time he resolutely carved out his own individual and definite way in life."

Tolstoy strikes a comic note in Levin's case as he does in Pierre's. It comes of the disparity between anxious, strenuous reflection and effortless intuition. Levin, like Pierre, finds himself returning to certitudes of childhood: "I have discovered nothing. I have merely found out what I knew. . . . I have rid myself of deception." Levin recognizes the certainty that he has lived by whenever he has not allowed reflection to unsettle him. As he looks up at the sky, he knows that he "cannot see it except as round and finite" although he knows that "space is infinite." Could the astronomers have charted the heavens if they had not taken the earth as fixed? Could they have measured all they did if they had not made their observations in relation to one meridian and one horizon? Is not man's moral awareness such a fixed point?

There is a striking resemblance between Levin's argument and that which governs Ludwig Wittgenstein's late work, *On Certainty*. One of Wittgenstein's problems is to set the limits of skepticism. "Doubt itself rests only on what is beyond doubt." "A doubt without an end is not even a doubt." Wittgenstein treats the question of a framework that is raised by Berlin: "I do not explicitly learn the propositions that stand fast [*feststehen*] for me. I can *discover* them subsequently like the axis around which a body rotates. This axis is not fixed in the sense that anything holds it fast, but the movement around it determines its immobility." But, Wittgenstein goes on, what I hold fast to is "not one proposition but a nest of propositions." These propositions provide the structure upon which all our empirical knowledge must rest or into which all our experience, including the experience of uncertainty, must be fitted. "That is to say, the *questions* that we raise and our *doubts* depend on the fact that some propositions are exempt from doubt, are as it were the hinges on which those turn." We must begin with such fixities: "If I want the door to turn, the hinges must stay put." For doubts, like all our uses of language, arise from "forms of life." "My *life* consists in my being content to accept many things."

Wittgenstein admired Tolstoy. He is said to have carried Tolstoy's brief version of the Gospels with him during the First World War, and he provided his friend, Norman Malcolm, when he in turn was a soldier, with a copy of Tolstoy's last major work of fiction, *Hadji Murad*. "I hope you get a lot out of it," he wrote Malcolm, "because there is a lot *in* it." Of Tolstoy himself, he wrote: "There's a *real* man, who has a *right* to write." He particularly admired the moral parables of Tolstoy's *Twenty-Three Tales*, perhaps out of the same desire for a morality at once clear and profound that made him enjoy Dr. Johnson's prayers and his life of Pope. We see this moral concern in his remarks on G. E. Moore, whose absence of vanity and innocence of nature Malcolm praised:

> There is . . . a *certain* innocence about Moore; he is, e.g., completely unvain. But as to its being to his *credit* to be childlike,—I can't understand that; unless it's also to a *child's* credit. For you aren't talking of the

innocence a man has fought for, but of an innocence which comes from a natural absence of temptation.—I believe that all you wanted to say was that you *liked*, or even *loved*, Moore's childlikeness. And that I can *understand*.

Wittgenstein was, in effect, recalling the rules for the use of praise or credit; he was telling Malcolm that in neglecting the element of moral effort or self-mastery he had used a word outside the language-game that was its home.

The conception of language-games recognizes that we have many overlapping structures of language, each somewhat arbitrary and conventional, each resting upon a distinctive kind of activity that it serves. These patterns of activity Wittgenstein called forms of life, and he used that phrase to refer to small-scale activities as well as to others that include a large portion of our existence. "Only in the stream of thought and life do words have meaning." As he says, "We remain unconscious of the prodigious diversity of all the everyday language-games because the clothing of our language makes everything alike."

Wittgenstein felt that "the problems arising through a misinterpretation of our forms of language have the character of *depth*. They are deep disquietudes; their roots are as deep in us as the forms of our language, and their significance is as great as the importance of our language."

Wittgenstein wrote *On Certainty* to meet the questions raised when G. E. Moore claimed to know the truth of such propositions as "Here is one hand, and here is another" or "The earth existed for a long time before my birth." Wittgenstein tries to show how empirical propositions, as they become part of the structure of beliefs or of the picture we inherit and take as our ground for doubts, serve a new function as well.

> The propositions describing this world-picture might be part of a kind of mythology. And their role is like that of rules of a game; and the game can be learned purely practically, without learning any explicit rules.
>
> It might be imagined that some propositions, of the form of empirical propositions, were hardened and functioned as channels for such empirical propositions as were not hardened but fluid; and that this relation altered with time, in that fluid propositions hardened, and hard ones became fluid.
>
> The mythology may change back into a state of flux, the river-bed of thoughts may shift. But I distinguish between the movement of the waters on the river-bed and the shift of the bed itself; though there is not a sharp division of the one from the other.
>
> But if someone were to say "So logic too is an empirical science" he would be wrong. Yet he is right: the same proposition may get treated

at one time as something to test by experience, at another as a rule of testing.

The consequences of Wittgenstein's position is a world without "sufficient reason," without absolutes or permanent grounds. "The difficulty is to realize the groundlessness of our believing": "Giving grounds, however, justifying the evidence, comes to an end;—but the end is not certain propositions' striking us immediately as true, i.e., it is not a kind of *seeing* on our part; it is our *acting* which lies at the bottom of the language-game." And Wittgenstein introduces a splendid architectural paradox: "I have arrived at the rock bottom of my convictions. And one might almost say that these foundation-walls are carried by the whole house."

Anthony Flew has drawn interesting parallels between passages in Tolstoy's A Confession (written shortly after Anna Karenina) and passages near the close of Wittgenstein's Tractatus. Running through Tolstoy's review of his religious life was his recognition of the misdirected effort to find in empirical science the kind of meaning that Wittgenstein makes clear it could not reveal. As Tolstoy put it, his mistake lay in that his "reasoning was not in accord with the question" he had put; for his question ("Why should I live? . . . [W]hat meaning has my finite existence in this infinite world?") "included a demand for an explanation of the finite in terms of the infinite, and vice versa." "I asked: 'What is the meaning of my life, beyond time, cause, and space?' And I replied to quite another question: 'What is the meaning of my life within time, cause, and space?' With the result that, after long efforts of thought, the answer I reached was: 'None.' "

In response to such questions Wittgenstein wrote:

> We feel that even when all possible scientific questions have been answered, the problems of life remain completely untouched. Of course there are then no questions left, and this itself is the answer.
>
> The solution of the problem of life is seen in the vanishing of the problem. (Is not this the reason why those who have found after a long period of doubt that the sense of life became clear to them have then been unable to say what constituted that sense?)
>
> There are, indeed, things that cannot be put into words. They *make themselves manifest.* They are what is mystical.

One is inclined to see in Pierre and Levin the truth of what Bertrand Russell wrote in 1919 about Wittgenstein: "He has penetrated deep into mystical ways of thought and feeling, but I think (though he wouldn't agree) that what he likes best in mysticism is its power to make him stop thinking." We may want to find a term other than *mysticism,* and we might want to alter "likes best" to "needs most," for the thinking of Pierre and

Levin is intense, exacting, and—so long as it pursues the questions it sets—endlessly frustrating.

INSIDE AND OUTSIDE

[W]hen we intend, we are surrounded by our intention's *pictures*, and we are inside them. But when we step outside intention, they are as mere patches on a canvas, without life and of no interest to us. When we intend, we exist in the space of intention, among the pictures (shadows) of intention, as well as with real things. Let us imagine we are sitting in a darkened cinema and entering into the film. Now the lights are turned on, though the film continues on the screen. But suddenly we are outside it and see it as movements of light and dark patches on a screen.

Wittgenstein's discussion of our being inside or outside intention's pictures is comparable to H. L. A. Hart's treatment of the difference between an internal and external view of rules.

The internal view is enclosed, one might say, within the authority of the rules, accepts their claim, and acts in conscious awareness of them. "But whatever the rules are, whether they are those of games, or moral or legal rules, we can, if we choose, occupy the position of an observer who does not even refer . . . to the internal point of view of the group. Such an observer is content merely to record the regularities of observable behavior in which conformity with the rules partly consists. . . ." He may be able to predict the behavior of a group without recognizing the power the rules have for it. "What the external point of view, which limits itself to the observable regularities of behavior, cannot reproduce is the way in which the rules function as rules in the lives of those who normally are the majority of society."

One may speak of the game or the social structure as an institution, and of the normative claims of rules as institutional facts. The detached observer, who does not participate in the life of the institution, may so describe action as to make it seem ludicrous or outrageous, and this is frequently the way in which the satirist works. He strips from complex behavior those implicit norms (or intentions) that help to explain it and renders instead the external gestures which the norms induce. The effect may be one of moral horror, as when Lemuel Gulliver describes a soldier as "a Yahoo hired to kill in cold blood as many of his own species, who have never offended him, as possibly he can." So Tolstoy describes the beginning of war:

On the twelfth of June 1812, the forces of western Europe crossed the Russian frontier and war began, that is, an event took place opposed to human reason and to human nature. Millions of men perpetrated against one another such innumerable crimes, frauds, treacheries, thefts, forgeries, issues of false money, burglaries, incendiarisms, and murder as in whole centuries are not recorded in the annals of all the law courts of the world, but which those who committed them did not at the time regard as being crimes.

But the rules need not be the terrible claims of patriotism and so-called just war. They may be those of artistic convention. In *War and Peace*, Natasha Rostov attends the opera in a state of mind that prevents her from making an appropriate response: "She saw only the painted cardboard and the queerly dressed men and women who moved, spoke, and sang so strangely in that brilliant light. She knew what it was all meant to represent, but it was so pretentiously false and unnatural that she first felt ashamed for the actors and then amused at them." And Tolstoy offers the deadpan vision of the alienated or uncomprehending spectator:

> many people appeared from right and left wearing black cloaks and holding things like daggers in their hands. They began waving their arms. Then some other people ran in and began dragging away the maiden who had been in white and was now in light blue. They did not drag her away at once, but sang with her for a long time and then at last dragged her off, and behind the scenes something metallic was struck three times and everyone knelt down and sang a prayer. All these things were repeatedly interrupted by the enthusiastic shouts of the audience.

With this, one may compare Flaubert's method in *Madame Bovary*. Here the novelist presents a mocking, external view of the opera (a performance of *Lucia di Lammermoor*) while showing Emma's fervent response. Her response is not simply an internal one; it is an internal view used as the occasion for fantasy. Her response is more than appropriate; she identifies Lucy's fictive life with her own, and the intensity of her response is all the more ludicrous for the external view Flaubert has given of the performance. The celebrated tenor Lagardy is performing, and we are given a brief account of his private life, for it is to the "sentimental fame" of Lagardy that Emma responds as much as to the role he performs.

> A skilled ham actor, he never forgot to have a phrase on his seductiveness and his sensitive soul inserted in the accounts about him. He had a fine voice, colossal aplomb, more temperament than intelligence, more pathos than lyric feeling; all this made for an admirable charlatan type, in which there was something of the hairdresser as well as of the bull-fighter.
> From the first scene he brought down the house. He pressed Lucy in his arms, he left her, he came back, he seemed desperate; he had outbursts of rage, then elegiac gurgling of infinite sweetness. . . . Emma

bent forward to see him, scratching the velvet of the box with her nails. Her heart filled with these melodious lamentations. . . . [T]he voice of the prima donna seemed to echo her own conscience, and the whole fictional story seemed to capture something of her own life. But no one on earth had loved her with such love.

If Natasha remains at too great a psychic distance from the opera's fictions, Emma leaves too little distance. Flaubert insists upon the physical presence of the theater. The velvet of the box is made the more real by the very obliviousness with which Emma scratches it. Flaubert's field of vision includes details that are incongruously solid. They resist and mock the fantasies of his heroine.

Tolstoy is profoundly concerned with the moments when we move from an internal to an external view. Probably the best known instance in *Anna Karenina* occurs as Anna returns from Moscow after her encounter there with Vronsky:

As soon as the train stopped at Petersburg and she got out, the first person to attract her attention was her husband. "Goodness, why are his ears like that?" she thought, looking at his cold, distinguished figure and especially at the cartilages of his ears, pressing up against the rim of his round hat. Catching sight of her, he walked toward her, pursing his lips in his usual sarcastic smile, and looking straight at her with his large, tired eyes. As she met his fixed and tired gaze, her heart contracted painfully with a sort of unpleasant sensation, as though she expected to find him looking different. She was particularly struck by the feeling of discontent with herself which she experienced when she met him. It was that old familiar feeling indistinguishable from hypocrisy which she experienced in her relations with her husband; but she had not been conscious of it before, while now she was clearly and painfully aware of it.

The ludicrous sight of Karenin's ears seems to precipitate a new way of looking at him. He ceases to be a familiar presence, someone seen as all but part of herself. Instead, he has become a distinct figure, seen from a distance and very much from the outside. The observation of his ears is not, of course, the cause of what follows; it is simply the first detail registered by a new analytic view made possible through the withdrawal or absence of the usual feelings. Because it is a mere physical detail of no great consequence, it serves all the better to trigger a new way of looking at Karenin and, by the end of the paragraph, of seeing in retrospect and being able at last to identify a feeling that always shadowed their relationship. Anna has moved from the inside to the outside of her marriage. A few pages later she tries to disavow this change, and now the ears become an impediment:

" 'All the same, he's a good man; upright, kind, and remarkable in his own sphere,' Anna said to herself when she had returned to her room, as though defending him against someone who had accused him and maintained that one could not love him. 'But why do his ears stick out so oddly? Has he had a haircut?' " In this instance, we have seen Anna moving from an internal to an external view of her marriage. But we can see another movement as well, toward the inside of a new relationship with Vronsky. At their first meeting, Anna expresses her concern for the widow of the railway guard killed at the station. Vronsky hurries off to make a large donation. There is no reason to think that he means Anna to learn of it; but she does, and it troubles her. "She felt there was something in this incident that had to do with her, something that should not have been." Her power over Vronsky dismays her, for his gift to the widow is the creation of a new relationship, and the action becomes, to a small degree, a claim upon her. If she were entirely indifferent to Vronsky, she might not feel so keenly that they now share a bond she should repudiate—if that were not to make too much of it. Later, in Petersburg, Anna assumes the power that Vronsky has been urging upon her. When he speaks of love during their meeting at the Princess Betsy's Anna stops him: " 'Please remember that I've forbidden you to utter that word, that odious word,' said Anna with a shudder; but at once she felt that by that very word 'forbidden,' she had shown she admitted that she had certain rights over him, and by this very fact was encouraging him to speak of love." Later, as she leaves, she returns to this: " 'Love,' she repeated slowly, speaking inwardly to herself, and suddenly . . . she added: 'The reason why I dislike the word is because it means too much to me, much more than you can understand,' and she glanced into his face."

Tolstoy's characters move in and out of such frames, from participation to detachment and back again, slipping out of a structure or watching it dissolve about them. Beneath or within these institutional structures—families, regiments, provincial councils, theological systems—lie those activities, those forms of life, that are the scene and source of vitality. Tolstoy, whatever his moral concerns or perhaps most of all *in* his moral concerns, was a vitalist. We have the phrases that Pierre speaks or hears or imagines in *War and Peace:* "Life is God. Everything changes and moves and that movement is God." We can see this vitalism in the fierce, often clumsy, energy of Levin's search for meaning in his life. We can see it, too, in Anna. In the moments after the first consummation of their love, she is appalled to hear Vronsky speak of their happiness. The word is too trivial for what she feels. "She felt at that moment she could not express in words the feeling of joy, shame, and horror at this entry into a new life, and she did not want to talk about it, to profane this feeling by inexact words."

FORMS OF LIFE AND DEATH: "WAR AND PEACE"

Nicholas Rostov moves from the inside of one form of life to the inside of another when, after informing his father of his enormous gambling debt, he returns to the regiment. There, "bound in one narrow, unchanging frame, he experienced the same sense of peace, of moral support, and the same sense of being at home here in his own place, as he had felt under the parental roof. But here was none of all that turmoil of the world at large." He is free of difficult choices and awkward explanations; one had only to do "what was clearly, distinctly, and definitely ordered." (This is very much the appeal of military life for Vronsky as well.)

It is not, however, so simple as Nicholas might wish. He is troubled when the emperor fails to grant his petition in Denisov's behalf. Nicholas is even more profoundly troubled by the mutual esteem the emperor and Napoleon display at the Peace of Tilsit. Nicholas doesn't know quite what disturbs him, and the disturbance takes the form of vivid memories rather than reflection, memories he has repressed in his state of hopefulness:

> Terrible doubts arose in his soul. Now he remembered Denisov with his changed expression . . . and the whole hospital, with arms and legs torn off and its dirt and disease. So vividly did he recall that hospital stench of dead flesh that he looked around to see where the smell came from. Next he thought of that self-satisfied Bonaparte, with his small white hand, who was now an Emperor, liked and respected by Alexander. Then why those severed arms and legs and those dead men? . . . He caught himself harboring such strange thoughts that he was frightened.

Rather than allow himself to acknowledge such thoughts, Nicholas drinks heavily and rebukes a fellow officer who expresses the thoughts that trouble Nicholas himself. The officer provides him with an occasion to fight down his doubts. How can you judge the Emperor's actions! While the fellow officer protests that he has never criticized the emperor, Nicholas continues: "If once we begin judging and arguing about everything, nothing sacred will be left! That way we shall be saying there is no God—nothing!" Nicholas comes in from the frontiers of disbelief; he has been made all too much aware of the medium, of the assumptions and presuppositions he is terrified of losing; and he regains assurance with a mixture of wine and rationalization.

Nicholas's mother, the Countess Rostov, provides us with a good instance of someone who has moved outside the life she has always lived. She has lost her young son Petya and her husband:

She ate, drank, slept, or kept awake, but did not *live*. Life gave her no new impressions. She wanted nothing from life but tranquillity, and that tranquillity only death could give her. But until death came she had to go on living. . . . She talked only because she physically needed to exercise her tongue and lungs. . . . What for people in their full vigor is an aim was for her . . . merely a pretext.

One of the most consistent ways in which Tolstoy treats these forms of life we take for granted is in his account of military command. The tenor of his argument throughout is that the plans of commanders have little relevance to what occurs. There are too many imponderables, there is too vast a field to encompass. Those like Kutuzov who recognize the nature of this vast play of forces can at least learn to work with them. When Kutuzov listened to battle reports, he attended not to the words spoken or the facts reported, but to "the expression of face and of voice of those who were reporting." He knew how few sane choices could be made by a commander and how much depended on "that intangible force called the spirit of the army." Kutuzov, therefore, listens and watches with a "concentrated quiet attention," for he recognizes the true framework which it is not customary to acknowledge. He knows military operations from the inside.

A commander in chief, Tolstoy observes, "is never dealing with the beginning of any event." He is "always in the midst of a series of shifting events and so he never can at any moment consider the whole import of an event that is occurring. Moment by moment the event is imperceptibly shaping itself, and at every moment . . . the commander in chief is in the midst of a most complex play of intrigues, worries, contingencies," etc. The general may give orders so as to make whatever must happen seem to have been brought about by his will, but, Tolstoy insists, the sense of freedom which we have and must act upon should not delude us into thinking we have greater powers than we do. "Only unconscious action bears fruit, and he who plays a part in an historic event never understands its significance. If he tries to realize it his efforts are fruitless." Most events represent the convergence of wills unknown to each other, of circumstances which are never sufficiently recognized. It is only when an event is past that we can see it completely. Just as Kuruzov listens for what the voice rather than the words reveals, so again when he addresses the troops, they do not hear his words, but they understand his "feeling of majestic triumph combined with pity for the foe and consciousness of the justice" of the Russian cause.

We see Kutuzov, then, improvising a series of tactical retreats, allowing the French forces to occupy Moscow, watching them founder in their ill-conceived retreat. He does not play the game of dazzling strategy and glorious victory; only he, in fact, knows that the Battle of Borodino was a victory for the Russians and the turning point in Napoleon's expedition. Kutuzov has his own game, if that is the word for it; he is like the patient defendant who keeps prudently deferring a trial until the plaintiff litigates himself into insolvency. For his game is not winning a lawsuit but defeating the plaintiff; and sapping the plaintiff's will or his fortune is less costly and risky than confronting him in court. This is perhaps an unattractive account of Kutuzov's method, but one must think of him as a defendant who believes so completely in the justness of his cause that he does not need to declare it or defend it in a court.

Kutuzov is a man who exhibits little distinction of manner; he is corpulent and untidy, in some ways resembling both Pierre and Karataev. What he shares with them is an unheroic, even antiheroic, manner. Tolstoy is full of sympathy for the soldier's patriotic feeling, but he tends to celebrate the greatness that is thrust upon men, stability to endure and wit to improvise. There is no better instance than Prince Andrew's snatching up the fallen standard at Austerlitz as Napoleon had done at the Bridge of Arcola, and leading an improbable charge against the French. "Forward, lads! he shouted in a voice as piercing as a child's." The final simile is telling; there is a wonderful naivety about his action, and yet he is followed by a battalion in the face of the cannon which the French have captured and are about to turn around. As Andrew lies wounded on the battlefield, even the standard missing, he hears Napoleon remark of him, "That's a fine death!"

Prince Andrew is the antithesis of such unheroic figures as Pierre and Kutuzov. And, like all the Bolkonskis in the novel, he has turned away from life. We first encounter him at Anna Schérer's soirée, where the deadliest sin is to be natural and where Andrew gives the impression of having found everyone, but most of all his wife, "so tiresome that it wearied him to look at or listen to them." Later in private conversation Pierre sees a new aspect of Andrew, a passion of nervous excitement and morbid criticism. Andrew feels himself trapped by marriage, consigned to the role of a court lackey, caught in a narrow circle of gossip, ceremony, and triviality. He is about to go to war as a means of escape.

Throughout the novel we see Andrew looking for something to believe in with heroic devotion and abandon, but always prepared, at the least threat to the perfection of that faith, to withdraw into sardonic disenchantment. There is some part of him that is drawn to the glories of power; he enjoys helping other young men to win the success which his pride cannot accept for himself. He is ready to admire a court official like Speranski, but equally ready to be disenchanted. There is about Prince Andrew something of the Byronic hero who yearns for a greatness he can trust, but who is always afraid of being taken in and ready to meet every occasion with irony. This is a pride that seems superior, but proves, as the novel unfolds, less robust, less intelligent, than Pierre's often clumsy and childish tenacity. As he lies on the battlefield, Andrew concentrates upon the "lofty sky, not clear yet still immeasurably lofty." Yes, he thinks, "all is vanity, all falsehood, except that infinite sky." This is the peace of abstention, the repose of a mind that cannot be deceived because it has chosen emptiness (or one might call it purity). So, when Napoleon stoops over him to admire what he takes to be a hero's corpse, he seems to Andrew "a small, insignificant creature compared with what was passing now between himself and that lofty, infinite sky with the clouds flying over it." It is once again "the lofty, equitable, and kindly sky" that makes Napoleon's joy in victory seem nothing but "paltry vanity," a "short-sighted delight at the misery of others." The loss of blood and the apparent nearness of death make Andrew think of "the insignificance of greatness, the unimportance of life . . . and the still greater unimportance of death. . . ." How good it would be, he thinks, if "everything were as clear and simple" as it seems to his devout sister, but he cannot pray either to an "incomprehensible God," the "Great All or Nothing," or "to that God who has been sewn into this amulet by Mary." All that is great is incomprehensible, all he can comprehend is unimportant.

I think we can see a pattern here—an intense idealism that demands more certainty than life can afford, a readiness to turn at the least threat of uncertainty to a cynical disdain. Both are forms of withdrawal from the actual, whether impatience to redeem and transfigure it or scorn for its inadequacy and betrayal. We see only the sense of betrayal in his treatment of his wife, and her reproachful face on her deathbed leaves him feeling guilty for having failed to love her. (We do not know why he married her or how he saw or imagined her then.) He can say to Pierre that there are only two evils in life: remorse and illness. "The only good is the absence of those evils." Pierre is not persuaded. "To live only so as not to do evil and not to have to repent is not enough. I lived like that, I lived for myself and ruined my life." His phrase "lived for myself" is a commentary on Andrew's defensiveness, and Andrew accepts it. He has, he says, tried to live for others, in the search for glory; but he has become calmer now that he lives only for himself of for those few people who are, so to speak, extensions of himself, his family.

Pierre is not discouraged by Andrew's mixture of realism and cynicism, and Andrew comes to respond to Pierre's insistent faith with a "radiant, childlike, tender look," as if he could see once more in the "high, everlasting sky" what he had seen as he lay wounded at Austerlitz. It awakens in turn something slumbering in himself, "something that was best within him." He is prepared for a new ideal form of life, which he is about to find in Natasha.

Before he comes to that, he encounters once more the ancient oak on his estate which seems to tell him of the changelessness and futility of life: a "stupid, meaningless, constantly repeated fraud! . . . There is no spring, no sun, no happiness!" And Andrew withdraws from life again into a restful, mournfully pleasant, rather sentimental "hopelessness." It is always at such a moment that a Tolstoyan hero encounters a force of renewed life. When he sees Natasha he wonders, "What is she so glad about? . . . Why is she so happy?" The delight Natasha finds in her life is mysterious to him, and once he overhears her intense reponse to the beauty of the night, the ancient oak is transfigured. In his own seizure of an "unreasoning springtime feeling of joy and renewal" he is at last ready to give up living for himself alone.

There is a significant intertwining of two series of events, Andrew's attachment to Natasha and his regard for Speranski. He has found in Speranski the ideal of a perfectly rational and virtuous man, and he feels for him an admiration like that he had once felt for Napoleon. But just after the ball at which Natasha dances so radiantly, and where Andrew begins to love her, he finds himself seeing through Speranski's artifices and condescension. All of his hard work on the Legal Code now seems useless and foolish. He turns all the more eagerly to a world of personal feeling. As Natasha sings, Andrew finds himself choked with tears. For what? he wonders, and concludes: "The chief reason was a sudden, vivid sense of the terrible contrast between something infinitely great and illimitable within him" (one thinks of the illimitable, overarching sky) and "that limited and material something that he, and even she, was. This contrast weighed on and yet cheered him while she sang." This reconciliation of the infinite and the immediate becomes an opening up of freedom and responsibility; he believes at last in "the possibility of happiness."

When Andrew learns of Natasha's relation with Anatole and has accepted the breaking of their engagement, we find him defending Speranski, who has fallen from power, against the charges of others. He finds relief from his other grief and anger in argument, and when he learns from Pierre of Natasha's illness, he voices his regret and smiles very much like his father, "coldly, maliciously, and unpleasantly." He has once again withdrawn into a defensive pride and, so to speak, seceded from life.

Prince Andrew, like Nicholas Rostov, loses himself in his regiment; his hatred for his past emerges whenever he meets a former acquaintance. Then he grows "spiteful, ironical, and contemptuous." As he returns to the estate at Bald Hills, he encounters two small peasant girls who have carried plums from the hothouse in their skirts and hide when they see Andrew. He tries to spare their feelings, and for a while they involve him in a shared life: "A new sensation of comfort and relief came over him when, seeing these girls, he realized the existence of other human interests entirely aloof from his own. . . ." It is too much to sustain. When he sees the soldiers bathing nearby in a pond, splashing happily and laughing, he feels a sudden disgust with their naked bodies and his own. It is a feeling he does not understand, and it contravenes that moment of involvement he felt in the girls' pleasure. It seems like a withdrawal from everything alive in others and himself, a cruel asceticism which is a sentence upon his own life.

We see that again in the cold white light which seems to descend over all reality upon the eve of the Battle of Borodino. It is a fierce light "without shadow, without perspective, and without distinction of outline." He welcomes it as clear daylight and truth as opposed to the lantern-slide images that have deceived him all his life. (He is outside the forms of life he once accepted, and the figure is close to Wittgenstein's.) All that has claimed him for life now seems "simple, pale, and crude in the cold white light of this morning. . . ." He thinks with special bitterness, which is also an unacknowledged yearning, of his romantic belief in Natasha. It is hard to extirpate altogether the sense of himself: he looks at the sunlit row of birches and thinks, "That all this should still be, but no me." And in the process the trees and all the scene about him become "terrible and menacing."

In retrospect one sees Prince Andrew's fluctuations between life and some form of externality—aloofness or detachment or defensiveness—some form, that is, of death. His trust in life is insufficient, in part because he brings to it tyrannical ideals; but even those may be a means of assaying its impossibility so that he may justify his retreat. Some of course of Andrew's attitudes are such as Tolstoy held, or had held, or would hold; they were always a part of him and they are given their life here in opposition to the attitudes of Pierre and Natasha, which were no less his own.

If Andrew fluctuates between two forms of life—between withdrawal into ascetisicm and expansion into incautious love—his father tries to impose the pattern of the life now denied him, in exerting his command upon his plain, unloved, and pious daughter. And Mary, in turn, tries to shape her life after the example of Jesus, in a constant putting of others before her. Some part of Mary fights this continual self-abasement; there is enough force of life in her to demand some fulfillment, however frighteningly the demands present themselves.

Pierre, in contrast to the Bolkinskis, ties ceaselessly to bring himself within the frame of life, enduring humiliation, accepting entrapment. "All this had to be and could not be otherwise," he reflects when the proposal he has not yet quite made is accepted by Hélène's father. "It is good because it's definite and one is rid of the old tormenting doubts." Pierre is often a comic figure, in part because he behaves repetitiously, in part because he is without pride, a man wholly open to what he finds in himself, somewhat like Boswell or Tolstoy himself in his curiosity about his feelings and his powers. He engages in a succession of self-deceptions. He feels, as an initiate into Freemasonry, "that he had been vicious only because he had somehow forgotten how good it is to be virtuous." He soars into visions of his future benevolence, persuaded by his warm feeling that he has already attained moral perfection. Later, his steward stages performances by grateful serfs who shower Pierre with gratitude.

But increasingly, even as he falls repeatedly into illusion, Pierre finds forms of active goodness, as in his reassurance of Natasha at the time of her disgrace, his delicacy in speaking with her during his illness, his participation in the battery's activities at Borodino, his rescue of a child. Even his demented plan to assassinate Napoleon is conceived as rescue and service for his fellow Russians. Natasha accepts his kindness without gratitude: "it seemed so natural for him to be kind to everyone that there was no merit in his kindness."

As a prisoner Pierre sheds the qualities that have made him seem foolish; the experience of captivity is one he assumes, so to speak, for the other characters in the novel. For while Andrew and Natasha undergo great change, Pierre's is the change which most fully combines thought and feeling, and which seems to arise from the deepest engagement with reality. He is freed of tormenting doubts; he has lost that freedom which once made the choice of occupation indissolubly difficult. He is reduced to a life where the very qualities that had made him seem clumsy in society now become appropriate and all but make him seem a hero.

His response to the landscape and the sky about him shows his difference from Prince Andrew. He sees the sun rising, making everything "sparkle in the glad light"—the cupolas and crosses of the convent, the hoarfrost on the grass, the distant hills and the river. Pierre feels "a new joy and strength in life such as he had never known before." It is at night in the brilliance of a full moon that Tolstoy presents one of those sacra-mental moments that are so essential to his sense of life. Pierre achieves a transcendence which is not a separation or withdrawal like Andrew's but a moment of ecstatic inclusiveness—the bivouacs and campfires, the forests and fields visible in the distance. "And further still, beyond those forests and fields, the bright oscillating limitless distance that lured one to its depths. Pierre glanced up at the sky and the twinkling stars in its faraway depths. 'And all that is me, all that is within me, and it is all I.' " He smiles at the effort men have made to imprison his soul, and then he lies down to sleep "beside his companions."

As Pierre finds freedom in imprisonment and learns what can be endured, he realizes "the full strength of life in man," he gains the power to control his attention and direct his thought. When Karataev is executed Pierre can concentrate his attention upon the French soldiers who have shot him. In another moment of defamiliarization, he recognizes one of them as the man who had burned his shirt while drying it two days before and had aroused laughter among them. At each moment that his mind turns in grief to Karataev, a consoling memory from the past deflects his attention. The inability of the mind to close in upon its suffering seems in one view helpless passivity before its associations, in another a genius for survival.

"INEXORABLE LAW"

Tolstoy's intensity is not simply the effect of brilliant gesture or image. In fact, Proust dismisses observation altogether:

> This is not the work of an observing eye but of a thinking mind. Every so-called stroke of observation is simply the clothing, the proof, the instance, of a law, a law of reason or of unreason, which the novelist has laid bare. And our impression of the breadth and life is due precisely to the fact that none of this is the fruit of observation, but that every deed, every action, being no other than an expression of law, one feels oneself moving amid a throng of laws—why, since the truth of these laws is established for Tolstoy by the inward authority they have exercised over his thinking, there are some which we are still baffled by.

One can see what Proust means in those mordant ironies through which Tolstoy looks beyond his characters' vision and instantiates laws in epigram. We see Anna "calling to mind Karenin with every detail of his figure, his way of speaking, and his character, and making him responsible for everything bad she could find in him, forgiving him nothing because of the terrible thing she had done to him." Much later there is a terrible parallel when she has had her last quarrel with Vronsky: "All the cruelest things a coarse man could say she imagined him to have said to her, and she did not forgive him for them just as if he had really said them."

Or we have Anna telling Vronsky of her pregnancy. He has been troubled by all the subterfuges both of them, not without shame, have had to practice; and he has begun to feel "revulsion against something: against Karenin, against himself, against the whole world—he was not sure which." Anna's son Seryozha, in his own uncertainties, has made Vronsky feel ill at ease and aroused in him once more "that strange feeling of blind revulsion which he had experienced of late." And with Anna's news, Vronsky turns pale and lowers his head,—Anna thinks with gratitude that he understands the full significance of the event. "But," Tolstoy proceeds, "she was wrong in thinking that he understood the significance . . . as she, a woman, understood it. At this news he felt the onrush of that strange feeling of revulsion for someone; but at the same time he realized that the crisis he had wished for had now come." One must suspect that some of Vronsky's revulsion is for Anna and for the power she has over him; that is a possibility she cannot allow herself to entertain until later. Again, at the steeplechase before Vronsky's fall, Anna is outraged by Karenin's protracted conversation with an important colleague. "All he cares about is lies and keeping up appearances," she thinks, without considering "what exactly she wanted of her husband or what she would have liked him to be. Nor did she realize that Karenin's peculiar loquaciousness that day . . . was merely an expression of his inner anxiety and uneasiness." In each of these cases there is a false estimation or an irrational judgment; Anna is too guilty or eager or bitter to see what the author discloses. In each case there is cause enough for Anna's misapprehension, but Tolstoy's immediate ironic rectification has the effect of invoking what Proust calls his laws of reason and unreason.

As soon as characters seem to obey laws of which they are unaware, the implications become ambiguous. Are they too much obsessed to see what is really there? Or are they too deeply committed to make a cool canvass of fact? Is Anna's obliviousness a form of self-absorption and fantasy, or is it the integrity of a woman who "must live her feelings right through"?

Against her intensity we can set those compromises and dissonances that mark most lives. The novel opens with the dissolution of a family structure. It is a temporary dissolution, but the restoration will never be complete. Stiva Oblonsky awakens at eight o'clock as always; but, as he stretches out his feet for his slippers and his hand for his dressing gown, he realizes that he has slept on the sofa: for his wife Dolly has learned of his affair with the former governess; and when she expressed her horror, Oblonsky's face quite involuntarily "smiled its usual kind and, for that reason, rather foolish smile." It is the smile that Stiva regrets rather than the adultery, for the smile had the force of a blow for his wife. She responded with bitter words and has refused to see him.

Stiva is pained at his wife's grief. He has persuaded himself that she has pretended not to know of his infidelities, and in fact that is the attitude Dolly will assume thereafter, "letting herself be deceived, despising him, and most of all herself, for that weakness." On the occasion of this first discovery, she is divided between the need to take strong action and the pull of habit and convention. She feels outrage at the sight of his pity because it is so visibly less than love; but she is more troubled by the fear of estrangement. Stiva recognizes the "usual answer life gives to the most complicated and insoluble questions": to live from day to day and to lose oneself in the "dream of life."

While the Oblonskys' marriage is not a very happy one and will never get better, it is, at any rate, a structure of habits and responsibilities which, however imperfectly realized, is still a refuge from the intolerable. But it is imperfectly realized. We see this in Stiva's treatment of his children. When his daughter embraces him, he holds her and strokes her neck as he asks after her mother. Stiva knows that he does not care so much for his son, and he always tries therefore to treat both children in the same way. But his son senses the effort and responds to it rather than its pretense. When Stiva asks if her mother is cheerful, his daughter knows that there has been a quarrel and that her father is fully aware of her mother's disturbance but pretends that he is not. She blushes for him. He perceives that and blushes in turn.

We see the persistence of Stiva's neglect when Dolly takes the children to their country cottage in order to save expenses. Stiva has gone to Petersburg to further his career, and he has taken almost all the money in the house. He was asked by Dolly to have the cottage put in comfortable shape. He looked to the externals but neglected essential repairs. Nor was this the lack of the will to be a "solicitous father and husband." He has meant well, or at least has meant to mean well; but the roof still leaks, the cattle have been loose in the garden, there are no pots and pans, there are not enough milk and butter and eggs. The bailiff whom Stiva chose for "his handsome and respectful appearance" is of no help at all. Dolly is in despair until her old servant Matryona sets everything right, and gradually Dolly recovers her spirits and recaptures her great pride in her children.

On a fine spring day after much preparation of their clothes, Dolly takes her children to communion. The occasion requires that Dolly dress beautifully so as "not to spoil the general effect" and she is pleased with the admiration that she and her six children elicit from the peasants in church. And the children behave beautifully. The smallest, Lily, takes the sacrament and delightfully repeats, in English, Oliver Twist's words, "I want some more, please." It is a day of all but unclouded joy. Dolly feels both love and confidence. Near the river where they have all gone bathing, she falls into conversation with the peasant women. Dolly finds it hard to leave these women, "so absolutely identical were their interests." All the world about her seems for once to belong to Dolly, to reflect her own feelings and to embrace her with affection and admiration.

The rapture cannot be sustained. As they return to the cottage, Levin is waiting. He has come at Stiva's urging, but he does not want Dolly to feel that Stiva has foisted responsibility on him. Dolly not only perceives that, but she is touched by the "fine perception and delicacy" with which Levin tries to spare her the shame of her husband's neglect. Here as with the exchange of blushes between Stiva and his daughter, there is a second-order response, a response to a response. Tolstoy uses it characteristically to emphasize the implicit meanings that are shared within a form of life, but perhaps become more oblique and difficult as the form is compromised.

Dolly wants Levin to know that Kitty is coming to visit her. She has suspected that he proposed and was rejected, and now, as she senses his anger, she tries to meet it with an account of Kitty's suffering. The more precisely Levin recalls that rejection, the more uncharitable he becomes and the more determined not to see Kitty. Dolly tells him he is absurd, but she says it with tenderness. She creates a distraction by addressing her daughter in French and requiring that Tanya answer in French. This, as now everything about the family, strikes Levin as disagreeable. "Teach French and unteach sincerity," he thinks to himself, not imagining that Dolly considered that danger for a long while before deciding it was worth the cost of some sincerity for her children to learn French. Levin, disenchanted, prepares to leave. The disenchantment spreads like a cloud.

The children have begun to fight, and for Dolly a "great shadow seems to have fallen over her life." She "realized that these children of hers . . . were not only quite ordinary, but even bad, ill-bred children, with coarse, brutal propensities, wicked children in fact." She voices all her sorrow to Levin, and he reassures her that all children fight. But he is no longer sincere. He thinks as he leaves, "No, I won't try to show off and talk French with my children."

Both Dolly and Levin have feelings that are spontaneous, deep, and pervasive. Their world must, in Wittgenstein's phrase, 'wax or wane as a whole. As if by accession or loss of meaning." Wittgenstein's point is that our will cannot alter the facts of the world, only its limits or boundaries; it can affect our world only by making it wholly different. Tolstoy gives some of his characters an intensity of feeling that wholly alters their world. The process if faintly ludicrous even as it is touching, as in this case.

These instances may be seen as acute observation of motive and manners, as the necessary consequences of laws Tolstoy traces and confirms, as the meeting point of thematic concerns and their convergence in events of depth and resonance. Proust chooses to stress the second, to see particulars as "simply the clothing, the proof, the instance, of a law." This is in part a tribute to the sense of necessity Tolstoy gives his world; his "apparently inexhaustible fund of creation," as Proust calls it, does not need to spend itself in merely clever observations. The necessity which Proust ascribes to laws in Tolstoy he accounts for in other ways that are no less apt in his discussion of George Eliot:

> Another striking thing is the sense of gravity attached to an evil intention or to a failure of resolution, which because of the interdependence of mankind spreads its fatal repercussions in every direction; and another, the sense of the mysterious greatness of human life and the life of nature, the solemn mysteries in which we play a part while knowing no more about them than does the growing flower. . . .

This concatenation of lives in fatal repercussions resembles what George Eliot calls "undeviating law," "invariability of sequence," or the "inexorable law of consequences"—patterns of order which we can recognize and to which we must submit.

The capacity for submission, for what George Eliot calls "patient watching of external fact" and "silencing of preconceived notions," is a readiness to allow possibilities their emergence, a reluctance to delimit experience to what is governable and explicable. This may be a withdrawal from visible but not from conceivable relevance, and it risks the acceptance of details, events, "observations" which may threaten as well as exemplify laws. George Eliot found the "highest form" in the "highest organism, that is to say, the most varied group of relations bound together in a wholeness which again has the most varied relations with all other phenomena." We tend, today, to want to demystify a term like *organism*, which by definition represents an incalculable unity. We may recognize that the novelist often uses a few bold inconsistencies which are suggestive enough to demand of him and of us a new and more arduous effort to explain and unify. Tolstoy's boldness is so nicely judged that we are persuaded of the implicit lawfulness and consequently look for it in greater depth. I want to consider two instances.

Kitty Shcherbatsky, like Levin and Anna and even more than her sister Dolly, cannot live a half-life or dismiss her grief over Vronsky's betrayal. We see her falling into illness that has no physical cause. She is examined by a specialist whose self-importance may be measured by his indifference to his patient's embarrassment. Kitty's mother, the Princess Shcherbatsky, feels guilty about Vronsky, and she means to be abject before the doctors. They in turn consult with each other to decide which treatment of Kitty will best satisfy her imperious mother. Dolly, who is present, asks their mother if Kitty's shame and grief are due in part to her regret that she has refused Levin, but the old princess is appalled at the thought that she is to blame for having encouraged Vronsky, and she grows angry with Dolly. Nor is she alone in her response. Kitty throws off her sister Dolly's pity with anger and cruelty: "I've enough pride," she cries, "never to let myself love a man who does not love me." And when Dolly ignores the thrust and talks directly about Levin, Kitty is all the more furious: "I shall never, *never* do what you're doing—go back to a man who has been unfaithful to you, who falls in love with another woman." Dolly is crushed by her sister's cruelty, and Kitty at last breaks down in tears. Each understands the other's feelings, and Kitty knows that she has been forgiven.

She can speak then of her changed world, so much like the one Anna will create as the climate of suicide: "everything has become odious, disgusting, and coarse to me, myself most of all. You can't imagine what disgusting thoughts I have about everything." Later, at the German watering place Kitty tries to achieve entire selflessness and idealism, only coming at last to realize that she has misjudged and injured others in order to sustain her aspiration. She finally dismisses her role of ministering angel as a sham. "Let me be bad, but at least not a liar, not a humbug," she cries, and she realizes that she has been "deceiving herself in imagining that she could be what she wished to be." She returns to Russia cured, "calm and serene." Kitty's pride leads to difficulties both before her marriage and after; but it is a principle of vitality. Her independence and resistance to Levin's will is a far greater thing than Dolly's bitter resignation.

Vronsky is a character who shows so much growth in the early parts of the novel that we are not quite prepared, in spite of sufficient warning, for his limitations in what follows. We first see him as an immature libertine, a brilliant and wealthy officer charmed by the innocence and adoration of a young girl of high society (all of his love affairs have been outside it). "He could not possibly believe that what gave such genuine pleasure to him, and above all to her, could be wrong." But he has no affection for the conventions of family life, and the role of husband seems "alien, hostile, and above all, ridiculous." His initial shallowness is to be seen in his "pleasant feeling of purity and freshness" at the Shcherbatskys', "partly due to the fact that he had not smoked all evening, and with it a new feeling of tenderness at her love for him." Even when Vronsky has become a great deal more serious, his sense of well-being finds its immediate expression in a consciousness of his body. "It gave him pleasure to feel the slight pain in his strong leg, it was pleasant to feel the muscular sensation of movement in his chest as he breathed." And Tolstoy enforces an incongruity: "the same bright and cold August day which made Anna feel so hopeless seemed exhilarating and invigorating to him and refreshed his face and neck, which were still glowing after the drenching he had given them under the tap." Somehow the face and neck seem awkwardly specific and trivial, just as the pride he feels after his first meetings with Anna seems touching but naive: "He looked at people as if they were things. A nervous young man . . . sitting opposite began to detest him for that look."

Vronksy's love for Anna makes him a far more serious and courageous man. He tends, it is true, to return easily to his old world of habit, and the first part of the novel ends on a somewhat ominous note, as habit recaptures the Vronsky we have so far seen in Moscow or on the train: "As always when in Petersburg, he left the house not to return till late at night." Unlike Anna, he has a role both in his regiment and in the society he frequents that gives him a secure sense of rightness; the role of a man pursuing a married woman had "something grand and beautiful about it and could never be ridiculous." He has not yet had to leave the world he has known in order to enter this new world that their love creates. The first real test of Vronsky is the steeple chase. He has, as we have seen, been troubled by the deceptions he has had to practice and has felt a sudden revulsion at the news of Anna's pregnancy. In the race a moment of doubt disables his customary, assured command of his horse, and through a terrible error he breaks the back of Frou-Frou, the nervous mare he is riding. Worst of all perhaps is the rage to which his remorse and frustration lead: he kicks the dying horse in the belly before he realizes fully what he has done. Much later, when Anna rejects his warning and insists upon going to the opera, where she will surely be snubbed, Vronsky is left behind in outrage. "And why does she put me in such a position?" he exclaims, and he upsets the table that holds soda and brandy. He tries to steady the table but only overturns it, and, finally, in his vexation, he kicks it over.

Between these two events Vronsky has attempted suicide. As a man who has always needed a clear code of rules, who had an essential role in the regiment that is his only family, he finds himself suddenly humbled by Karenin's forgiveness. The forgiveness leaves Vronsky feeling "ashamed, humiliated, guilty . . . kicked out of the normal way of life. . . . Everything that had seemed so firmly established, all the rules and habits of his life, suddenly turned out to be false and inapplicable." Vronsky finds himself, as it were, outside the forms of life, without purchase or balance, awed and disgraced by the generosity and dignity of Karenin. "They had suddenly exchanged roles. Vronsky felt Karenin's greatness and his own humiliation." He has lost the grandeur of the lover, and he has lost Anna; and in that moment the love that had begun to wane altogether revives. His attempt to kill himself fails, and he has prepared instead to undertake a "flattering and dangerous mission to Tashkent" when Anna recovers and returns to him. He must resign not only the new post but his comission as well; he sets about shaping new forms of life with Anna. The new forms remain unreal; they have no rooted existence, they make no earnest demand, they carry no necessity.

ENDINGS

One way to speak of the contrast between the story of Levin and that of Anna is the expansion of Levin's life to include more and the painful contraction of Anna's life as she is excluded from those forms which have formerly sustained her. She and Vronsky have made in Italy one halfhearted attempt to create new forms, and in the sixth part of the novel that attempt is renewed in more plausible but more radically flawed forms. The sixth part of *Anna Karenina* is the most elegant in design. We move between two estates with Dolly, from Levin's to Vronsky's; and the final section brings both landlords to the provincial elections. There is, moreover, the ludicrous dandy Veslovsky, who appears at both estates. Dolly and her children are staying with Levin and Kitty. Her own country house is now, through Oblonsky's neglect, "completely dilapidated"; and Oblonsky is happy to send his family off to the country, where he can pay them occasional short visits.

With Kitty and Dolly is their mother, the princess, and the three women make raspberry jam together. Kitty feels a new relationship with her mother, something closer to equality, as they talk—three married women—about the likelihood of Varenka's receiving a proposal from Levin's brother, Koznyshev. Dolly thinks back to Stiva's courtship. Kitty asks her mother how her own marriage was settled, in what gestures or words agreement was reached. "And," Tolstoy goes on, "the three women thought about one and the same thing." It is one of those moments that Tolstoy manages with distinctive power. There is not the dissolution of membranes between people so that they become, as in Virginia Woolf, for a moment one stream of feeling. In Tolstoy, people, often locked in their own memories, participate in a common form of life.

So with a possible marriage. Koznyshev remarked with regret at Levin's wedding that he was "past all that." Varenka is a mature and selfless woman who might comfort that rather complacent intellectual. To his younger brother Levin, Koznyshev seems to lead only a spiritual existence. He is "too pure and high-minded a man" to come to terms with reality. And Kitty in turn insists that Varenka is "all spirit." There isn't, she says, "so much of this reality in her as there is in me." But the proposal fails because neither person quite wants it, and all the trivia that somehow rush to Varenka's lips have behind them her resistance to the exposure and risk of a new relationship. Koznyshev has pressed beyond his comfortable rationalization—his fidelity to the long-dead Marie. He is at the point of proposing but ready to withdraw, all too easily thrown off. And so they go on talking about mushrooms. The ludicrous, Chekhovian banalities become their defenses. "And the moment those words were uttered, both he and she understood that it was all over, that what should have been said would never be said, and their agitation, having reached its climax, began to subside."

Each of them represents a kind of half life in the novel. Varenka's conventionality and denial of life once seemed to Kitty saintliness. Koznyshev's intellectuality and condescension have had the power to shake Levin's confidence. But, in fact, each of these characters helps to define the vitality of the central figures, who risk everything because they cannot endure something less than life. Later, as the children have their tea, everyone avoids talking of what might have happened. Koznyshev and Varenka feel "like children who have failed their examinations and have to stay behind in the same class or who have been expelled from school for good."

Levin finds the Shcherbatsky element—Kitty's family—gaining domination on his estate, and he is annoyed that Stiva brings with him an unknown guest, Veslovsky. Levin's displeasure begins to spread. It is, on a very small and comic scale, like Kitty's sense of defilement after Vronsky's desertion or Anna's final vision of corruption before her suicide. The deep, pervasive feelings of these characters shape and color their world. The process can be ludicrous when it is not awesome; and Levin rather preposterously sees falsehood everywhere. Dolly doesn't really believe in Stiva's love even if she looks pleased that he's there; Koznyshev only pretends to like Oblonsky. Varenka is a plaster saint with her eye on a marriage partner. And Kitty is clearly flirting with Veslovsky. The last is more than Levin can endure, and he speaks to Kitty of the "horror and the comic absurdity" of his situation. Unlike Vronsky, she is "glad of the force of love for her which found expression in his jealousy." With her reassurance Levin takes Stiva and Veslovsky on a shooting party, where Levin finds his recovered spirits lowered again by their frivolity and by Veslovsky's clumsiness. Nothing goes right until finally Levin goes off by himself and brings down his birds. But Levin can have no peace until he sends Veslovsky packing.

The principal contrast of the sixth part hinges on Dolly's visit to Anna and Vronsky. Her sudden release, the children left behind, from responsibilities and concerns leaves her, during the ride, free to think about her life, to enjoy a measure of self-pity and then to daydream about a life like Anna's: "She wants to live. God has put that need into our hearts. Quite possibly I should have done the same." A "mischievous smile wrinkled her lips, chiefly because while thinking of Anna's love affair, she conjured up parallel with it an almost identical love affair with an imaginary composite man who was in love with her. Like Anna, she confessed everything to her husband. And Oblonsky's astonishment and embarrassment at the news of her unfaithfulness made her smile." For a moment Dolly, of all people, brings Emma Bovary before us. "As is quite often the case," Tolstoy observes, "with women of unimpeachable moral conduct who are rather tired of the monotony of a virtuous life, she not only condoned from afar an illicit love affair but even envied it." In Dolly's case, the effect upon Stiva must count for much.

But while Dolly finds Anna more beautiful than ever, she comes to see Anna's unhappiness as well, her inability to love her daughter, her use of contraception (a new and shocking idea for Dolly, who dreads another pregnancy), and her dependence on morphine. Vronsky has made his family estate into a little court where he is surrounded by a respectful cabinet and where he plays at life again (as he has in Italy with painting), now building a hospital. Dolly is disenchanted. The room she is given reminds her in its luxury "of the best hotels abroad." Everything in it is new and expensive, not least the "smart lady's maid" before whom Dolly is ashamed to display her "patched dressing jacket," proud as she has been of the "patches and darns" at home. She is surprised to find everyone busily at play, "grown-up people carrying on a children's game in the absence of children." Dolly feels as if she is "taking part in a theatrical peformance with better actors than herself" and as if her own performance is spoiling the show. Anna is an assiduous hostess, creating unity among her guests, putting up with Veslovsky's flirtation. But Anna regrets Dolly's leaving; for the feelings that Dolly has raised, however painful, Anna recognizes as "the best part of her inner self" and a part that is being "rapidly smothered by the life she [is] leading."

Among the topics discussed at Vronsky's table is the value of rural councils and magistrates. Dolly cites Levin's scorn for these public institutions, and Vronsky replies with a vigor meant to defend his own interest in them as well. Anna observes that Vronsky has already become, in the six months they have spent on his estate, a member of five or six such institutions. "And I fear," she adds, "that with such a multiplicity of official duties, the whole thing will become a mere form." There is asperity in her tone; clearly she resents Vronsky's frequent absences to attend these meetings, just as he feels the need to assert his freedom by going. Tolstoy treats the electoral meetings at Kashin as an ugly farce, which Levin loathes but Vronsky greatly enjoys. Vronsky, in fact, resolves to stand himself in three years if he and Anna are married by then, "just as when winning a prize at the races he felt like taking the jockey's place himself next time." The meetings at Kashin present a world of rhetoric and political manipulation. Vronsky is pleased by the "charming good form" he finds in the provinces. Only "the crazy fellow who was married to Kitty Shcherbatsky" had talked a lot of nonsense "with rabid animosity." Perhaps the typical figure at such an occasion is the amiable Sviazhsky, who stands for so much of the world Tolstoy is presenting in the novel: "Sviazhsky was one of those people who always amazed Levin because their extremely logical, though never original, ideas were kept in a watertight compartment and had no influence whatever on their extremely definite and stable lives, which went on quite independently and almost always diametrically opposed to them. . . ." Whenever Levin presses Sviazhsky on a point that reveals an inconsistency, he sees a "momentary expression of alarm in Sviazhsky's eyes which he had noticed before whenever he had tried to penetrate beyond the reception rooms of

Sviazhsky's mind." When Levin is troubled by his own insincerity or his failure to face the truth in matters of religion, it is with the feeling that there is "something vague and unclean in his soul." He sees himself in the position "for which he found fault with his friend Sviazhsky."

When Levin finally meets Anna in Moscow, he is altogether charmed by her seriousness, her beauty, and her intelligence. After a day of largely senseless talk, he is moved by her naturalness and lack of self-consciousness. Levin is moved to make a witticism about French art, which has had so far to go in its return to realism: "They saw poetry in the very fact that they did not lie." Anna's face lights up with pleasure. What gives the episode its sadness is not Kitty's jealousy afterwards, but the disclosure that Anna has "done all she could . . . to arouse in Levin a feeling of love." Seductiveness is perhaps the only behavior she allows herself any more with Vronsky, and with other men as a matter of course. The obvious contrast is with Natasha at the close of *War and Peace:*

> She took no pains with her manners or with delicacy of speech, or with her toilet. . . . She felt that the allurements instinct had formerly taught her to use would now be merely ridiculous in the eyes of her husband. . . . She felt that her unity with her husband was not maintained by the poetic feelings that had attracted him to her, but by something else— indefinite but firm as the bond between her own body and soul.

At the end we see Anna surrendering to powers of destruction, in her savage torture of herself and Vronsky, in her sad effort to stir the pitying Kitty to jealousy. Her world fills with hatred and disgust; everyone she sees is vicious or filthy. The breakdown of mind creates a stream of consciousness, and the rage of her last hours is the form her vitality takes. Unlike her husband, who finds consolation in fashionable superstition, she finds herself outside all forms of life.

In the last part of the novel, at first suppressed, Tolstoy shows the mindless rush of Slavic patriotism and war hysteria. We enter that stream with Koznyshev when his book wins ridicule and early oblivion. He turns to the Slav question and the Serbo-Turkish war. He sees the excitement as "frivolous and ridiculous," but he admires its power. "The soul of the nation," as he puts it, has "become articulate." And so the intellectual devotes himself to a "great cause and forgot to think about things in his book." Vronsky has volunteered to fight for Serbia, taking a whole squadron at his own expense and evidently looking for death. Oblonsky has come into his long-sought post and is giving a farewell party for another volunteer, the unspeakable Veslovsky. Only Levin stands outside this new whirl of mindlessness, hoping to solve his own problems, insisting that war in itself is evil. "It's not only a question of sacrificing oneself," he observes to his brother, "but of killing Turks." In reply Koznyshev glibly cites, "I came not to send peace but a sword," quoting "the passage from the Gospels that had always perplexed Levin more than any other, just as if it were the most comprehensible thing in the world."

Tolstoy seems to reverse George Eliot's movement, as we see it in Dorothea Brooke's coming to awareness, moving outward from the self to include the multifarious and independent world. For Tolstoy the hero must recover the immediate. To borrow Wittgenstein's terms again, "The aspects of things that are most important for us are hidden because of their simplicity and familiarity." What Tolstoy's heroes must uncover, in short, is the framework itself of which Isaiah Berlin has written; they must dissolve false problems and find their way back to what they have always known. The emphasis must rest then upon the forms of life which we overlook or distort or deny, and those forms may be as far back as we can or should go. The language-game rests in the end upon our activities: "it is not based on grounds. It is not reasonable (or unreasonable). It is there—like our life." "What has to be accepted, the given, is—so one could say—*forms of life.*"

Characters like Anna are tragic figures because, for reasons that are admirable, they cannot live divided lives or survive through repression. We can see throughout the last part of the novel how profoundly Anna feels the need to hold Vronsky's love since theirs is not a life given shape by institutional forms—it has no necessities but their happiness, and there are no forms within which to make their love a sanctity. There seems no clear line at last between Anna's wish to believe in Vronsky's love and her readiness to believe that it no longer exists. The torture she inflicts is a reflex of self-pity she begins to suffer, and there are moments when she seems irrationally to wish to be proved right by Vronsky's rejection of her love. We sense this in her despair. Yet before she throws herself under the train, Anna crosses herself. And the familiar gesture, one of the forms of her early life, arouses a series of memories of her childhood and girlhood until "the darkness that enveloped everything for her was torn apart, and for an instant life presented itself to her with all its bright past joys."

Chronology

1828   Lev Nikolayevich Tolstoy is born on August 28, at Yasnaya Polyana, his father's estate 80 miles south of Moscow, to Nikolay Ilich Tolstoy and Maria Nikolayevna Tolstaya. Tolstoy has three older brothers and, later, a younger sister.

1830   Tolstoy's mother dies on August 4.

1837   Tolstoy's father dies on June 20.

1844–47   Tolstoy attends the University of Kazan. He enters in the department of Turkish-Arabic studies, but transfers to the law faculty in 1845. He leaves the University without having graduated, and returns to Yasnaya Polyana, where he attempts to initiate social reform among the peasants.

1851   On May 2 Tolstoy leaves for the Caucasus with Nikolay, his oldest brother, and participates in the Caucasian campaign.

1852   Tolstoy officially joins the army.

1853   Tolstoy sends the manuscript of *Childhood* to Nekrasov, editor of the *Contemporary*, on July 3. *Childhood* is published in the *Contemporary* on September 6. Turgenev praises *Childhood* in a letter to Nekrasov.

1854–57   Tolstoy is a frequent contributor to the *Contemporary*, publishing several stories and short novels, including *Boyhood* (1854), "Sevastopol in August, 1855" (1856), *The Two Hussars* (1856) and *Youth* (1857). The critical reception of his work is enthusiastic.

1858   Tolstoy finishes *Three Deaths* and works on *The Cossacks*, then stops writing and devotes himself to farm work during the summer.

1859   Tolstoy publishes *Three Deaths* and *Family Happiness*; the critical response is less enthusiastic. In October, he founds an experimental school for the peasant children of Yasnaya Polyana.

1860   Tolstoy continues teaching at Yasnaya Polyana until he leaves for western Europe on June 25. His brother Nikolay dies on September 20.

1861	Tolstoy returns to Russia on April 12. He publishes *Yasnaya Polyana,* an educational journal. On May 27, he quarrels with Turgenev and challenges him to a duel.
1862	Tolstoy proposes to Sofia Andreyevna Bers on September 14; they are married on September 23.
1863	Tolstoy publishes *The Cossacks.* On August 3, his first son is born.
1864–69	Tolstoy writes and publishes *War and Peace.* The work provokes heated critical debate.
1873–76	Tolstoy writes *Anna Karenina.* The novel is published in serial form in the *Russian.* Tolstoy does not enjoy writing it, and struggles to produce each installment. The novel is very popular and the critical reaction is generally favorable.
1877	Tolstoy has an increased interest in religion and spirituality.
1878	Tolstoy and Turgenev are reconciled.
1882	Tolstoy learns Hebrew and reads the Old Testament. He publishes *Confession.*
1883	Turgenev writes to Tolstoy from his deathbed, urging him to continue writing fiction.
1884–86	Tolstoy writes and publishes *The Death of Ivan Ilych,* to positive critical response.
1887	Tolstoy publishes *The Power of Darkness,* a play which seriously offends the Tsar.
1889	*The Kreutzer Sonata.*
1895	*Master and Man.* Chekhov makes his first visit to Yasnaya Polyana on August 8.
1899	Tolstoy publishes a final version of *Resurrection,* which he has been writing for more than ten years.
1902	Tolstoy finishes *Hadji Murad.*
1902–10	Tolstoy's relations with his wife are increasingly bad. On the night of October 27, 1910, he decides to leave her. He falls ill on the train and is taken off at Astapovo, where he dies on November 7.

Contributors

HAROLD BLOOM, Sterling Professor of the Humanities at Yale University, is the author of *The Anxiety of Influence, Poetry and Repression* and many other volumes of literary criticism. His forthcoming study, *Freud: Transference and Authority,* attempts a full-scale reading of all of Freud's major writings. A MacArthur Prize Fellow, he is the general editor of *The Chelsea House Library of Literary Criticism.*

GYORGY LUKACS, Hungarian philosopher and literary critic, developed a Marxist system of aesthetics opposing political control of artists and defending humanism. His books include *The Theory of the Novel* and *Studies in European Realism.*

THOMAS MANN, German novelist, received the Nobel Prize in literature in 1929 for *Buddenbrooks.* His other works include the novels *Doctor Faustus, Death in Venice* and *The Magic Mountain,* as well as a number of literary, philosophical and political essays.

VIKTOR SHKLOVSKY was a major modern Russian literary theorist and critic and the author of *Third Factory.*

PHILIP RAHV is an American literary critic who emigrated from the Ukraine as a child. One of the founders of *The Partisan Review,* he wrote on the role of the intellectual and the artist in society. He is the author of *Image and Idea* and *Literature and the Sixth Sense.*

GEORGE STEINER is Professor of Comparative Literature at the University of Geneva and an Extraordinary Fellow of Churchill College, Cambridge. His books include *After Babel, The Death of Tragedy, Language and Silence* and *On Difficulty.*

SIR ISAIAH BERLIN, O.M. is former Master of Wolfson College at Oxford. He is the author of *The Hedgehog and the Fox, Against the Current: Essays in the History of Ideas, Four Essays on Liberty* and *Russian Thinkers.*

R. P. BLACKMUR was Professor of English and Chairman of the Gauss Seminars at Princeton University. He is the author of *Language as Gesture: Essays in Poetry, The Double Agent* and *The Expense of Greatness.*

BARBARA HARDY is a lecturer of History and Literature at Harvard University. Her books include *Effects of Travel in English Renaissance Dramatic Literature* and *East and West in the Renaissance*.

JOHN BAYLEY is Professor of English at Oxford University and the author of *An Essay on Hardy, Keats and Poetry* and *Shakespeare and Tragedy*.

W. GARETH JONES has written several articles on Tolstoy.

GARY SAUL MORSON teaches in the department of Slavic Languages at the University of Pennsylvania. He is the author of *The Boundaries of Genre: Dostoevsky's 'Diary of a Writer' and the Traditions of Literary Utopia*.

EDWARD WASIOLEK is Professor of Russian and Comparative Literature at the University of Chicago. He is the author of *Dostoevsky: The Major Fiction*.

W. W. ROWE is the author of *Nabokov's Spectral Dimension*.

NATALIA KISSELEFF is Assistant Professor of Slavic Languages and Literature at the State University of New York at Albany.

ROBERT WEXELBLATT teaches literature and philosophy at Boston University.

MARTIN PRICE is Sterling Professor of English at Yale University. His books include *Swift's Rhetorical Art: A Study in Structure and Meaning*; he has also edited a number of works on seventeenth- eighteenth- and nineteenth-century literature.

Bibliography

Arnold, Matthew. "Count Leo Tolstoy." In *Essays in Criticism, Second Series*. New York: MacMillan, 1906.

Bayley, John. *Tolstoy and the Novel*. New York: Viking, 1966.

Berlin, Isaiah. *The Hedgehog and The Fox: An Essay on Tolstoy's View of History*. New York: Simon and Schuster, 1953.

Bulgakov, Valentin. *The Last Year of Leo Tolstoy*. Translated by Ann Dunnigan. New York: Dial Press, 1971.

Christian, R. F. *Tolstoy: A Critical Introduction*. Cambridge: At the University Press, 1969.

Dostoevsky, F. M. *The Diary of a Writer*. Translated and annotated by Boris Brasol. New York: Charles Scribner's Sons, 1949.

Eikhenbaum, Boris. *The Young Tolstoy*. Translation edited by Gary Kern. Ann Arbor, Mich.: Ardis, 1972.

———. *Tolstoy*. 3 vols. Ann Arbor, Mich.: Ardis, 1982.

Gibian, George. *Tolstoy and Shakespeare*. The Hague: Mouton, 1957.

———. "Two Kinds of Human Understanding and the Narrator's Voice in *Anna Karenina*." *Orbis Scriptus* 92 (1966): 314–22.

Gorky, Maxim. *Reminiscences*. Translated by S. S. Koteliansky and Leonard Woolf. Richmond, England: Hogarth Press, 1920.

Hagan, John H., "A Pattern of Character Development in *War and Peace*." *Slavic and East European Journal* 13 (January 1963): 17–49.

———. "Ambivalence, in Tolstoy's *The Cossacks*." *Novel* 3 (1969): 28–47.

Jackson, Robert L. "Chance and Design in *Anna Karenina*." In *The Disciplines of Criticism: Essays in Literary Theory, Interpretation and History*. Edited by Peter Demetz, Thomas Greene, and Lowry Nelson. New Haven: Yale University Press, 1968.

James, Henry. *The Art of the Novel*. New York: Charles Scribner's Sons, 1934.

Jones, Malcolm V. "Problems of Communication in *Anna Karenina*." In *New Essays on Tolstoy*. Edited by Malcolm Jones. New York: Cambridge University Press, 1978.

Jones, W. Gareth. "George Eliot's *Adam Bede* and Tolstoy's Conception of Anna Karenina." *Modern Language Review* 61 (1966): 73–81.

Lawrence, D. H. *Reflections on the Death of a Porcupine and Other Essays*. Philadelphia: The Centaur Press, 1925.

Lubbock, Percy. *The Craft of Fiction*. New York: Viking, 1957.

Lukacs, Gyorgy. *Studies in European Realism*. Translated by Edith Bone. New York: Grosset and Dunlap, 1964.

Mann, Thomas. "*Anna Karenina.*" In *Essays of Three Decades.* Translated by H. Lowe-Porter. New York: Knopf, 1965.

Matlaw, Ralph, ed. *Tolstoy: A Collection of Critical Essays.* Englewood Cliffs, N.J.: Prentice-Hall, 1967.

Maude, Aylmer. *The Life of Tolstoy.* 2 vols. London: Constable, 1908.

Muir, Edwin. *The Structure of the Novel.* New York: Harcourt, Brace and Company, 1929.

Poggioli, Renato. "A Portrait of Tolstoy as Alceste." In *The Phoenix and the Spider.* Cambridge, Mass.: Harvard University Press, 1957.

Rolland, Romain. *Tolstoy.* Translated by Bernard Miall. London: T. F. Unwin, 1911.

Shestov, L. *Dostoevsky, Tolstoy, and Nietzsche.* Athens, Ohio: Ohio University Press, 1969.

Simmons, Ernest J. *Leo Tolstoy.* New York: Vintage Books, 1960.

———. *Introduction to Tolstoy's Writings.* Chicago: The University of Chicago Press, 1968.

States, Bert O. "The Hero and the World: Our Sense of Space in *War and Peace.*" *Modern Fiction Studies* 11 (1965): 153–64.

Steiner, George. *Tolstoy or Dostoevsky: An Essay in the Old Criticism.* New York: Knopf, 1959.

Steward, David D. "*Anna Karenina:* The Dialectic of Prophecy." *PMLA* 79 (June 1940): 266–82.

Troyat, Henri. *Tolstoy.* Translated by Nancy Amphoux. New York: Doubleday, 1967.

Vogue, E. M. de. *The Russian Novel.* Translated by H. A. Sawyer. New York: Doran, 1914.

Wasiolek, Edward. *Tolstoy's Major Fiction.* Chicago: The University of Chicago Press, 1978.

———. "The Theory of History in *War and Peace.*" *Midway* 2, vol. 9 (1968): 117–35.

Woolf, Virginia. "The Russian Point of View." In *The Common Reader.* New York: Harcourt, Brace and Company, 1925.

Zweers, Alexander. *Grown-up Narrator and Childlike Hero: An Analysis of the Literary Devices Employed in Tolstoy's Trilogy, "Childhood," "Boyhood," and "Youth."* The Hague: Mouton, 1971.

Acknowledgments

"Tolstoy and the Attempts to Go Beyond the Social Forms of Life" by Gyorgy Lukacs from *The Theory of the Novel: A Historico-Philosophical Essay on the Forms of Great Epic Literature* by Gyorgy Lukacs, copyright © 1971 by The Merlin Press. Reprinted by permission.

"Goethe and Tolstoy" by Thomas Mann from *Essays of Three Decades* by Thomas Mann, copyright © 1947 by Alfred A. Knopf, Inc. Reprinted by permission.

"Parallels in Tolstoy" by Victor Shklovsky from *Twentieth-Century Russian Literary Criticism* edited by Victor Erlich, copyright © 1975 by Yale University Press. Reprinted by permission.

"Tolstoy: The Green Twig and the Black Trunk" by Philip Rahv from *The Short Novels of Tolstoy* selected and with an introduction by Philip Rahv, copyright © 1946 by The Dial Press. Reprinted by permission.

"Tolstoy and Homer" by George Steiner from *Tolstoy or Dostoevsky: An Essay in the Old Criticism* by George Steiner, copyright © 1959 by George Steiner. Reprinted by permission.

"Tolstoy and Enlightenment" by Isaiah Berlin from *Mightier Than the Sword* by Charles Morgan, J. B. Priestley, et al., copyright © 1964 by The English Centre. Reprinted by permission.

"The Dialectic of Incarnation: Tolstoy's *Anna Karenina*" by R. P. Blackmur from *Eleven Essays in the European Novel* by R. P. Blackmur, copyright © 1964 by R. P. Blackmur. Reprinted by permission.

"Form and Freedom: Tolstoy's *Anna Karenina*" by Barbara Hardy from *The Appropriate Form: An Essay on the Novel* by Barbara Hardy, copyright © 1970 by Barbara Hardy. Reprinted by permission.

"*What Is Art?*" by John Bayley from *Tolstoy and the Novel* by John Bayley, copyright © 1966 by John Bayley. Reprinted by permission.

262 • ACKNOWLEDGMENTS

"A Man Speaking to Men: The Narratives of *War and Peace*" by W. Gareth Jones from *New Essays on Tolstoy* edited by Malcolm Jones, copyright © 1978 by Cambridge University Press. Reprinted by permission.

"The Reader as Voyeur: Tolstoy and the Poetics of Didactic Fiction" by Gary Saul Morson from *Canadian-American Slavic Studies*, copyright © 1978 by Charles Schlacks, Jr. and Arizona State University. Reprinted by permission.

"*Resurrection*" by Edward Wasiolek from *Tolstoy's Major Fiction* by Edward Wasiolek, copyright © 1978 by The University of Chicago. Reprinted by permission.

"Some Fateful Patterns in Tolstoy" by W. W. Rowe from *Nabokov and Others: Patterns in Russian Literature* by W. W. Rowe, copyright © 1979 by Ardis. Reprinted by permission.

"Idyll and Ideal: Aspects of Sentimentalism in Tolstoy's *Family Happiness*" by Natalia Kisseleff from *Canadian Slavonic Papers*, copyright © 1979 by Canadian Slavonic Papers. Reprinted by permission.

"Symbolism in *The Death of Ivan Ilych*" by Robert Wexelblatt from *The Massachusetts Review*, copyright © 1980 by The Massachusetts Review, Inc. Originally entitled "The Higher Parody: Ivan Ilych's Metamorphosis and the Death of Gregor Samsa." Reprinted by permission.

"Tolstoy and the Forms of Life" by Martin Price from *Forms of Life* by Martin Price, copyright © 1983 by Yale University Press. Reprinted by permission.

Index